Calling on God

Sacred Jewish Teachings

For Seekers of All Faiths

By Pamela Frydman

Prefaced by Wali Ali Meyer & Scott Sattler, M.D.
Article by Zalman Schachter-Shalomi & Netanel Miles-Yepez

Star of David Cover Art by Art Rich Sigberman
Cover Design by Kerima Furniss
Interior Illustrations by Zubin Nur Westrik
Photo of author by Ellen Shireman

Pronunciation and melodies for the practices in this book are available at www.rebpam.com.

Published by Wild Earth Press

ISBN (Print Version): 978-0-9839844-1-2
ISBN (eBook): 978-0-9839844-9-8

.

WILD EARTH PRESS
P.O. Box 15
Arcata, CA 95518
www.wildearthpress.com

To Reb Zalman

Whose teachings, vision,
Support and love
Have opened a path for these practices

Table of Contents

ILLUSTRATIONS

Openings

Acknowledgements

I offer heartfelt thanks to all those mentioned in the text and footnotes, whose teachings and inspiration have guided me in the writing of this book; in particular, Rabbi Zalman Schachter-Shalomi, to whom this book is dedicated; Joe and Guin Miller, of blessed memory; Rabbi David Wolfe-Blank, of blessed memory; Murshid Wali Ali Meyer, Pir Shabda Khan; Hakim Sauluddin; and Aslan Scott Sattler, M.D.

I offer heartfelt thanks as well to:

Murad Malvin Finkelstein, C.A. for his inspiration and collaboration in contemplating and organizing the manuscript;

My editors:
•Rabbi Zalman Schachter-Shalomi, founder of the Jewish Renewal Movement and co-founder of the Inayati-Maimuni Tariqat, the first Jewish order of Sufis to our knowledge;
•Ofelia Alayeto, Ph.D., author of *Sofia Casanova, Spanish Poet, Journalist and Author*:[1] and
•Scott Sattler, M.D.;
•Rabbi Dennis Beck-Berman;

Reb Zalman for permission and encouragement to present his teachings in the book, and for guiding the transliteration; and Reb Zalman and Netanel Miles-Yepez for permission to reprint the article in Appendix F;

Pir O Murshid Zia Inayat-Khan, Murshid Hidayat Inayat-Khan and Sheikha Hamida Verlinden for their help with the researching of "May the blessing(s) of God rest upon you" found in Chapter 26;

Michael Baugh for musical accompaniment during the evolution of many of the practices in this book;

The singers and musicians whose recitation and chanting is available on the Internet at http://rebpam.com/. The names of those who helped with the recordings are listed on the website.

Zubin Nur Westrik for her illustrations on the section dividers (See <http://www.heartslight.net/> and <http://www.peaceplace.nl/>); and Amara Wahaba Karuna for the original heart and wings into which Zubin Nur added the six pointed star;

Rich Sigberman for the gift of his painting that adorns the book's cover.
See <http://www.sigsart.com/>;

Kerima Furniss for her cover design.
Please see ww.wildearthpress.com;

Josh Baugh for his consultation on the illustration design and formatting of the charts, and for his love and support throughout the writing and production process.

With blessings and gratitude,

Pamela Frydman

---

1 Ofelia Alayeto, *Sofia Casanova, Spanish Poet, Journalist and Author* (Scripta Humanistica, 1992).

Introduction

This book is divided into four sections: **Openings, Teachings, Practices and Appendices**.

The **Openings** section contains a Key to Pronunciation of non-English words—most particularly, Hebrew, Aramaic and Yiddish.

The **Teachings** section includes information about Jewish history and a guide for how to perform the practices in the Practice section. Some practices may also be found in the Teachings section.

The **Practices** section, together with the Index and Guide to Sacred Phrases, includes over one hundred spiritual and religious practices.

The **Appendices** include a Glossary of Terms, the Index and Guide to Sacred Phrases and an article discussing Reb Zalman's translation of the Sufi Invocation into Hebrew.

Musical recordings and pronunciation of sacred phrases are available at http://rebpam.com/.

* * * * * * *

Mystical Judaism—like all spiritual paths—is based upon experiences and not premises. The sacred phrases in this book may be chanted or spoken. Most may also be recited in silence in the mind and on the breath. Many of the practices may also be done while walking. The Hebrew Bible, prayer books and a vast variety of rabbinic commentaries contain a wealth of sacred words and phrases. The hundred or so practices in this book are but a beginning. There are countless other Jewish sacred phrases and melodies that may be found in other books and articles, and on CD's and the Internet.

In the Hebrew Bible, neither the Song of Songs nor the Book of Esther[2] mentions G-d. One might say that G-d is hidden in these texts, and there are many rabbinic commentaries that support such a view. One might also say that Esther and Song of Songs demonstrate G-d's all pervading presence in every character, scene and object. G-d is not just hiding in the drama in order to guide it from within, but rather, G-d is dwelling within, and is the very presence and reality in every thought and action.

In this Introduction, and in a few other places in this book, I write God's name as G-d,[3] because, according to Jewish tradition, when we write or speak G-d's name, we are responsible for our thoughts and actions, and we need to check to make sure that we are not taking the name of G-d in vain, either intentionally or inadvertently. This is discussed in the section entitled, "Third Commandment" in Chapter 9. In the chapters and appendices of this book, I write out the names of G-d without hyphens

---

2 The Book of Esther is read in the synagogue on the Jewish festival of Purim. Chapter 3 of this book contains a teaching from the Book of Esther. The Song of Songs is read in the synagogue on Shabbat Pesach (the Sabbath that falls during Passover).

3 When we read, some of us pronounce the words in our mind. One of my editors asked, "how do I pronounce "G-d" while I'm reading?" I would say that if you are familiar with the use of "G-d," then pronounce it in your mind the way that feels most comfortable. If you are not familiar with the use of "G-d," then I would pronounce it as "God."

and without changing key letters.[4] **It is my intention that this book be treated and used as one uses a Bible or prayer book—with utmost decorum and proper intention, for study and prayer, and for the sake of heaven.**

May we be graced with spiritual awakening, and tools that help us to help those who depend upon us, as we continue to unravel the mysteries on the path to spiritual realization in the footsteps of our ancestors and the mystics and sages of all time.

With love and blessings,

Pamela Frydman
May 20, 2012
28 Iyyar 5772[5]
43rd Day of the Omer,[6] Chesed Sheb'malkhut

---

4 There are examples in Chapter 9 of changing letters to avoid the possibility of taking G-d's name in vain.
5 The date 28 Iyyar 5772 is the twenty-eighth day of the Jewish month of Iyyar in the Jewish year 5772. The Jewish calendar is described in Appendix E.
6 The Torah tells us to count seven weeks from Passover to Shavu'ot. Passover is the anniversary of Israelite freedom from slavery, and Shavu'ot (the Feast of Weeks) is the anniversary of receiving the Ten Commandments at Mount Sinai. This counting of seven weeks is known as "counting the omer." Omer means "sheaf." On the second day of Passover, the Israelites would bring a sheaf of barley to the Holy Temple in Jerusalem to give thanks for the spring harvest. They would count the days from their bringing as "first day of the omer (sheaf)," "second day of the omer," etc. They would count for forty-nine days, and on the fiftieth day, they celebrated Shavu'ot, the Festival of Weeks. Many Jews continue to count the omer today. May 20, 2012 was the forty-third day of the omer.

Key to Pronunciation

The sounds in this Key to Pronunciation are pronounced at http://rebpam.com/.

* * * * * * *

Bold for Pronunciation – In the Index and Guide to Spiritual Practices as well as occasionally in the chapters in the Practices section, a word may appear partly in regular type and partly in bold. When this is the case, the accent is on the syllable in bold.

Proper Names – For the names of teachers and others whose stories and teachings are included in these pages, if the person's name was originally spelled in Hebrew, Yiddish or Aramaic, I have spelled the person's name in English in the way that it is most commonly found in written sources. It is my hope that doing so will render these names recognizable to those familiar with the person, and also to render the name easily searchable in libraries and on the Internet.

* * * * * * *

Below is a Key to Pronunciations for individual sounds. The Index and Guide to Sacred Phrases in Appendix C and the Glossary of Terms in Appendix A also contain information on pronunciation.

ch – represents the Hebrew letter "chet" and is pronounced like "ch" in the name of the famous musical composer "Bach."

kh – represents the Hebrew letter "khaf." Kh is also pronounced like "ch" in the name of the musical composer "Bach."

h – represents the Arabic letter het as in the Arabic divine qualities rahman and rahim, meaning mercy and compassion. Making this sound is like breathing out a puff of air from the back of the throat.

k – represents the Hebrew letters "kaf" and "koof," both of which are pronounced like "k" in "kite," "kiss" and "kitten."

a – pronounced like the "o" in "hot."

e – pronounced "eh," like the "e" in "pet" except when it is followed by "y." In that case, "ey" is pronounced like "ay" in "say."

i – pronounced like "ee" in "beet."

o – pronounced like "o" in "hole."

u – pronounced like "u" as in "rule."

uh – pronounced like "u" in "usher," "cut," "but" and "hut."

Key to Pronunciation

ey – pronounced like "ay" in "say." (Please note: Generally, "e" is pronounced like "e" in "pet," except when it is followed by "y." In that case, "ey" is pronounced like "ay" in "say.")

ay – also pronounced like "ay" in "say."

ai – pronounced like "i" in "bite," "mite" and "kite."

' – This apostrophe or single quotation mark between letters in Hebrew and Aramaic words means that there is an ever-so-slight pause between the preceding letter and the letter that follows.[7]

Unusual Spelling

YaH – In accordance with the custom of Rabbi Zalman Schachter-Shalomi, and at his request, I have used a capital "Y" for the Hebrew letter yod, and a capital "H" for the Hebrew letter hay in the divine name "YaH." The "a" in the divine name YaH stands for the Hebrew vowel kamatz. Chart 5 includes all of the Hebrew vowels.

Shechina and Shekhinah – The English word for the feminine indwelling presence of G-d is spelled "Shechina." However, to conform with the Key to Pronunciation above, the Hebrew is spelled "Shekhinah" in this book. The Aramaic for "Shechina" is "Shekhintay," which literally means "God's Shekhinah." As stated earlier in this Key to Pronunciation, "kh" in Hebrew and Aramaic words is pronounced like "ch" in the last name of the great musical composer Johann Sebastian Bach.

Bold for Pronunciation – In the Index and Guide to Spiritual Practices as well as occasionally in the chapters in the Practices section, a word may appear partly in regular type and partly in bold. When this is the case, the accent is on the syllable in bold.

* * * * * * *

If you cannot offer your sincere heartfelt prayers,
then offer your empty agnostic ones,
for God in His mercy (also) accepts counterfeit coin.

Jelaluddin Rumi

* * * * * * *

Sometimes people get the mistaken notion
that spirituality is a separate department of life,
the penthouse of existence.
But rightly understood,
it is a vital awareness that pervades all realms of our being.

Brother David Steindl-Rast

* * * * * * *

---

7 This apostrophe or single quotation mark sometimes depicts the vowel "shva" when it is "shva nah," as opposed to "shva nakh," which is silent. It is also used to depict the consonants ayin and alef in the middle and end of words, and sometimes it simply divides consonants to help the non-Hebrew/Aramaic speaker know how to pronounce the word.

Preface

By Wali Ali Meyer

This excellent book is designed to serve those fortunate human beings whose lives have been touched by the Divine Presence, and who yearn to feel the Divine Presence more. The Jewish religion that many of us, myself included, received in the synagogue had no interest in the mystical dimension, and the conception of God and our relationship with God that were presented seemed to be missing something essential.

The fact that our experience of Judaism was this way demonstrated that there was a need for renewal of the depth of the tradition. The forms of worship and religious education that the religion had taken missed delving into our love relationship with the Source of all, and our deepest yearnings for union with the beloved.

Calling on God contains within it a kind of articulation of the profound nature of God, and it uses the Hebrew language and the traditions of Judaism as a ground for this mystical teaching. That alone should make it recommended reading for Jews who wish to more deeply realize the soul of their own religion without having to take leave of Judaism in a search for tangible practices of self-realization and the nature of existence.

Meeting this kind of need was what gave birth to the Jewish Renewal Movement. Murshid Samuel Lewis stood as a pioneer in bringing forth keys for renewing the spiritual life of the Jewish religion, and Rabbi Pam makes reference to this many times in her superb text. Her book is both for those who want a more esoteric Judaism and those who just want a way as lovers of God to prayerfully use Jewish Hebrew practices.

Martin Buber wrote that there has been an aversion among Jews to the practice of repeated invocation of single holy Names or phrases in Jewish communities for centuries. Long prayers are repeated, but not a single Name of God over and over. This can be contrasted with the mantric practice of millions of Hindus and Buddhists and the Zikrs of the Sufis. Part of the resistance to such practice in Judaism was expressed theologically by doctrines that focused on man's impure nature and fear that this limitation would stain any attempt to directly invoke the divine mystery. While this may be an effort to protect the pristine nature of God from the obscurations of the human ego, I believe that it exaggerates human isolation from God. And overcoming that isolation through realization of our real nature is the very purpose of the spiritual path.

Rabbi Pam offers repetition, breath, walking, song, and dance practice in the Sufi manner to Hebrew practices, all with great respect for the Jewish tradition. She accentuates to some degree the importance of repeated Names and phrases, and she does it ever mindful of the beliefs and feelings of members of Orthodox, Ultra Orthodox and Conservative Jewish communities, as well as the practices and sensitivities of Reform, Reconstructionist and Renewal Judaism. This is a significant contribution to awakening the heart of Judaism in our time and totally aligned with Murshid Samuel Lewis' prophetic type warning that the Jewish people had given up the protection of the Divine Name that God had given them, and needed to return to the practice.

Rabbi Zalman Schachter-Shalomi's guiding wisdom is a steady presence throughout this book. He, like Murshid Samuel Lewis, was one of the first Jews in America to inwardly receive from the Source an inner impulse to renew the heart of the Torah as an answer to the need of the age. And like Sam, he reached out to other spiritual traditions not in simply an ecumenical way, but intuitively, knowing that there was a common source of all in what the Sufis call "The Mother of the Book," the silent and all-potent ultimate reality.

The fact that there was a palpable need for Jewish renewal can be illustrated in a story that I love to tell. In 1974, Rabbi Zalman and Pam (not yet a rabbi, nor even a rabbinic student) organized a "Dharma and Torah" symposium in Berkeley, California. It was well attended. On the panel were leaders and senior students from many different spiritual traditions. There was a senior monk from the Zen Mission Society, one from the Christian Holy Order of Mans, one from the Sikh tradition, three or four Sufi teachers, including me, Reb Zalman, someone from Rabbi Shlomo Carlebach's House of Love and Prayer, and a few others I can't remember now. At a certain point in the program, it became clear that every single panel member was originally Jewish! The children of Abraham were definitely asserting their need to find God in whatever form might be more available to them.

There is a great deal in this book to learn, appreciate and practice. There are profound presentations on the masculine and feminine aspects of the Divine Being. There are Dances of Universal Peace and healing practices. There is an exploration of Hebrew and Aramaic Divine Qualities as inter-related families such as the Qualities of Eternity, Strength and Love, in the same manner as the treatment of the Ninety-Nine Names of Allah in *Physicians of the Heart*.[8] The inner meanings that underlie Jewish religious understanding are suggested in the same way that the Sufis have done with Islam. There is a guide to pronunciation and a website to hear the Names and sacred phrases pronounced.

Murshid Samuel Lewis suggested a better translation than, "I am that I am," for ehyeh asher ehyeh—God's self descriptive words to Moses at the burning bush. Murshid Sam said ehyeh asher ehyeh means the eternal movement of the One and only being. I believe that is happening in our time to reawaken the heart of Judaism, Christianity, and Islam as part of the One and Only Being's all-compassionate activity.

I have known Rabbi Pam for more than three decades, first as a seeker, a student, a Sufi mureed, a Sufi teacher, as one called back to study deeply her own religious roots, as a rabbinic student, a Rabbi, and as a friend. She has named and honored many teachers and influences in her book. Let us just take a few breaths to honor her for her life and her work.

Love and Blessings,

Wali Ali Meyer

---

8 Wali Ali Meyer, Bilal Hyde, Faisal Muqaddam and Shabda Kahn, *Physicians of the Heart, a Sufi View of the Ninety-Nine Names of Allah* (San Francisco: Sufi Ruhaniat International, 2011).

Preface

By Scott Sattler, M.D.

I grew up in an Ohio Christian community in the 1950's and my first exposure to Judaism was in Presbyterian Sunday school. I learned that some of the Bible's books were also Jewish holy books, and I remember reading the story of Abraham, the son of an idol merchant, who as a child questioned the belief system of his father because he strongly felt that the entire universe was the work of a single Creator. I recall thinking "of course!" for this teaching resonated with my own inner sense of truth. I also remember learning that Abraham, through his wife Sarah and their son Isaac, gave rise to the tribes of Israel and thus to the Jewish religion, from which Christianity emerged. Interestingly, the fact that Jesus was Jewish was not emphasized much.

A decade later I found myself living with an Islamic family in Turkey as an American Field Service (AFS) exchange student. My host mother was a history teacher and taught me Turkish world history. This was my first introduction to the Muslim world. From her I learned that Abraham was not only the father of Judaism and thus Christianity, but also the grandfather of the religion of Islam, as the tribes of Arabia stem from Abraham and Hagar and their son Ishmael even as the tribes of Judea stem from Abraham and Sarah and their son Isaac and their grandson Jacob. I also learned that the Qur'an contained much wisdom, as well as many stories of Abraham, Moses, Jesus and Mary—more, in fact, on Mary the mother of Jesus than did our own Christian Bible. But most of all, by living with this wonderful family, I learned that their hearts were made up of the same stuff as mine. We laughed and loved and cried and enjoyed nature, music, friends and family, just as did the folks back in Ohio. The Gediks were clearly 'family,' and they still are, some forty-eight years later.

During my college and post-graduate years I sought out the wisdom in Buddhism and Hinduism as well, even to the point of living for a while at Swami Muktananda's ashram in Ganeshpuri, India. After medical school at Stanford, my first job as a practicing physician found me on the Hoopa Indian reservation and gave me the chance to taste Native American spirituality. Through these experiences I grew to realize that hidden beneath their formal religious dogma, the root wisdom of each of these traditions was essentially identical to the others, only shaded with differing cultural nuance. I also realized that the aboriginal literature of Black Elk, Chief Seneca and Tecumseh resonated with the same core truths, as did the wisdom teachings of Christianity, Islam and Hinduism. When my wife and I moved from Hoopa to Eureka, California in 1982 we began to search for a spiritual community that reflected this attunement, and we found the First Congregational UCC Church. The pastor at that time delighted in quoting Buddha from the pulpit. He gave refreshingly good sermons and he never seemed to get around to preaching the "Jesus is the only way" dogma that I heard as a child.

Not long thereafter, I met the Universal Sufis whose teachings stemmed from and expanded upon a line of wisdom schools going back to the time of the ancient Egyptians. Hazrat Inayat Khan (1882-1927), a master musician and Sufi teacher, had first brought the principles of Universal Sufism from India to the west (United States, Europe and Russia) in 1910. In 1967, forty years after the passing of Hazrat Inayat Khan, the eclectic Sufi and Zen master Murshid Samuel L. Lewis (1896-1971), who had studied with Hazrat Inayat Khan and Zen master Nyogen Senzaki, was called upon on the inner planes to take on the role of spiritual leader of hippies in San Francisco. His subsequent work led to the development and widespread teaching of the Dances of Universal Peace and the creation of the Sufi Ruhaniat International, an order of Universal Sufism originally based in the San Francisco Bay Area, and now maintaining centers around the world. I first met the Ruhaniat in 1983 and was delighted by the fact that they focused with great intensity upon the unifying thread which runs through the world's various religious traditions and that they shared and taught spiritual practices taken from all these traditions when those practices spoke to their hearts. Within this Sufi sangha, this spiritual community, there are Sufis like me who were raised Christian and still relate to that path. We sometimes call ourselves 'Crufies', Christian Sufis. There are also many Buddhist Sufis (Bufies) and a ton of Jewish Sufis (Jewfies). All in the sangha feel perfectly free to hold their own religious beliefs, for there is clear consensus that there can be no coercion or compulsion on the spiritual path.

I must confess, however that within this dynamic, eclectic sangha of Universal Sufism, I often found it difficult to grasp the deeper aspects, the core teachings, of the Jewish path. When I attend Bar and Bat Mitzvahs or other Jewish services in my community I truly delight in the beauty, open-heartedness and joy of Jewish worship, for it is palpable during these gatherings, but my inherent Hebrew deficiency clearly marginalizes my experience.

I could almost hear The Divine Being giggling when Rabbi Pamela, a dear friend whom I met through the Sufis in 1983, asked me if I would help her edit the manuscript of *Calling on God*. She wanted an editor who was neither Jewish nor involved in the path of Judaism. While my brain told me that I simply didn't have time to fit this into my schedule, the voice of my heart told me that this task was indeed mine to take on, and that if I looked closely and deeply at it, I would realize the truth of this. So I looked, and it did.

It is difficult to describe the happiness and joy I felt reading this manuscript. Rabbi Pamela has precisely addressed those issues that inadvertently distance non-Jews from a fuller resonance with the Judaic sense of spiritual truth, and by doing so she has opened a clear window into the heart and soul of Judaism. The glossary she provides is a Rosetta stone for the non-Jew. Her explanation of the adab, the spiritual politeness, surrounding the use of the various Hebrew names of God is a must-read for those of us who speak before eclectic gatherings such as the Dances of Universal Peace and multi-faith assemblies. Her clarification of the structure of the Jewish sacred text is most helpful. Her sharing of the sacred phrases given by Moses and their incorporation into sung and spoken practices opens a wide door into the Zikr remembrance practices so beloved by the Sufis. She goes on to share many of Judaism's sacred healing practices, given to help individuals and the world's need for healing. There is also discussion and clarification of Kabbalah, Gematria, the Jewish calendar and the Hebrew alphabet.

In short, this book is a precious gift for all those drawn to the spiritual path, those lovers of wisdom who have fallen awake to the soul's longing to be known. Rabbi Pamela, steeped in Judaism since birth and a student of universal Sufism for almost four decades, has laid forth her Judaic heritage and opened it to our common language for all to see. More than that, Rabbi Pam takes the reader deep into the experiential commonality shared by Sufis and Jews and people of other faith traditions by unveiling a host of spiritual practices common to our communities in all but language. With this guidance she specifically lifts the reader above the differences and distinctions that currently divide the family of Abraham and shows us the Oneness of the Divine, the unity that is the essence of the Abrahamic transmission.

Love and Blessings,

Scott Sattler, M.D.

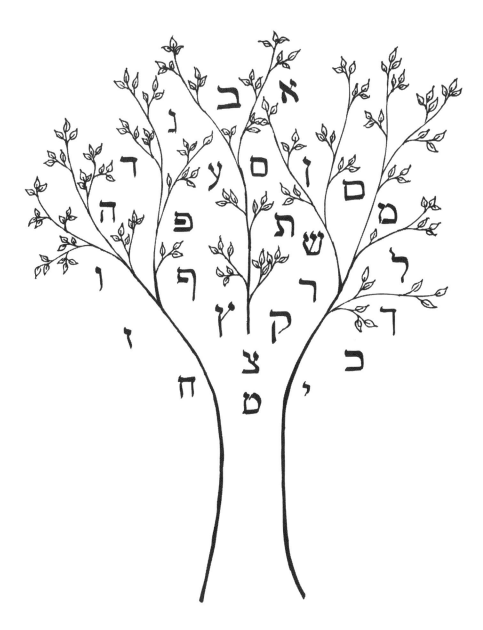

Teachings

This decorative tree is called the Ashrey Tree after the Ashrey prayer that contains sequential lines beginning with each letter of the Hebrew alphabet except nun. This is discussed in Appendix H.

Chapter I

From Sacrifices to Davvenen: A History of Jewish Worship

In Judaism, the day begins on the previous evening, in attunement with the first recounting of creation in the Torah,[9] in which it says "it was evening, it was morning" and then the number of the day. For example, "it was evening, it was morning, the first day," and so on.[10] There are three daily Jewish worship services, which are held in the evening, morning and afternoon. The evening service is called ma'ariv from the Hebrew word erev, meaning evening. The morning service is called shacharit from the Hebrew word shachar, meaning dawn. And the afternoon service is called mincha, meaning gift. The morning and afternoon worship services are considered to take the place of the morning and afternoon sacrifices that—according to the Torah—were given by God to Moses, and carried out by the Israelite priests in ancient times.

In addition to these two daily sacrifices, the Torah tells us that God required an additional sacrifice on the Sabbath and holy days.[11] God also instructed the Israelites in other sacrifices, such as offerings of thanksgiving, free will, and repentance from sin and guilt. The Torah tells us that God instructed Moses and the Israelites about the sacrifices while they were wandering in the wilderness following their freedom from slavery.[12]

The Hebrew word for sacrifice is korban. The root of korban is karov. Karov means close, and korban means that which brings us close. **The intention of the sacrifices was for the Israelites to become close to God, or to return to closeness with God after straying from the path.** When the Israelites completed forty years of wandering in the wilderness, they crossed the Jordan River and entered the land of Israel. They brought with them the mishkan, a portable sanctuary that they had built in the wilderness according to God's instructions, and they continued their sacrificial rites. The Aron Kodesh—Holy Ark—first contained the Ten Commandments, and later the Torah. The Aron Kodesh was kept at Shiloh, and later at Kiryat Ye'arim, until King David brought it to Jerusalem in the tenth century B.C.E.[13] The First Holy Temple was built under the direction of David's son, Solomon. The priests offered sacrifices in the Holy Temple until the Babylonians destroyed it in 586 B.C.E. and took the Jewish people into captivity.

---

9 The Torah—also known as the Five Books of Moses—consists of the first five books of the Hebrew Bible described in Appendix B. In brief, the Torah contains 613 mitzvot—commandments—that are the basis of traditional Jewish life, together with stories about the creation of the world, the founding fathers and mothers of the Jewish people and numerous other peoples, Israelite slavery in Egypt; freedom from slavery, the parting of the sea, and the forty years of wandering in the wilderness—including receiving the Ten Commandments at Mount Sinai, and learning how to build a portable sanctuary that was assembled and used when the Israelites camped, and disassembled and carried when they wandered from place to place. At the end of the Torah, the Israelites are camped on the eastern shore of the Jordan River, prepared to enter the Land of Israel. Moses speaks to the Israelites for thirty-seven days and then he passes from this world. Deuteronomy, the fifth book of the Torah, contains his talk, his passing and burial, and the Israelites mourning and eulogizing him.
10 Genesis, Chapter 1.
11 On the new moon, the Sabbath and holy days, we have an additional worship service called musaf. Musaf means "additional" and is included in our worship in place of the additional sacrifices that were offered on these special days in the portable sanctuary in the wilderness, and later in the Holy Temple in Jerusalem.
12 Leviticus, Chapter 1, ff.
13 B.C.E. is an abbreviation for "Before the Common Era." B.C.E. is used by Jews, Hindus and others who do not count time from the birth of Jesus. (B.C.E. is used in place of "B.C." and C.E. is used in place of "A.D.")

Approximately fifty years later, in 538 B.C.E., King Cyrus united the Persians and Medes, and conquered Babylonia. King Cyrus—called Khusro in his native language—is believed to have been a Zoroastrian. It says in the Biblical Book of Chronicles that God roused the spirit of Cyrus, and Cyrus gave the Jewish people permission and encouragement to return to Jerusalem to rebuild the Temple and resettle the land.[14] Many did return, settled in the land, and rebuilt the Temple; but many others continued to live in Babylonia and elsewhere.

During the period of the Second Holy Temple, the priests once again offered daily sacrifices, additional sacrifices for the Sabbath, new moons and festivals, and sacrifices for special purposes. Individual and communal prayers evolved along side the sacrifices during the Second Temple period. After the Romans destroyed the Second Temple in 70 C.E., individual and communal worship evolved further and replaced the sacrificial rites, together with the practice of charity and deeds of loving kindness.

In Yiddish,[15] worship is called davvenen. When we davven, we focus on the words, pronunciation and meaning of our prayers, as well as on the nusach—the formulation of chanting or melody. In Hindu terms, we would call Jewish davvenen a jnana practice.[16] Davvenen has tremendous spiritual benefit for those who engage in it deeply, but because of its nature, real davvenen is available only to those with sufficient knowledge, capacity and commitment.

One may davven in Hebrew, or in any other language, but in general, the ability to read Hebrew in the original or in transliteration is central to davvenen. Davvenen is, therefore, not generally "user friendly" to those who cannot read Hebrew letters or Hebrew transliteration. However, one may nevertheless attend Jewish worship and enjoy the music, teachings and explanations, as well as the good feeling. Many also attend Jewish worship as guests for special occasions, such as a bar or bat mitzvah,[17] a baby naming or a synagogue celebration that precedes or follows a marriage[18]—called an Aufruf[19] or Shabbat Hatan.[20]

---

14 II Chronicles 36:22-23.

15 See the definition for "Yiddish" in the Glossary of Terms.

16 Jnana is of the mind or the intellect, and bhakti is of the heart. Also see "Jnana" in the Glossary of Terms.

17 "Bar" means "son" in Aramaic. Mitzvah means "commandment" in both Aramaic and Hebrew. Bar mitzvah is the attainment of religious adulthood by a Jewish young man; bat mitzvah is the similar attainment for a young lady. Bar mitzvah and bat mitzvah denote that the young person is now responsible for his or her own religious and spiritual practice.

18 There are many types of Jews. For purposes of delineating countries of origin, Hebrew pronunciation, foods, customs and ceremonies worship, we often speak of Ashkenazi, Sephardi and Mizrahi Jews, which are defined in the Glossary of Terms. The footnotes below describe the Ashkenazi, Sephardi and Mizrahi traditions for celebrating a marriage in the synagogue.

19 "Aufruf" is Yiddish, meaning "called up" and refers to the Ashkenazi custom of the groom being called to the Torah in the synagogue on the Sabbath before his wedding. While at the Torah, both groom and bride are blessed in honor of their upcoming marriage. In Conservative/Masorti, Reform/Progressive, Liberal, Reconstructionist and Renewal congregations, the bride may also be called to the Torah; and where gay and lesbian marriages are performed, two brides or two grooms may be called to the Torah.

20 "Shabbat Hatan" is Hebrew, meaning "Sabbath of the Groom" and refers to the Sephardi and Mizrahi custom of calling the groom to the Torah and blessing the bride and groom. Shabbat Hatan is held on the Sabbath after the marriage.

Davvenen is a very important part of Jewish religious and spiritual practice, and, as mentioned above, it was part of the replacement for the ancient sacrifices. However, the rabbis of the Talmud[21] were clear that prayer and practice, in and of themselves, do not entirely replace the sacrifices, and that how we treat one another must also be a part of the mix. Below are two Talmudic teachings on the subject. This first teaching is from the Jerusalem Talmud[22]:

> Rabbi Shmuel bar Nachmani said, "The Holy One said to [King] David: 'Solomon, your son, is building the Temple. Is this not for the purpose of offering sacrifices there? The justice and righteousness of your actions are more precious to Me than sacrifices.' And how do we know this? 'To do what is right and just is more desirable to Adonai[23] than sacrifice.[24]'"

This second teaching is from *Avot d'Rabbi Natan*[25]:

> Once, Rabban[26] Yochanan ben Zakkai was walking with his disciple, Rabbi Yehoshua, near Jerusalem after the destruction of the Temple. Rabbi Yehoshua looked at the Temple in ruins, and said: "Alas for us! The place that atoned for the sins of the people Israel[27]—through the ritual of animal sacrifice—lies in ruins!" Then Rabbi Yochanan ben Zakkai spoke to him these words of comfort: "Do not grieve, my son. There is another equally meritorious way of gaining atonement even though the Temple is destroyed. We can still gain atonement through deeds of lovingkindness." For it is written: "Lovingkindness I desire, not sacrifice."[28]

---

21 The *Talmud* is introduced in Chapter 2 of this book.
22 *Brachot* 2:1 [Jerusalem Talmud, *Tractate Brachot*, chapter 2, verse 1.] Quoted from the translation in *Siddur Sim Shalom for Weekdays* (New York: The Rabbinical Assembly; The United Synagogue of Conservative Judaism, 2005) 9.
23 Adonai is a Hebrew name of G-d.
24 "To do what is right and just is more desirable to Adonai than sacrifice" is from *Proverbs*, chapter 21, verse 3.
25 *Avot D'Rabbi Natan* 4:5. Quoted from the translation *Siddur Sim Shalom for Shabbat and Festivals* (New York: The Rabbinical Assembly; The United Synagogue of Conservative Judaism, 1998) 68. Additional Note: *Avot D'Rabbi Natan* is one of a series of books known as the Minor Tractates (Masekh'tot Ketanot). The Minor Tractates are not officially part of the Talmud, but they are generally included in the publication of most editions of the Talmud.
26 Rabban is a form of the title rabbi.
27 The "people Israel" (am Yisrael in Hebrew) means the Jewish people. The Jewish people are also called B'nay Yisrael, meaning Children of Israel.
28 "Loving kindness I desire, not sacrifice" is from Hosea 6:6. "Loving kindness" is generally written as two words, or a hyphenated word according to grammarians. I generally use it as two words in the text of this book. However, "lovingkindness" is sometimes spelled as one word with no hyphen in Jewish Bibles and prayer books, such as *Siddur Sim Shalom*, from which the above quote is cited.

Chapter 2

Jewish Sacred Texts

The Hebrew scriptures are known as Tanakh. Tanakh is an acronym; "T" stands for Torah; "N" stands for Nevi'im, meaning Prophets; and "K" stands for Ketuvim, meaning Writings. Appendix B contains a list of the books of the Tanakh and a brief description of each. **The Tanakh is called the "Written Torah," and all other Jewish spiritual and religious teachings are called the "Oral Torah."**

The word "Torah" shares its linguistic root with the Hebrew words moreh and morah, meaning male and female teacher; horeh and horah, meaning male and female parent; and hora'ah, meaning teaching. Thus, the Torah is the "Teaching of the Divine Parent." Nevertheless, Torah is more commonly translated as "the Law," and the Jewish people are known as the People of the Book, with "Book" implying "Book of Laws," because, as mentioned previously, in addition to countless stories, the Torah contains the 613 mitzvot (commandments), which form the basis of Jewish law.[29]

The early rabbis and sages hoped—and intended—to keep the Oral Torah as a fluid transmission recited from mouth to ear, and transmitted from heart to heart. This would have allowed the Oral Torah to evolve from generation to generation as a living breathing renewing body of sacred wisdom and spiritual and religious teaching and guidance. However, the persecution of Jews during the Roman occupation undermined the transmission of the Oral Torah and threatened Judaism with extinction. To counter the threat of extinction, the rabbis and sages began and continued a process of writing down and codifying the Oral Torah.

During the Roman occupation, study of Torah was forbidden upon pain of death and retribution against one's family. Many Jews were tortured and murdered for being caught studying Torah. The spouse might also be murdered, and the children might also be punished, such as a daughter being consigned to a brothel. The Romans also forbade the ordaining of rabbis. The punishment for ordaining a rabbi included murdering the ordaining rabbi, the newly ordained rabbi, and all the residents of the city where the ordination took place, as well as the destruction of the city and all of its buildings and adjacent properties.[30] It was the hope and intention of the Roman Empire that these policies would eradicate Judaism.

Rabbi Yehudah ben Bava lived in the second century of the Common Era. He and his colleagues knew that it would be impossible for Judaism to continue without spiritual teachers so they trained candidates for the rabbinate in secret. Rabbi Yehudah ben Bava and others took five or six trained candidates and ordained them at a low point in a valley half way between two mountains that lay between the cities of Usha and Shefaram. The site was chosen because there were no people living in the valley or on the mountains and they hoped that there would be no destruction of Jewish cities or murdering of Jewish residents should the ordination be discovered.

---

29 In a vacuum, it may seem that 613 mitzvot (commandments) is a large and onerous number. Consider, however, that the California Constitution is so voluminous, and contains so many laws, that it fills an entire room in Sacramento (California's capital). Similarly, the Revenue and Taxation Code of most countries contains more than 613 laws and sub-laws.

30 *Avodah Zarah* 8b [*Babylonian Talmud*, Tractate *Avodah Zarah* (Idol Worship), page 8, side b.] Also *Sanhedrin* 14a.

Shortly after the ordination, Roman troops appeared on the hilltops, and those gathered for the ordination realized that their presence had been detected. "Run my children," said Rabbi Yehudah. "What about you?" asked his disciples. "I will lie still like a stone not overturned," said Rabbi Yehudah. Miraculously, the five or six newly minted rabbis escaped. It says in the Talmud that the Romans cast three hundred iron spears into Rabbi Yehudah ben Bava's body, making it like a sieve.[31] Out of deference to the great Rabbi Yehudah ben Bava, the Talmud does not mention the names of the others who joined him at the ordination, nor does it further recount their fate. Rabbi Yehudah ben Bava and his colleagues risked their lives in the hope that the newly minted rabbis would survive and serve the next generation.[32]

As Jewish spiritual teachers faced torture and death at the hands of the Romans, they continued to adhere to the spiritual principles by which they had lived. This is illustrated in the story of Rabbi Yehudah ben Bava above and in that of Rabbi Hanania ben Teradion below.[33] According to the Talmud,[34] Rabbi Hanania ben Teradion sat and studied Torah, publicly gathered assemblies and kept a scroll of the Torah in his bosom. The Romans arrested Rabbi Hanania, wrapped him in the Scroll of the Torah from which he studied, placed bundles of branches around him and set the branches on fire. They then placed over his heart tufts of wool that had been soaked in water so that he should not die quickly.[35]

Rabbi Hanania's daughter[36] exclaimed, "Father, oh that I should see you in this state!" Rabbi Hanania replied, "If it were I alone being burnt, it would have been a thing difficult to bear; but now that I am burning together with the Scroll of the Torah, he who will have regard for the plight of the Torah will also have regard for my plight." Rabbi Hanania's disciples called out, "Rabbi, what do you see?" Rabbi Hanania answered, "The parchments are being burned,[37] but the letters are soaring on high."

"Then open your mouth," cried the disciples to Rabbi Hanania, "so that the fire may enter you." Rabbi Hanania replied, "Let Him who gave me take me away, but one should not injure oneself." Rabbi Hanania's Executioner then said to him, "Rabbi, if I raise the flame and take away the tufts of wool from over your heart, will you cause me to enter into the world to come?" "Yes," said Rabbi Hanania. "Then swear unto me," said the Executioner, and Rabbi Hanania swore it. The Executioner then raised the flame and removed the tufts of wool from over Rabbi Hanania's heart, and his soul quickly departed. The Executioner then jumped and threw himself into the fire. And a bat kol [a divine feminine voice] was heard exclaiming, "Rabbi Hanania ben Teradion and the Executioner have been assigned to the world to come." When Rabbi Yehudah HaNasi[38] heard this story, he wept and said, "One may acquire eternal life in a single moment, another after many years."

---

31 *Sanhedrin* 14a. Also *Avodah Zarah* 8b. (The story is told in both Tractates of the *Babylonian Talmud.*)
32 Rabbi Yehudah ben Bava was approximately 80 years old at the time of these ordinations.
33 Rabbi Hanania ben Teradion is referred to both as Hanania and Hanina.
34 *Avodah Zarah* 18a. [*Babylonian Talmud, Tractate Avodah Zarah*, page 18, side a.]
35 The Talmud tells us that the sentence included the torture and murder of Rabbi Hanania ben Teradion, the slaying of his wife, and the placing of one of his daughters in a brothel. *Avodah Zarah* 18a.
36 This is believed to be another daughter of Rabbi Hanania ben Teradion. Perhaps it was the famous Beruriah, the wife of Rabbi Meir, who was a scholar in her own right.
37 The Torah is written on parchment made of the hide of a kosher animal. Each piece of parchment is like a very large sheet of paper, such as the kind used by architects. When the writing of a Torah scroll is completed, the parchments are sewn and taped together to form a scroll, and rolled onto two wooden handles, called atzay chayyim, meaning trees of life.
38 Rabbi Yehudah HaNasi (Judah the Prince) was the redactor of the Mishna as explained later in this chapter.

In light of the calamities that befell Rabbi Yehudah ben Bava, Rabbi Hanania ben Taradion and many other scholars and sages—and in light of the fear that these calamities instilled—Judaism was in danger of extinction. Rabbis feared that it would be impossible to sustain the Oral Torah for a later resurgence of Judaism without writing it down. They were caught in a quandary. Not writing down the Oral Torah put Judaism at risk of extinction, and writing down the Oral Torah put the spiritual teachers of the time at risk of torture and murder. So they waited and studied and taught the Written Torah and the Oral Torah in secret, and scholars and students were caught from time to time, tortured and killed.

Rabbi Yehudah HaNasi ("Judah, the Prince") was a great Torah scholar, a strong community leader, and a man of great personal wealth. He was respected in the Jewish community and among the Roman authorities. When the Roman Emperor Hadrian died in 139 C.E.[39] there was an improvement in the treatment of the Jewish community. Toward the end of the second century C.E., Rabbi Yehudah HaNasi befriended the Roman authorities and there are legends that he consulted with Roman authorities on matters of Roman state policy.[40]

Rabbi Yehudah HaNasi knew that darker times lay ahead and there was a danger that the oral tradition would be forgotten due to the persecution of those who studied it. To avert such danger, Rabbi Yehudah HaNasi compiled the Mishna, which is a series of brief teachings that illuminate and clarify the laws and stories of the Written Torah, and their application to daily life and practice. The Mishna was completed in approximately 200 C.E.

The Talmud

The Mishna was written in Hebrew. Over the centuries, two commentaries on the Mishna were written in Aramaic interspersed with Hebrew. Both commentaries are known as the Gemara. One Gemara was written in Tiberias, a city located on the banks of the Sea of Galilee in Northern Israel, and is known as the Palestinian Gemara. Due to continued Roman persecution, the Palestinian Gemara was never completed. The incomplete Palestinian Gemara, written in Aramaic, together with the Mishna, written in Hebrew, is known as the Jerusalem Talmud or the Palestinian Talmud. The Jerusalem Talmud was published in the fourth century C.E.

The second Gemara was written and compiled in the Academies at Sura and Pumpedita—and elsewhere—in Babylonia, which is part of modern Iraq. The scholars of the Babylonian Gemara included descendants of those who did not return to Jerusalem after the Persians conquered Babylonia, descendants of those who returned to Babylonia from Israel and elsewhere over the centuries, and descendants of some who escaped the Roman occupation. The Babylonian Gemara written in Aramaic, together with the Mishna in Hebrew, is known as the Babylonian Talmud. The Babylonian Talmud was published toward the end of the sixth century C.E.

---

39 As explained in an earlier footnote, C.E. stands for "Common Era" and B.C.E. stands for "Before the Common Era." These terms are used by Jews, Hindus and others who do not count time from the birth of Jesus. (C.E. is used in place of "A.D.," which stands for Anno Domini, meaning "year of our Lord." B.C.E. is used in place of "B.C.," which stands for "before Christ.")

40 *Encyclopaedia Judaica* (Jerusalem: Keter Publishing House, 1996), Vol. 10, 367-71. Rabbi Berel Wein, *Echoes of Glory, The Story of the Jews in the Classical Era 350 B.C.E. to 750 C.E* (Mesora Pubns Ltd., 1995) 224. Cited by Rabbi Ken Spiro, "Crash Course #39: The Talmud," *Aish HaTorah*, August 4, 2001, August 11, 2011 <http://www.aish.com/jl/h/cc/48948646.html>.

Over the centuries, numerous scholars wrote commentaries on the Talmud. A traditional page of Talmud has Mishna and Gemara in the middle of the page with various commentaries in the margins surrounding it. These include the commentaries of Rashi, who lived in France in the eleventh century, Maimonides who lived in Spain and Egypt in the thirteenth century, and a commentary known as Tosafot, meaning "additions," compiled from the teachings of a number of scholars. Rabbi Adin Steinsaltz, a Chabad Rabbi based in Jerusalem, has recently completed a new column of commentary on the Talmud that includes a translation of the Aramaic into Hebrew in order to render the Gemara accessible to modern Hebrew speakers. Rabbi Steinsaltz has also translated the Talmud into English. There are many other English translations, as well as translations into other languages.

Other Rabbinic Literature

As mentioned earlier, the Jewish people are known as the People of the Book. In the centuries during and after the commentaries on the Talmud were crafted, Jewish scholars, mystics and sages transmitted teachings to their students and followers. Some wrote down their teachings while others had their teachings recorded by students. Many such commentaries are written in Hebrew interspersed with Aramaic. There are also commentaries written in Arabic, Spanish, Italian, English and other languages spoken where mystics and scholars lived and taught.

Codes

As mentioned at the beginning of this chapter, the Written Torah contains 613 mitzvot, or commandments. These mitzvot are discussed, interpreted and expanded upon in the Talmud and its commentaries as well as elsewhere in rabbinic literature. The Shulchan Arukh, meaning Set Table, was compiled by Rabbi Joseph Caro in the fifteenth century C.E. and is a kind of encyclopedia of Jewish law that draws upon previous sources from the Written Torah forward. The Shulchan Arukh is considered to this day to be a standard in the codification of Jewish Law. There are many other texts on Jewish law written by Maimonides and others that—together with the Shulchan Arukh—are called codes of Jewish Law, or simply "codes" for short.

Mystical Texts

A number of Jewish mystical texts have appeared over the centuries. There is a small book, known as the *Sefer Yetzirah* (the Book of Formation, or the Book of Creation), attributed by some to Abraham, the father of Judaism, and by some to Rabbi Akiva. The *Sefer Yetzirah* pairs the letters of the Hebrew alphabet with names of God, planets, constellations and parts of the human body. (See Appendix D.)

Sefer HaBahir may be translated as Book of the Clarity or Book of the Illumination. *Sefer HaBahir* is a short mystical text published in the first century C.E. Many attribute the text to Rabbi Nehunia ben HaKana whose teachings are also found in the Talmud. However, according to historians, it is likely that *Sefer HaBahir* is actually a compilation of the teachings of many mystics, including Rabbi Nehunia ben HaKana and some of his students. *Sefer HaBahir* is one of the earliest, if not *the* earliest, Jewish written reference that openly discusses the transmigration of souls, or reincarnation.[41]

---

41 Aryeh Kaplan, *The HaBahir* (York Beach, Maine: Samuel Weiser, Inc., 1989), 70-72, 77-78. The foregoing page numbers from Rabbi Kaplan's book are references to *Sefer HaBahir*, Part One, paragraphs 184 and 195.

In the Mishna, it says that Reb Nehunia ben HaKana used to say a prayer as he entered the Beit HaMidrash (House of Study), and a short prayer as he left it. They asked Reb Nehunia ben HaKana about these prayers and he explained: "When I enter [the House of Study], I pray that no offence should occur through me, and when I leave, I give thanks for my portion."[42]

The *Zohar* (Book of Splendor) is a multi-volume mystical commentary on the Torah written in Aramaic interspersed with Hebrew. The *Zohar* is attributed to Rabbi Shimon bar Yochai and his contemporaries and is one of the most complex and valuable texts of Jewish Kabbalah. Rabbi Shimon bar Yochai lived in the second century C.E. during the Roman occupation, and he and his contemporaries are quoted at length in the *Zohar*. There are many scholars who believe that the *Zohar* was written in the second century and hidden for over a thousand years until it appeared in Spain in the twelfth century. Because of its late appearance however, and also because of references in the text that may be attributed to knowledge of later resources within and beyond Judaism, many scholars assert that the *Zohar* was written around the twelfth century by mystics who withheld their own identity and presented the teachings in the name of their ancient teachers, whom they channeled. The modern Jewish scholar and mystic, Daniel Matt, is in the process of retranslating the *Zohar* into English. He has already published several volumes with commentary and hopes to complete the translation of the entire *Zohar* during his lifetime.[43]

In the thirteenth century, Rabbi Abraham Abulafia wrote a number of mystical texts. His work was of particular interest to Murshid Samuel L. Lewis[44]—whom those in the Sufi Ruhaniat International call Murshid Sam—possibly because Abulafia was known to have been in contact with Sufi mystics of his time. One of the practices given by Rabbi Abulafia is discussed in Chapter 8 of this book.

There are also many other texts that describe, define and provide a window into Jewish mysticism and Kabbalah.

---

42 *Mishna Brachot* 4:2 [Mishna on Blessings, chapter 4, second mishna]. Also *Brachot* 28b. [*Babylonian Talmud (Gemara), Tractate Brachot*, page 28, side b.]

43 *The Zohar*, Pritzker Edition, Volume 1, Daniel Matt, editor (Stanford, California: Stanford University Press, 2004).

44 Murshid Samuel L. Lewis was raised in a Reform Jewish family. He became a mystic, studying Sufism, Buddhism and many other spiritual paths, and he was the founder of the Sufi Ruhaniat International.

Chapter 3

Rekindling Judaism After the Holocaust

In the Biblical Book of Esther[45] it says "Layehudim hayeta orah v'simcha v'sasson viyeqar," which means the Jewish people had light and happiness and joy and preciousness. At the end of the Sabbath, the ritual of Havdallah is performed with a candle, wine—or other liquid—and spices. During Havdallah, participants begin a shift from the consciousness of restful other worldliness to the consciousness of work, school and engaging in tikkun olam—helping to make the world a better place.

Shabbat is the Jewish Sabbath, which begins on Friday evening at sundown and continues until after dark on Saturday night. Shabbat is a spiritual retreat in the midst of life in the world, when we are invited to experience our divinity and enjoy earthly delights in the same time and space. It is a time to experience unity between God transcendent and God in creation while spending time with loved ones and friends. It is a time to study for its own sake without writing down the fruits for later;[46] a time to pray and sing without having to watch the clock in order not to be late; a time to walk without destination; to dance without escorting a bride and groom; to take a break from grieving even when the loss is fresh; and to taste a world where one does not need to worry about how the rent or mortgage will be paid.

During Havdallah, as we prepare for the upcoming week, we recite the above phrase from the Book of Esther, and we add "keyn tih'yeh lanu," so may it be for us. The Jewish people had light and happiness and joy and preciousness; so may it be for us. Reb Nachman of Breslov said, "mitzvah gedolah lih'yot b'simcha tamid," which means it is a great mitzvah (commandment) to always be in [a state of] joy. It is noteworthy that Reb Nachman himself suffered from depression. So practicing joy—which Reb Nachman is said to have practiced himself, and given to his disciples and the world—was a challenge for him; it did not come easily.

Reb Nachman taught that when a difficult time arises, the only thing to do is be happy. Guin Miller used to say that joy is the natural state.[47] In the late 1960's and early 1970's, Murshid Samuel Lewis was with his young disciples, many of whom have evolved over the years to become spiritual teachers and guides in the Sufi Ruhaniat International and elsewhere. As the festival of Simchat Torah was approaching,[48] Murshid Sam would say, "We need more simchas and less Torah!" (Simchas is Yiddish for joyous occasions.) Murshid Sam's quip was apt since Simchat Torah is a time to dance, sing, carouse and celebrate. Yes, we do read from the end of the Torah and the beginning of the Torah

---

45 Esther 8:16.

46 There are many sacred Jewish texts that were written by one of the disciples of a great teacher. The disciple would hear a talk on the Sabbath or a festival and wait to write down the teachings at the conclusion of the holy day. These remembered teachings might be interspersed with teachings that the master gave on ordinary days when notes could be taken.

47 Guin Miller (1904-1992) and her husband Joe Miller (1904-1992) were spiritual teachers at the San Francisco Lodge of the Theosophical Society for many decades. There were also Buddhist Dharma Masters and ministers in the United Church of Christ. Joe was also a student of Christian Qabbalah and he served as a spiritual uncle to the teachers of the Sufi Ruhaniat International.

48 Simchat Torah, which literally means "Joy of Torah" is a festival that falls at the end of the seven day autumn festival of Sukkot, and its accompanying Shmini Atzeret (literally "eighth [day] of gathering").

to symbolize that Torah study is continuous; no sooner do we come to its end, than we begin to read it again. However, beyond festival worship and chanting from the Torah, there are no sermons, no classes, and no long discussions on Simchat Torah. Instead, there is dancing and singing and drinking and carousing and being silly.

In the 1990's, there was a synagogue not far from where I live where members wore raincoats on Simchat Torah morning and when the words "mashiv haruach umorid hagashem" were recited, they would take out their squirt guns and spray one another. "Mashiv haruach umorid hagashem" means, "Who brings the wind and causes the rain to fall." This is a prayer that we recite every day during every Amidah (silent devotion), beginning with the day before Simchat Torah and continuing until Passover, because, in the northern hemisphere, that is the season when we need a great deal of precipitation for the plants to grow and the land to be nurtured by moisture.[49]

The Amidah is one of the most spiritually focused and serious times during davvenen (Jewish worship), requiring even more presence and focus than the recitation of the Shema.[50] Right there, during the Amidah on Simchat Torah,[51] members of this mainstream synagogue recite "mashiv haruach umorid hagashem" and then they take out their squirt guns and have a water fight!

When I was purchasing our first Torah scroll for Or Shalom Jewish Community,[52] the scribe, an Ultra Orthodox Jew, told me that if the Torah were ever damaged due to wine or wear, he or one of the scribes in his company would be glad to repair it for us. "Damaged by wine?" I asked, chuckling. "On Simchas Torah!" he said, "Remember! We make Kiddush right there at the Torah!"[53]

Murshid Sam's teaching about more simchas (joyous occasions) and less Torah was a double entendre. Murshid Sam lived through the Holocaust, and he prayed mightily for the souls who were suffering through torture, starvation and death. The Judaism of the years after World War II had become dry and brittle, forced and fraught with paradox. Six million Jews had been murdered, along with six million others. The six million others included two million Polish Catholics, seventy-five percent of the world's Roma and Sinti population,[54] and hundreds of thousands of Seventh Day Adventists,[55] gays and lesbians, the physically, mentally and emotionally disabled, political dissidents, and those who risked their lives to hide and save Jews and others.

---

49 During the rest of the year, we acknowledge G-d as "morid hatal," which means "Who causes the dew to fall."

50 In modern Jewish worship, many participants focus most carefully and deeply when reciting the Shema. However, there are many who focus even more carefully and deeply during the Amidah. There are teachings in the Talmud and elsewhere to support this hierarchy of practice. In Sufi terms, one might say that the Shema is a Zikr and the Amidah is a practice of worshipping in the state of Zat or Aklak Allah, which is, being—or acting as though we are—in the Divine Presence, or in the Abode of G-d.

51 As explained in Chapter 1 of this book, musaf—meaning addition—is the name of the worship service added after shacharit—the morning service—on the Sabbath, festivals and the new moon.

52 The author was the founding rabbi of Or Shalom Jewish Community in San Francisco.

53 Kiddush, meaning sanctification, is the practice of blessing and drinking wine or grape juice as part of the sanctification of the Sabbath or a festival. Kiddush is discussed in Chapter 24.

54 Roma and Sinti are two populations who were formerly known as Gypsies.

55 Seventh Day Adventists were singled out by the Germans for torture and murder, because they observe the Sabbath on Saturday, which coincides with the Jewish Sabbath.

The six million Jews included one and one-half million children, and eighty to ninety percent of the world's Jewish spiritual teachers. The world's Jewish population prior to the Holocaust was just under eighteen million, and Europe's Jewish population was approximately nine million. Thus, the overall loss of Jewish lives during the Holocaust had a tremendous impact on the Jewish community at large.

The greatest impact, however, was on Jewish spirituality. Many Jews had left Europe in the centuries prior to the Holocaust, looking for a better life. However, the promise of better livelihood and a safer environment free of persecution did not have the same draw for Jewish spiritual teachers as it had for other Jews. Many teachers were concerned that assimilation in the west would draw Jews away from their religious practice. Frequently, these teachers chose to stay in Europe to serve those who did not or could not leave. During the Holocaust, the Nazis often singled out Jewish leaders for arrest, torture and murder. There are also many stories of rabbis and other teachers who were offered documents and transportation to escape suffering before and during the war, but refused the opportunity and instead remained in ghettos, concentrations camps and elsewhere to help those around them to endure their suffering.

There was a rabbi in Baden bei Wien, a suburb of Vienna, who was beaten to death in front of his wife and four year old son for the crime of delivering food to wives and children who faced starvation because the husband, and primary bread winner of the family, had been sent to a concentration camp following the German annexation of Austria in 1938.[56] That rabbi's name was Moishele.[57] I learned his niggun[58] from Rabbi Daniel Lev who learned it from Rabbi Shlomo Carlebach, who learned it at age nine from Reb Moishele just a few days before Reb Moishele was killed.

In the years following the Holocaust, Jewish theologians were at a loss to explain how God could have allowed a tragedy of such magnitude. Why practice a faith that led to millions of men, women and children being murdered in mass graves and gas chambers? How does one practice joy when one cannot stop crying? In my own family, my father's mother and thirty-one of her children and grandchildren were murdered.[59] Not only did the Nazis and their collaborators humiliate, torture and kill, but they specifically chose Jewish holidays for mass killings and forced evacuations to concentration camps. Rosh HaShanah, Yom Kippur, Pesach and other holidays were Nazi favorites for atrocities, and they delighted in the desecration of Torah scrolls and other Jewish ritual objects. When the Nazis took over a town in Poland that had a large enough Jewish population to warrant the creation

---

56 The first concentration camps were constructed and became operational in 1933, shortly after Hitler came to power. By the time World War II began in 1939, tens of thousands of Jews, political dissidents and others had already been imprisoned and tortured. Some were murdered, some were freed, and some remained imprisoned when the war began.

57 According to Reb Zalman—who knew Rabbi Moishele personally—Reb Moishele Heschel was the son of Kopitchenitzer Rebbe, Rabbi Avraham Yehuoshua Heschel. Rabbi Avraham was a cousin of Professor Rabbi Abraham Joshua Heschel who served on the faculty of the Jewish Theological Seminary, and marched for the rights of people of color with Dr. Martin Luther King, Jr.

58 Niggun literally means melody in both Hebrew and Yiddish. In Hebrew, it is pronounced with emphasis on the last syllable, whereas, in Yiddish, it is pronounced with emphasis on the first syllable. To be a niggun, a song must have two distinct musical parts. When one sings a chant that has one musical part, one may continue to sing while spacing out, but with a niggun, one needs to pay attention to change ever upcoming change in melody. This helps us to bring our wandering mind back into focus.

59 My family lost over one hundred adults, teenagers and children during the Holocaust, including my paternal grandmother, aunts, uncles, first cousins and the siblings of my grandparents and their descendants.

of a ghetto, they rounded up the rabbis and other spiritual leaders, together with the President of the Jewish community, forced them at gun point into a Jewish community center, poured a flammable liquid around the perimeter and burned the building to the ground, together with the leaders, the Torah scrolls, prayer books and other religious objects while community members were forced, at gunpoint, to look on.

Where Torah scrolls were not burned, some scrolls were taken to camps where prisoners were forced to cut patterns from the lettering and sew them into the soles of shoes made for the Germans, so Germans could walk on the holy letters. My son Josh found one such Torah scroll on display at Yad VaShem in Jerusalem some months before his bar mitzvah. Unbelievably, the Torah was open to the beginning of the Book of Leviticus, which was Josh's parasha—the portion of Torah that he would read and discuss on his bar mitzvah. Josh chanted the words prior to the gaping, footprint shaped, holes and then he made his way through the section with the footprints, relying upon memory for the missing words, as I stood near him and wept.

In the village where my father was born and raised, men ages 15 to 45 and women ages 14 to 40 were rounded up and taken to concentration camps on Hoshana Rabbah, the last day of Sukkot, the festival when we build huts and eat and celebrate in them to remember the wandering in the wilderness that followed Israelite slavery. Two days later, on Simchat Torah, the Nazis came back and liquidated the ghetto, taking everyone to concentration camps except those whom they murdered on the spot. My paternal grandmother, for whom I am named, was killed on Simchat Torah.[60]

The Inayati Sufis were also deeply affected by the Holocaust, most particularly by the brutal torture and murder of Hazrat Inayat Khan's daughter, Noor-un-Nisa Inayat Khan, who was a British spy in Vichy France before being captured by the Germans. After endless brutality in prison, Noor-un-Nisa was deported to Dachau where she was again tortured and then shot.

Healing takes time. Many Holocaust survivors and families of the victims could not bring themselves to speak about their experiences following the war. After decades, and with a change in world culture about discussing these atrocities, many found their voice and gave video interviews. Tens of thousands of these videos were recorded by the Shoah Oral History Project, and are archived at the University of Southern California in Los Angeles and at Yale University in New Haven, Connecticut, as well as in Holocaust museums and on websites. These archives provide information and courage to historians and educators. Sadly, genocide was a major phenomenon of the twentieth century. Genocide continues, as of this writing, in the Democratic Republic of the Congo in central Africa, formerly called Zaire. Over four million have been murdered. There are nine million refugees. Rape is said to be as common as death. Who is speaking about it? Who even knows? May the people of the DRC soon have peace in their land and healing from their suffering. Indeed, may the people of all lands where tyranny rules soon have peace and healing.

The rekindling of the light of Judaism in the shadow of the Holocaust is a slow organic process—and there is tremendous progress—but it is no wonder that young Jews of the 1960's and 1970's left Judaism in droves for the spiritual paths of Sufism, Buddhism, yoga and meditation where joy abounds and spiritual teachers are filled with realization, faith and joy. There are also many Jews who continue to practice Judaism and explore spiritual alternatives simultaneously.

---

60 The story of my paternal grandmother's death is retold in Pamela Frydman Baugh, "A Blessing From My Grandmother," *Zeek Magazine,* online edition, October 2009 <http://zeek.forward.com/articles/115540/>.

Rabbi David Weiss Halivni was born and raised in Hungary and suffered at the hands of the Nazis. He wrote a book, which he concludes as follows:

> Prayer, like any other religious behavior, does not ask for change, even in the face of the terrible tragedy that eclipsed our generation; religiously we act as if we are still under the mantle of the Revelation at Sinai.[61] Nevertheless, personal emphasis and intention, [called] *kavannah,* is an indispensable accompaniment of prayer, and this accompaniment ought to be different today than in the past, prior to Auschwitz.
>
> In the past we extolled the glory of God's power over our limited powers.... Today, it is more suitable for us to add emphasis and *kavannah* to the [following] prayer[62] ... recited three times a day, [that reads]: "*We acknowledge* (that is the right translation) that You are the strength of our own life and our saving shield. In every generation we will thank You and recount Your graces for our lives that are in Your charge, for our souls that are in Your care." This prayer emphasizes God's closeness to us, an assurance that His alienation will not last forever....
>
> Only a prayer that pleads that God will retake the reign He forfeited for the sake of granting free will to sinful human creatures; only a prayer that pleads for the curtailment of God's ... withdrawal by means of which He was able to create a finite and corruptible world; only a prayer that acknowledges that God's purpose of creation is for us to worship Him, to obey Him, to be close to Him, only prayers like these may heal the terrible wound that recent history has inflicted on us and shorten the distance between the two major events in Jewish history: Sinai and Auschwitz. Amen.[63]

When Noor-un-Nisa Inayat Khan was about to be shot by her Nazi handlers in Dachau, she called out in French, "Vive la liberté!" This means, "Long live liberty!" Noor-un-Nisa was the daughter of one of the greatest Sufis of the twentieth century. The authors of her biography entitled, *The Spy Princess,*[64] say that her tormentors described her as different from any other prisoner, and fellow inmates spoke of her silence in the face of torture, and her calling out "abba"[65] softly during solitude, and her crying softly in the night. Her biographers speculate that Noor-un-Nisa was calling out to her father;[66] but abba is also a name of God, and I wonder if Noor-un-Nisa's strength and courage might have perhaps come from both calling upon the divine and upon her beloved father of blessed memory. In either case, Noor-un-Nisa's last words were not abba or a name of God; it was liberty that she called.

---

61 The "revelation at Sinai" refers to the Israelites receiving of the Ten Commandments and the Torah at Mount Sinai seven weeks after leaving Egypt and crossing the sea. The story is recounted in the Torah. *Exodus* 19:1-20:23.

62 "We acknowledge that You" is Rabbi Weiss Halivni's translation of "modim anachnu lach." These are the opening words of a prayer that appears toward the end of the Amidah/Silent Devotion. As we recite the phrase "modim anachnu lach," we bow in gratitude, and we continue with the words of the prayer that speak of our involvement with God and God's involvement in our lives.

63 David Weiss Halivni, *Breaking the Tablets, Jewish Theology After the Shoah* (Maryland: Rowman & Littlefield Publishers, Inc., 2001) 125-126.

64 Shrabani Basu, *The Spy Princess, The Life of Noor Inayat Khan* (The History Press Ltd., 2006) Prologue.

65 Abba means father.

66 Basu 61.

Rabbi Yitzchak Greenberg is a scholar, mystic and historian. Reb Yitz teaches that since the Holocaust, we must find God within, and realize that when we are suffering, it is God who is suffering, and when we have joy, it is God who is having joy. This teaching of Reb Yitz is closer to the spiritual goal of realizing our oneness with God, whereas Rabbi Halivni's teaching and Noor-un-Nisa's last words call out more from the human side of consciousness; suffering is human, even as we learn to overcome it through union with the divine.

Years ago, Hakim Sauluddin and Aslan Sattler traveled together to the site of the Bergen-Belsen Concentration Camp and found it to be very holy. Rabbi Aryeh Hirschfield, of blessed memory, said that when he visited Bergen-Belsen, he experienced a power and holiness that he had never experienced at any other time in his life.[67]

May we never experience the agony that leaves one feeling abandoned by the One who created and sustains us and brings us to this moment. May the memory of the six million Jews and six million others be a blessing for all time, together with the memory of the fallen soldiers and spies and innocents who lost their lives in that terrible war, and in all wars.

---

67 Verbal introduction to the "Healing Song," *Let the Healing Begin* by Rabbi Aryeh Hirschfield, cassette tape.

Chapter 4

Jewish Aramaic and Sacred Hebrew

Jewish Aramaic

Jewish Aramaic has evolved into separate dialects from the Aramaic studied and used in Aramaic speaking Christian communities over the centuries. Jewish Babylonian Aramaic is of the family of Eastern Aramaic.[68] Jewish Palestinian Aramaic is of the family of Western Aramaic.[69] Jewish Aramaic contains a great many words and linguistic patterns related to Hebrew. The Aramaic sacred words and phrases in this book are Jewish Aramaic.[70]

Sacred Hebrew

Hebrew is known as "leshon hakodesh," the holy tongue, and is the primary language of the Hebrew Bible and Jewish prayer. Because Hebrew is a holy tongue, Ultra Orthodox Jews—called haridim—do not use Hebrew for teaching or for ordinary conversations. Instead, they teach and hold ordinary conversations in Yiddish—or in the tongue of the country in which they reside—and they reserve Hebrew for prayer and study of the Written Torah and Oral Torah.

Clearly, there are other holy tongues used in scriptures and prayers by peoples of other faiths. Murshid Sam states in his writings that Hebrew, Arabic and Sanskrit are holy tongues. I have also heard it said recently, by an Ultra Orthodox (haredi) rabbi, that Yiddish is becoming a holy tongue (leshon kodesh) through its use over the years in the teaching and discussion of holy matters.

The Hebrew letters are considered to have a life of their own, and are associated with different energies. Pronouncing Hebrew letters one by one, and in combination, is considered to impart spiritual magnetism,[71] and that is one of the main reasons that Hebrew is called a leshon kodesh. Those who davven (worship) in Hebrew, as well as those who practice the recitation of Hebrew sacred phrases, are aware of this reality.

Because Hebrew is a leshon hakodesh, we may derive spiritual benefit from reciting a Hebrew word or phrase just once. When we davven, we move from word to word with very little repetition, and there is great spiritual benefit. In *Likutei Maharan*,[72] Rabbi Nachman of Breslov uses the analogy of each Hebrew letter being like a flower. As we formulate a word with our mouth and our intention, we create a bouquet of flowering letters. As we move from word to word, our phrases become larger bouquets.

---

68 A relevant dictionary for Jewish Eastern Aramaic is Michael Sokoloff, editor, *A Dictionary of Jewish Babylonian Aramaic of the Talmudic and Geonic Periods* (Ramat Gan, Israel: Bar Ilan University Press, 2002).

69 A relevant dictionary for Jewish Western Aramaic is: Michael Sokoloff, editor. *A Dictionary of Jewish Palestinian Aramaic of the Byzantine Period* (Ramat Gan, Israel: Bar Ilan University Press, 1990).

70 Another important Jewish Aramaic dictionary is Marcus Jastrow, editor. *A Dictionary of the Targumim, the Talmud Bavli and Yerushalmi, and the Midrashic Literature* (Brooklyn, New York: Traditional Press, Inc.). It is an older resource than Michael Sokoloff's dictionaries and does not delineate the dialects of Aramaic or Hebrew of the words its defines, but it is, nevertheless, a helpful resource for those studying Talmud and midrashic literature.

71 Spiritual magnetism is an expression meaning spiritual energy.

72 Rabbi Nahman of Breslov, *Sefer Likutey Maharan* (Book of Gleanings of Our Teacher Reb Nahman) (Jerusalem: Publishing Fund of the Chassidim of Breslov, 5738 – 1978).

With proper concentration, we may assemble and offer these flowering bouquets to God, letter by letter, word by word, and paragraph by paragraph, as we davven.[73]

One may also derive spiritual benefit by repeating a single Hebrew word or phrase just as one may derive benefit through the repetition of sacred words and phrases in Sanskrit, Latin and Arabic. Indeed, English is also becoming a sacred language. Those who recite the Sufi Invocation, and the Sufi prayers Saum, Salat, Nayaz and Khatum[74] in English, as well as those who recite Christian hymns or Buddhist Sutras in English may feel this keenly. The spiritual magnetism of these prayers may also be experienced when reciting them just once, and without any accompanying recitation in another language.

---

73 *Sefer Likutey Maharan.*
74 The prayer that Inayati Sufis call the Sufi Invocation as well as the prayers Saum, Salat, Nayaz and Khatum were given in English by Pir-O-Murshid Hazrat Inayat Khan, a native of India, who brought a universal form of Sufism to the West in 1910.

Chapter 5

Gematria and the Counting of Jewish Sacred Phrases

Each Hebrew letter has a numeric value. The Hebrew word chai—meaning life—is composed of the letters chet and yod.[75] The numeric value of chet is eight and yod is ten, so the numeric value of the word chai is eighteen. Jewish people sometimes give chai dollars, or multiples of chai dollars—or franc or Deutsche Mark or shekel or other currency—as charitable donations, or gifts for special and sacred occasions. The intention of giving chai or multiples of chai is that the gift or donation may carry the blessing of enlivening the giver or the recipient and or the organization that will derive benefit from it.

The study of Hebrew numerology is called gematria. Gematria is complex and well developed, with sacred phrases of all kinds from scripture and elsewhere being numerically equated with one another to identify commonality of meaning and intention, and to derive spiritual understanding. Gematria may be used to understand the relationship of one's name with sacred phrases of the same gematria. One may also use gematria to understand the relationship between phrases from the Written Torah and the Oral Torah that, on their face, may not seem related. Through gematria, one may thus gain an understanding of the spiritual interconnectedness of names, words, phrases and objects.

The Hebrew word for love is ahavah. Ahavah is spelled with the Hebrew letters aleph hay vayt hay. Aleph equals one, hay equals five, vayt equals two, and the last hay equals five; so the gematria for ahavah is thirteen. The gematria of the name for God that is spelled with the Hebrew letters yod and hay and vav and hay equals twenty-six. (Yod equals ten, hay equals five, vav equals six, and the last hay equals five.) So love plus love equals God. The love of two unites in the One. God is lover and beloved; love and lover; love and beloved. Or as the Sufis say, God is love, lover and beloved.

As noted above, chai means life. For the practices given in this book, I recommend that chai—valued at eighteen—or multiples of chai—be used for counting the number of repetitions of sacred phrases that one repeats at a given time or during a given practice session. Those schooled in gematria may have other numeric favorites that will prove valuable as well. If you are used to counting the repetition of sacred phrases in another tradition, you may want to use that number—or those numbers--when repeating the sacred phrases in this book.

If you would like to try reciting the sacred phrases in this book chai times, and/or multiples of chai, then I encourage you to string—or to purchase pre-strung—prayer beads with markers at every eighteenth bead. You may want to have a total of 108 beads, or just eighteen, or thirty-six or fifty-four, etc.[76] You may also use your knuckles and/or the pads of your fingers for counting. To do this, figure out in advance the way that you will use your fingers in counting, so you know when you have reached the number of repetitions you are seeking. Some Buddhists, Hindus and Sufis also count on their fingers instead of, or in addition to, counting with beads.

---

75 The "ch" in chai is pronounced like the "ch" in the name of the famous musical composer Bach.
76 See http://rebpam.com/ for links to suppliers of beads with markers at every eighteenth bead.

In juxtaposition to these recommendations about how many times to repeat a sacred phrases, I want to recount a story about Swami Ramdas,[77] whom Murshid Sam called Papa Ramdas. (Papa Ramdas' disciple and successor was Mother Krishnabai, whom Murshid Sam said, was the spiritually highest woman he ever met.) At Anandashram, devotees would recite the sacred Sanskrit phrase Om Sri Ram Jai Ram Jai Jai Ram thousands upon thousands of times. Once, a disciple asked Papa Ramdas how many times one needs to recite the phrase Om Sri Ram Jai Ram Jai Jai Ram before attaining enlightenment, or God realization. Papa Ramdas responded that to realize Ram, one need recite Om Sri Ram Jai Ram Jai Jai Ram only once.[78]

---

[77] Swami Ramdas was born Vittal Rao in India in 1884. He stepped onto the spiritual path in 1920 and eventually established Anandashram in Kerala, India. Swami Ramdas was also known as Papa Ramdas or Papaji. He passed from this world in 1963. Before his death, he appointed Mother Krishnabai as his successor. Mother Krishnabai, known as Mataji, ran the Anandashram until her death in 1989. Today, there are Anandashram centers in many parts of India.

[78] Ram is a name of G-d. Om Sri Ram Jai Ram Jai Jai Ram is Sanskrit. It means Hail Holy Ram, Victory to Ram, Victory, Victory to Ram.

Chapter 6

Shokkelen and Sacred Focus

Shokkelen

Shokkelen is the practice of swaying forward and back during Jewish davvenen (worship). When sitting, I shokkel by moving my head forward and back just a bit, together with my upper body. When I am standing, I shokkel by bending my upper body forward and back just a bit, and sometimes more than a bit. One may also shokkel from side to side, or in a circular motion.

When praying in private, the davvener (worshipper) may feel free to shokkel as much and as intensely as might feel appropriate, so long as the davvener and those around him or her are safe. In public, however, it is important to practice modesty and not call attention to the self during davvenen, since the point of davvenen is to commune with the divine, and attention to the self gets in the way.

Sacred Focus

The six-pointed star is known in Judaism as the Jewish star, or the Star of David. The six-pointed star is also sacred in the Hindu faith and is recognized as a sacred symbol by some other faiths as well. It consists of two triangles, one with a base at the bottom and pointing upward, and one with a base at the top and pointing downward. There is a beautiful rendition of the Star of David on the cover of this book.

The energy of the Star of David is valuable in understanding spiritual balance. One may move spiritual energy up or down during spiritual practice, such as from the crown to the heart, or from the heart to the crown, or from the crown to the throat and then to the heart.

In Judaism, we speak of ten sephirot (pronounced "sfee-rote" with the emphasis on the last syllable). Sephirot may be translated as spheres or emanations or qualities with which God creates the universe and brings all things into manifestation. There is a place in or around the human body where each sephirah may be perceived and experienced most keenly. Like gematria (Hebrew numerology), the study of the sephirot is well developed, and there is much to learn. In the case of the sephirot, the learning may take a lifetime. Appendix D contains an introduction to the ten sephirot, including the name of each sephirah in English and Hebrew, and the place where it appears on the Tree of Life.[79]

The heart sephirah is called tiferet. Tiferet encompasses the divine qualities of love, harmony and beauty, and is located in the area of the physical heart. The crown sephirah is called ketter—which means crown—and is located just above the head. The throat center is called da'at—meaning knowledge—and is located in the area of the throat.

---

79 The Tree of Life has a number of depictions in Judaism. The two wooden handles on a Torah scroll are called "atzay chayyim," meaning "trees of life" and it says in the prayer that we recite in front of the open ark after reading Torah "eytz chayyim hi lamachazikim bah, v'khol netivoteha shalom," which means that "it (i.e. the Torah) is a tree of life to those who hold fast to it," in other words, to those who adhere to its teachings. The Tree of Life is also a depiction, both in drawings and in the imagination, of the energies with which the universe was created, and which are found in all of creation. These energies or emanations are called sephirot, and are described in Appendix D.

Ketter and da'at (crown and knowledge—located above the head and in the area of the throat, respectively) are aspects of the same sephirah. When counting the ten sephirot, ketter and da'at are counted as one, even though they are located in two different places on the Tree of Life and in the human body. Ketter (crown) is transcendent, and experienced outside the body, beginning just above the head. Da'at (knowledge) is eminent—or of this world—and experienced in the area of the throat. One may say that da'at is applied ketter, or ketter manifest; and ketter is da'at transcendent.[80] Or in plain English, one may say that the energy above the crown of the head connects with the transcendent, and the energy of the throat connects with manifestation. That is why we can feel spiritual power and receive spiritual transmission when listening to others as they speak about spiritual matters, and that is why spoken words have so much magnetism. The Torah tells us in the first chapter of Genesis that God created the world by speaking.[81] In the New Testament, it says, "In the beginning was the word and the word was with God and the word was God."[82]

The sephirah of malkhut is connected with the feet. Pir-O-Murshid Hazrat Inayat Khan—who, as mentioned previously, brought a universal form of Sufism to the West in 1910—gave Inayati Sufis walking practices. Murshid Sam also gave a variety of walking practices. Many of the sacred phrases given in this book lend themselves well to recitation or thought while walking.

The practices in this book focus primarily on the sephirot of ketter, tiferet and malkhut, which are centered in the crown above the head (ketter), the throat (da'at, which is an aspect of ketter), the heart (tiferet), and the feet (malkhut).

---

80 I learned this teaching from Reb Zalman and Joe Miller.
81 In Chapter 1 of *Genesis*, it says, "And G-d said, let there be …., and there was …." for various stages of creation.
82 *John* 1:1. *The New Testament in Hebrew and English*, translated into Hebrew from the Greek by Yitzhak Zelikinson, prepared for publication with corrections and annotations by David Ginsburg (London: The Trinitarian Bible Society) 176. Additional Note: In Greek, it says that in the beginning was "logos." Logos is translated as word, but also has additional meaning. The English translation is generally "word." In the Hebrew translation from the Greek in the foregoing source, the Hebrew word is "davar" which means word and also has additional meaning.

Chapter 7

Midrash, Adab and Derech Eretz

Midrash

It is a Jewish custom and practice to retranslate, reframe, interpret, comment and draw parallels from one text to another, and from a text to one's experience, in order to derive meaning and understanding of words, phrases, stories, teachings and laws found in the Written Torah, Oral Torah,[83] prayer books, and life. These activities are commonly known as creating midrash,[84] and the person who creates the midrash is known as the darshan (masculine) or darshanit (feminine).

Sometimes midrash is taken as truth. Because a great rabbi, scholar or sage exclaimed a certain principle or understanding, many assume that it is the truth for all time, and perhaps it is. But then someone else expresses a different midrash about the same point or practice or understanding. That new midrash may also be true. The Talmud records and expounds upon diverse and contradictory midrashim (plural of midrash). In some instances, the Talmud tells us that Judaism holds by so and so's midrash and not the other midrashim. The beauty of the Talmud is that we can view the opinion and insight that carried the day together with the opinions and insights that did not carry the day.

In the *Zohar*, a mystical commentary on the Torah, diverse views are generally expressed side by side without being reconciled. Sometimes it states that a certain rabbi wept upon hearing the view of his colleague and then the one who wept expresses a different view.

Every stream of Judaism from Ultra Orthodox to Secular Humanist has renewed and revivified Judaism through the midrashim of its teachers and sages, rendering Judaism relevant for a particular time or location or condition of life.

Some Jewish people adhere to the view that the Torah is the word of God, while others view it as a composite of ancient literature canonized into one accepted version. The more we evolve spiritually, the more we are able to hold to our own view as a truth or as midrash, while making room for the truth and midrash of others. Blessed are those who are able to evolve their own midrash on scripture and life while making room for the midrash of others. And blessed is the one who lives by the Talmudic teaching of Ben Zoma, "Eyzehu khacham? Halomed mikol adam." "Who is wise? The person who learns from everyone."[85]

Hebrew has many names for God. The two most common God names in the Hebrew Bible and Jewish prayer are Elohim and the ineffable divine name spelled with the Hebrew letters yod and hay and vav and hay. In Kabbalah, we learn that the ineffable name refers to God on the level of Mercy, or as the

---

83 The difference between the written Torah and the oral Torah is discussed in Chapter 2.
84 According to Kabbalah, there are four levels on which scripture may be understood: the literal level, the parallel or allegorical level, the interpretive level and the level of spiritual experience. The allegorical level is known as remez, or hint. Remez is when one story or teaching reminds us of another, like our wedding ring reminds us of our beloved and our commitment to our beloved. The interpretive level is known as drash, and our interpretations are called midrash. For purposes of the discussions in this book, I use "midrash" to refer to both the parallel and interpretive levels.
85 Pirkei Avot (Ethics of our Fathers) 4:1.

Gate of Mercy; and Elohim is God on the level of Judgment or Discernment, or as the Gate of Judgment or Discernment. The ineffable name refers to God transcendent, beyond name and form, whereas Elohim refers to God transcendent and in manifestation. These Kabbalistic understandings of Elohim and the ineffable divine name are Kabbalistic midrash. Some of the teachings in this book concerning the divine names are historical or linguistic, but most are midrash. And, from a certain point of view, history is also midrash in that different historians view and interpret the same facts and circumstances differently. The same is true of academic pursuits in the sciences and humanities, including linguistics and the study of language.

There is a Sufi understanding that we cannot say the truth, but we can be the truth. Truth is not captured in words because everyone hears and understands words differently. We, ourselves, might say something or write something on a given day and mean it in a certain way. Then, on another day, we might read or listen to our own words and understand them differently. One might say that truth is. Truth exists. However, we are not able to capture truth and express it irrefutably. And to make room for the reality that divergent points of view may be true simultaneously, one might say that there are many truths and one may express *a truth*, but not *the truth* since the truth is constantly shifting for those who are evolving humanly and growing spiritually.

The blessing of midrash is that we can embrace it and refute it and move toward it and away from it, and the midrash nevertheless remains. In a certain supernal sense, the Torah itself is midrash. There is a mystical teaching that God created the Torah before the creation of the universe. How is this possible when the stories in Torah took place within creation and specific names and events are described? One midrash is that the real Torah is not what we find written on the parchment when we remove it from the ark in the synagogue and unroll it and read it. The real Torah exists beyond time and space. The Torah written on the parchment scroll in the ark and in books is a reflection of the real Torah.

The beauty of these midrashim is that we can accept the Torah and study the Torah and interpret the Torah without worrying about whether there is something wrong with us or something wrong with the Torah because we and the Torah disagree. For example, it says in the Torah that we should not work on the Sabbath and that violating the Sabbath is a capital offense. There is a story in Torah about a man who gathered sticks on the Sabbath and this was considered work and he was stoned for it.[86] One might say, "I don't accept that violating the Sabbath is a capital offense and I am offended that the story of the man being stoned for gathering sticks is in the Torah." The great sage known as Ben Bag Bag said "hafoch ba v'hafoch ba d'khola va," meaning turn it and turn it and everything is in it. What pleases us is in it. What offends us is in it. What we agree with is in it and what we disagree with is also in it. What I understand today is in it, and what I don't understand is also in it. I can read it and study it over and over and there is always more to learn, because what is in the Torah is part of God, and since I am created in the image of God, what is in the Torah is reflected in me. The words I read and study are a reflection of the truth in a form with which I can wrestle, and each wrestle leads me to a new understanding and that is my midrash for that moment.

Murshid Samuel Lewis' first successor, Moineddin Jablonski was fond of saying that today's realization is tomorrow's quicksand. Years after coining the phrase, Moineddin and I were discussing it when he quipped, "I'm no longer sure things move that slowly."

---

86 Numbers 15:32-36.

Adab and Derech Eretz

Derech eretz is a Hebrew expression, meaning respect. In the Mishna,[87] Rabbi Eliezer ben Azariah is quoted as saying, "If there is no Torah, there is no respect; if there is no respect, there is no Torah."[88] Adab is an Arabic word meaning respect. The practice of adab is a cornerstone of Islam and it is an important quality cultivated among Sufis. When visiting Mevlevi Sufis in Turkey in 1983, I was taught that when a person enters the mosque or prayer room or a room devoted to sacred study, one takes off the shoes and places them with the toes pointing into the room. Should a person do something offensive or inappropriate that the Sheikh[89] deems to be too offensive to reverse or to tolerate, the Sheikh turns the person's shoes with the toes facing the door. If one finds the toes of one's shoes facing the door, one understands that one is not welcome to return.

Spiritual teachers in the West tend to be more lenient and tolerant than teachers in the East, and we may tolerate much that would be considered intolerable elsewhere. Nevertheless, the Jewish notion of derech eretz, the Sufi notion of adab and the Western notion of respect and decency toward others are core to our religious and spiritual practice. These qualities are also important to the health of our communities and our capacity to join together meaningfully with people of our own faith and practice, as well as with people of other faiths and practices.

The practices in this book are offered for the personal use of the reader. If you wish to share these practices with others, please be sure to do so respectfully and with deference to the person with whom you wish to share them. In some settings, these practices may be welcome, whereas in other settings, they may be shunned. This is true of all religious and spiritual practices, and for that matter, it is true of the scriptures and sacred teachings and midrash of every faith. **As in medicine, so in faith: one person's cure may be another person's poison.**

If you are not a member of the Jewish community, and you are invited into the Jewish community to present or lead chanting or Zikr or Dances of Universal Peace or yoga or any other spiritual practice, it is important to demonstrate respect for your host and for Jewish tradition. If you wish to offer the practices in this book in a Jewish setting, regardless of whether it is your home setting or a place where you are a visitor, it is important to inquire of the spiritual leader as to what is acceptable in that setting. If you are the spiritual leader, then sensitivity to minhag hamakom (the custom of the place) is relevant. If you are a guest or student or member of a Jewish community or congregation where the spiritual leader says no to your leading certain practices—whether from this book or any source—it is important to consider that the reason for this decision may have to do with minhag hamakom and the fact that, in Judaism, minhag hamakom often takes precedent over all other standards of faith and practice.

Pir-O-Murshid Hazrat Inayat Khan said that for the mystic, religion is a form of spiritual recreation. It is important to remember that recreation is, by definition, not a forced activity. **If the practice or view you wish to share with others is oppressive to them, then no matter how lofty or pure or advanced your practice, and no matter how God realized your being, you are, nevertheless, engaging in an act of oppression and not an act of faith.**

---

87 Mishna is defined in the Glossary of Terms and discussed in Chapter 2.
88 *Pirkei Avot* 3:21. [Tractate Pirkei Avot (Ethics of the Fathers), Chapter 3, section 21.]
89 A Sufi Sheikh is a spiritual teacher.

Hakim Sauluddin teaches that one must obtain permission from a person before praying for his or her healing. This is a spiritual principle in Judaism as well, and is discussed in Chapter 22. If we must obtain permission to pray for the healing of someone who is not well, how much more so must we respect our hosts in Jewish and interfaith settings, and, indeed, in all settings, by learning what is comfortable for them, and by finding a way to present the teachings we have been given in a way that can be received and absorbed by those who have invited us to teach and lead.

The following is a story that I heard from Paul Reps, a spiritual teacher who was a friend of Samuel Lewis, and my own teacher, Wali Ali Meyer:

> During the Kamkura period, Shinkan studied Tendai six years and then he studied Zen seven years; then he went to China and contemplated Zen for thirteen years more.
>
> When he returned to Japan many desired to interview him and asked him obscure questions. But when Shinkan received visitors, which was infrequently, he seldom answered their questions.
>
> One day a fifty-one year old student of enlightenment said to Shinkan: 'I have studied the Tendai school of thought since I was a little boy, but one thing in it I cannot understand. Tendai claims that even the grass and trees will become enlightened. To me this seems very strange.'
>
> 'Of what use is it to discuss how grass and trees become enlightened?' asked Shinkan. 'The question is how you yourself can become enlightened. Did you ever consider that!'
>
> 'I never thought of it that way,' marveled the old man. 'Then go home and think it over,' finished Shinkan.

Paul Reps has passed on, but this story remains for us in perpetuity in a book entitled, *Zen Flesh, Zen Bones*.[90]

If people come to us and ask us to teach them or guide them or help them, then we may have responsibility to do so, depending upon our capacity and our station in life. But it is not our job to go around checking out what others are doing and it is not our place to try to find ways to impose our opinion or our practice or our good ideas upon others. Better to busy ourselves with the matter of our own spiritual awakening than with the question of how others can best be awakened into God realization unless those others are our students or congregants or counselees who are asking for our guidance. And even then, it is important to remember that, according to Judaism, every human is created in the image of God, and every person has his/her own spiritual path and connection with divinity. As we teach and guide, it is important to find ways to respect the God given free will of each individual.

---

90 Paul Reps and Nyogen Senzaki, *Zen Flesh, Zen Bones* (Shambhala, 1994), story 46.

Practices

Chapter 8

Hebrew Names of God

The teachings in Chapter 7 regarding midrash, adab and derech eretz are relevant to understanding and applying the teachings in this chapter.

Elohim

Elohim is a divine name that appears throughout the Hebrew Bible, the Talmud, the *Zohar*, other rabbinic literature and Jewish prayer books. Elohim is generally translated as "God," and refers to God transcendent and in manifestation. Elohim appears in the story of the six days of creation in Genesis,[91] in the Shema,[92] and in the Atah Har'eyta teachings of Moses,[93] discussed in Chapter 11. Elohim is a plural noun, although God is one. Eyl is a singular name of God consisting of the first two letters of Elohim—alef and lamed. A practice for reciting "Todah La'Eyl," meaning "thank you God," is described in Chapter 17.

Hebrew is a Semitic language, in which pronouns and prepositions are often embedded within a noun or verb. The divine name Elohim appears in a number of linguistic forms in scripture and prayers, such as Elohaynu, meaning "our God," Elohi and Eloha'ee, meaning "my God," Elohay or Elo'ah, meaning "God of," and Elohecha or Elohaychem, meaning "your God." Since sound is important in spiritual practice, there may be a difference of experience when reciting the different forms of Elohim. I believe that repetition of, and meditation upon, all the forms of Elohim may bring one toward spiritual realization.

I believe that the divine name Elohim is pronounced during worship and when reciting blessings and reading from scripture throughout the Jewish world. In some Jewish communities, the same pronunciation is used for Elohim during teaching, discussion and ordinary conversation. However, in many Jewish communities, the pronunciation Elokim is used during teaching, discussion and ordinary conversation as part of exercising care to not inadvertently use God's name in vain.

The Divine Root Name

The ineffable name of God is spelled with the Hebrew letters yod and hay and vav and hay. This ineffable name has been discussed and contemplated throughout Jewish history. Nothing that we say or write can describe God either adequately or completely, and there is no correct pronunciation of the ineffable name of God.

This ineffable name consisting of the letters yod and hay and vav and hay derives from the verb "to be." In both ancient and modern Hebrew, the verb "to be" appears in the past tense and future tense. However, in the present tense, the verb "to be" is understood and does not actually appear in writing or when speaking.

---

91 *Genesis*, Chapter 1.
92 *Deuteronomy* 6:4.
93 *Deuteronomy* 4:35 and 39.

Rabbi Zalman Schachter-Shalomi translates the ineffable divine name as "IS-ness." Murshid Samuel Lewis translated the ineffable divine name as "constantly becoming," and there are many rabbis who also translate it as "becoming" or "constantly becoming." Joe Miller, who was steeped in Christian Qabbalah, used to say, "God is. It's not that God is this or God is that. God just is, and we are, and all you have to do is be. You don't have to be something. Just be."

There are a number of appropriate ways to refer to the ineffable divine name of God in ordinary speech and when teaching, explaining and discussing the divine in Jewish settings. One appropriate pronunciation is Shem Havayah, which means the "Ha-va-ya-h Name," or the name that includes the sounds "ha," "va," "ya" and "h." Another is HaShem, which means "The Name." Yet another is Shem HaMeforash, which means the explicit name or the explained name or the clear name.[94]

In some Jewish settings, Adoshem is also used in ordinary speech. However, there are some Orthodox teachers who have made the determination that Adoshem is not appropriate for ordinary speech. Adoshem is a combination of Adonai and HaShem. Adonai is generally translated as Lord, and one might translate Adoshem as "the Lord Name."

For purposes of this writing, I have translated Shem HaMeforash as the "Root Name" and I refer to the ineffable divine name as the **"Divine Root Name"** in order to remind the reader that **this name of God is at the root of the Jewish understanding of God.**

The Divine Root Name may be permutated, such that the ordering of the letters changes. For example, there are twelve months in the Jewish calendar and each month attunes to the four letters of the Divine Root Name in a different order. This is explained in Appendix E and depicted on Chart 3. There are mystical prayer books that display the letters of the Divine Root Name in different orders in the margins for different aspects of Jewish worship.[95] Rabbi Abraham Abulafia assigned different Hebrew vowels to the consonants of the Divine Root Name and we believe that he and his students intoned them. This is discussed in Chapter 10.

Make no mistake: God is One. There are many meanings ascribed to the Divine Root Name, and there are many understandings of these meanings, and there are also many other Hebrew names of God, and there are also names of God in every other human language, faith and culture. However, there is only One Being. Adonai Echad. God is One. Eyn Od Milvado. There is nothing but Him. (If you wish to say "there is nothing but Her," you would say "Eyn Od Milvada.")

The Divine Root Name is considered ineffable, because it is impossible to describe God in human language. It is also considered ineffable in order to avoid using the power of the name for selfish motives or misguided altruistic motives. The Divine Root Name was originally pronounced by the High Priest in the Holy of Holies in the Tabernacle—the portable sanctuary in the wilderness—and later in the Holy Temple in Jerusalem. Although there is much conjecture, no one in this day and age knows for sure how the High Priest pronounced the Divine Root Name. Many Jewish, Christian and other scholars refer to the Divine Root Name as Yahweh. Some refer to the Divine Root Name as Jehovah, and, as we know, there is a branch of Christianity called Jehovah's Witnesses.

---

94 Reuben Alcalay, *The Complete Hebrew-English Dictionary, New Enlarged Edition* (Tel Aviv: Chemed Books, 1996) 1448-9.
95 *Ohz HaT'filah, Siddur Shacharit Shel Chol im Leket Kitzur Kavanot HaAri z"l, v'chuleh* (Petach Tikvah, Israel, 5767), and *Ohz HaT'filah, Siddur T'filot Shabbat im Leket Kitzur Kavanot HaAri z"l, v'chuleh* (Petach Tikvah, Israel, 5767). These two prayer books are entirely in Hebrew.

Emmet Fox refers to the Divine Root Name as YHWH in his *Five Books of Moses*. Murshid Samuel Lewis wrote and pronounced the Divine Root Name as Ya-hu-va (hyphens intended).

The names Shem Havayah, HaShem and Shem HaMeforash—and in some settings, Adoshem—are proper pronunciations of the Divine Root Name in the Jewish community during teaching, discussion of spiritual topics and ordinary conversation. During worship services (often called davvenen), and when chanting from the Bible during worship, and when reciting a blessing—such as before study of scripture, before and after eating and drinking, or after relieving oneself—the normative pronunciation of the Divine Root Name is "Adonai." Since the letters of the Divine Root Name do not add up to the pronunciation of Adonai or HaShem or Adoshem or Shem Havayah or Shem HaMeforash, one may say that the pronunciation of the Divine Root Name in any of these ways is midrash. Similarly, the terms ineffable name of G-d and Divine Root Name are also midrash.

As mentioned in the foregoing paragraph, during Jewish worship and the recitation of Jewish blessings, as well as during the formal reading of scripture, the Divine Root Name is traditionally pronounced Adonai. Adonai literally means "Lord." The Conservative and Reform Movements generally translate the Divine Root Name as "Lord"[96] in the Jewish Publication Society Bible[97] that is widely used in their respective Biblical publications. The Divine Root Name is also generally translated as "Lord" in traditional Conservative and Reform prayer books, as well as in some Jewish Renewal prayer books. "Lord" is also the translation of the Divine Root Name in the King James Bible and in many other Christian translations of the Bible as well. There is a further discussion in Appendix H entitled, "The Relationship Between Adonai and the Divine Root Name."

The English word Lord is related to the Old English hlafweard, meaning loaf ward or "the one who guards the loaves,"[98] that is to say, the person responsible for providing sustenance to the people in the form of bread. Bread was a most basic food in ancient times, and in many places in the world, it still is.

In the *Zohar*,[99] it states that Adonai is one of the names of the Shechina, the feminine indwelling presence of God, or God in manifestation.

Rabbi Shefa Gold, a Reconstructionist and Renewal rabbi, summed up her understanding of "Lord" in a song she wrote in which she says, "My heart belongs to the Lord, Who doesn't Lord it over me."[100]

---

96 The Torah was translated into Greek by seventy scholars. Their translation is known as the Septuagint. The Septuagint translates the Divine Root Name as Kyrios, which means Lord. In the Vulgate, the Divine Root Name is translated as Dominus, which also means Lord.

97 *JPS Hebrew-English Tanakh: The Traditional Hebrew Text and the New JPS Translation*, second edition. (Philadelphia: The Jewish Publication Society, 1999). Tanakh means Bible and is an acronym. "T" stands for Torah, meaning teachings; "N" stands for nevi'im, meaning prophets; and "K" stands for Ketuvim, meaning writings. The books of the Tanakh are described in Appendix B.

98 *Online Etymology Dictionary*, August 2011 <http://www.etymonline.com/index.php?term=lord>. With gratitude to Scott Sattler for pointing me to this etymology.

99 *Zohar* I,101a and elsewhere. The *Zohar* is a mystical commentary on the Torah discussed in Chapter 2 of this book.

100Shefa Gold wrote a song entitled, "No More Big Daddy," circa 1984 and recorded it on one of her early albums. The chorus of the song is: "No More Big Daddy. The Monarchy is dead. I take responsibility for the Devils in my head. My love is like a circle that spins to set me free. My heart belongs to the Lord who doesn't Lord it over me."

Although Adonai is the generally accepted Jewish pronunciation of the Divine Root Name when reciting blessings and during worship and the formal reading and chanting of scripture, in many Jewish communities, it is not appropriate to recite the name Adonai in ordinary conversation because it puts one at risk of taking the name of God in vain as described in Chapter 9.

If you belong to a Jewish community, or a Jewish family where Adonai is used in ordinary conversation, then it is, of course, fine to use it there. If not, however, then out of respect for Jewish custom and practice, when speaking about God in ordinary conversation, it is best to refer to the divine name as HaShem or Adoshem or Shem Havayah or Shem HaMeforash or the ineffable name or the ineffable name of God or another respectful expression, such as Divine Root Name.

HaShem

The Artscroll Series has published a multi-volume set of the Bible with translation by respected Orthodox rabbis. The original Biblical text and translation are accompanied by extensive commentaries. In the Artscroll Series, the Divine Root Name is generally translated as HaShem and Elohim is generally translated as God.[101] As mentioned above, HaShem means "the name" and is a common pronunciation of the Divine Root Name in ordinary Jewish speech. HaShem is a placeholder name of God that has acquired spiritual magnetism through use.

YaH

YaH is a name of God that appears from time to time in the Hebrew Bible and Jewish liturgy. The divine name YaH is found in both Hebrew[102] and Jewish Aramaic.[103] It is part of the Hebrew word Halleluyah, which is found in a number of psalms in the Biblical Book of Psalms. Hallel means "praise," hallelu means "let us praise" and halleluyah means "let us praise God." (See Chapter 15 for practices using Halleluyah.)

YaH consists of the Hebrew consonants yod and hay. "Y" stands for yod. "H" stands for hay. And "a" stands for the vowel kamatz that appears under the yod in both Hebrew and Jewish Aramaic. The Hebrew consonants and vowels are depicted in Charts 4 and 5 in Appendix H.

While YaH may be considered a divine name in and of itself, it also consists of the first two letters of the Divine Root Name and is written in Hebrew and Jewish Aramaic with a mappiq in the hay. The mappiq is a dot that appears in a letter to indicate that some other letter or letters have been removed from the linguistic root from which the word is derived. An example of this in is the apostrophe that appears in the English words "can't" and "don't" to represent letters that have been removed to form these conjunctions.

---

101 The *Artscroll Tanach Series, A Traditional Commentary on the Books of the Bible* (New York: Mesorah Publications, Ltd.)

102 The following are examples of verses from the Hebrew Bible that also appear in Jewish Prayer and contain the divine name YaH: *Exodus* 15:2 (Song of the Sea, part of daily morning worship); *Isaiah* 12:2 (part of the ceremony of havdallah at the end of the Sabbath), *Psalms* 115:17 and 18 (fourth psalm of Hallel recited on the new moon and festivals), *Psalms* 115:18 (part of Ashrey recited daily morning and afternoon); and *Psalm*150:6 (part of daily morning worship).

103 A common example of YaH in Aramaic liturgy is YaH Ribon Olam, a zemer (poem sung during Sabbath meals) by Rabbi Israel Ben Moses Najara who lived in the sixteenth and early seventeenth century. Rabbi Israel was born and raised in Damascus where his father Moses was a rabbi. Israel himself served as a rabbi in Gaza. *Encyclopaedia Judaica* (Jerusalem: Keter Publishing House, 1996), Vol. 12, 798.

I believe that the appearance of the mappiq in YaH both in the Bible and Jewish liturgy is indicative of the fact that the authors view YaH as a shortened form of the Divine Root Name. While the Divine Root Name is generally pronounced Adonai during Jewish worship and the formal reading of scripture, the divine name YaH is pronounced YaH both during worship and the reading of scripture.

Rabbi Zalman Schachter-Shalomi is a Holocaust survivor who risked his life as a teenager to make his way out of a detention camp in Vichy France to obtain a ram's horn from a butcher shop from which he fashioned a shofar[104] for the community of prisoners to use on Rosh HaShanah, Jewish New Year.[105] After being released from detention camp, Zalman and his family immigrated to the United States via Puerto Rico. Zalman studied in Yeshivas Tomchei Temimim, an Ultra Orthodox Chassidic Yeshiva[106] run by Chabad, the sect of Lubavitcher Chassidim. Zalman was ordained as a rabbi at Yeshivas Tomchei Temimim. Over the years, his religious and spiritual understanding and practice became eclectic and universal and he is considered to be the founder of the Jewish Renewal Movement.[107] His students refer to him affectionately as Reb Zalman.

Reb Zalman has evolved the practice of pronouncing the Divine Root Name as "YaH" rather than Adonai during worship, the reciting of blessings and the formal reading of scripture. He evolved this practice in response to contemplating the reality that Adonai contains the root "din," meaning Judgment, and the Divine Root Name embodies the attribute of divine compassion.

Reb Zalman writes and pronounces the Divine Root Name as "YaH" in daily blessings, worship services, when reading or chanting scripture during worship, and in other sacred settings. To render the two consonants yod and vav transparent to the reader in English, and to acknowledge the connection between the Divine Root Name and the divine name YaH, Reb Zalman developed the practice of capitalizing the "H" at the end of YaH. **While copy editing the manuscript for this book, Reb Zalman requested that I represent YaH with a capital "H" and I have done so.**

In ordinary conversation, as well as when teaching, Reb Zalman generally refers to the Divine Root Name as HaShem or Adoshem or Shem HaMeforash or Shem Havayah or God.

Rabbi Alan Lew, of blessed memory, evolved Zen Buddhist meditation into a Jewish practice. Rabbi Lew pronounced YaH for the Divine Root Name in prayers and chants that he prepared and shared before and after sitting meditation.[108] When singing a portion of a Psalm or other prayer as a niggun

---

104 A shofar is a ram's horn, which is used on Rosh HaShanah (Jewish New Year) and Yom Kippur (the Day of Atonement) and during the month leading up to Rosh HaShanah. See Glossary of Terms.

105 Using a wire from the wires available in the detention camp, Zalman bored a hole into one ram's horn and accidentally penetrated the side of the horn. Learning from his experience, he worked on the second horn and created a shofar. This story and others will appear in a book on the Holocaust, slated for release by the author in approximately 2013.

106 A Yeshiva is a seminary.

107 Reb Zalman dates the founding of Jewish Renewal to 1962 when he was part of Chavurat Shalom in Boston, which experience delighted, challenged and stretched, and where he met some of his lifelong friends and colleagues. See https://www.aleph.org/ and http://www.ohalah.org/ for additional information on the Jewish Renewal Movement.

108 Makor Or means "Source of Light," and is the name of a Jewish meditation program founded by Rabbi Alan Lew at Congregation Beth Sholom in San Francisco where he served as senior rabbi for many years. Rabbi Lew co-led Makor Or with Zen Center Abbot Zoketsu Norman Fischer. During Rabbi Lew's lifetime, Makor Or became part of the Taube Center for Jewish Life at the Jewish Community Center of San Francisco. As of this writing, Makor Or remains part of the Taube Center for Jewish Life and is run by Zoketsu Norman Fischer and Rabbi Dorothy Richman. Congregation Beth Sholom maintains a meditation program called Makom Shalom, meaning "Place of Peace."

(spiritual melody) during worship services, Rabbi Lew also pronounced the Divine Root Name as YaH. For example, he was very fond of singing a niggun to the following phrase from Psalm 92: Mah Gadlu Ma'asekha YaH, Me'od Amku Mach'shevotekha,[109] which may be translated as "How vast are your works, oh God, your thoughts are very deep," or "How grand are your deeds, oh God, your designs are beyond our grasp."

Except as described above, however, Rabbi Lew pronounced Adonai for the Divine Root Name during worship services and the formal reading of scripture and also when reciting blessings before and after meals. In settings outside of prayer and worship, and outside of meditation—such as while teaching or writing a poem or writing a book about spirituality—Rabbi Lew referred to the Divine Root Name as HaShem or Adoshem or Shem HaMeforash or Shem Havayah or God.

Eyn HaChayyim

The founder of the Jewish Reconstructionist Movement, Rabbi Mordecai Kaplan, of blessed memory, was trained and ordained as an Orthodox rabbi. Rabbi Kaplan was eventually shunned by the Orthodox for his innovations, which included carrying the Torah into the women's section of the synagogue, and bringing girls to the bimah (pulpit) to become bat mitzvah. Bat mitzvah for girls is an ancient ritual given in the Talmud,[110] but until the twentieth century, bat mitzvah was celebrated during a festive meal or in other settings outside of formal Jewish worship. In 1922, Rabbi Kaplan invited his daughter Judith to recite the Torah blessings and read a selection from a book of Torah while standing on the bimah with the open Torah scroll on a table just a short distance away. Judith Kaplan was, as far as we know, the first girl in human history to become bat mitzvah on the pulpit.[111]

After Rabbi Kaplan was rejected by the Orthodox community, he affiliated with the Conservative Movement. Over time, the Reconstructionist Movement evolved among Rabbi Kaplan and his followers.

Reconstructionist and Renewal prayer books are among the most innovative in their use of God language, both in terms of the Hebrew divine names, and the translations of the divine names. The Reconstructionists use the formulation of Hebrew blessing, "N'vareykh Et Eyn HaChayyim," which may be translated as "we will bless the source of life"[112] or "we will blessing the wellspring of life." Eyn HaChayyim is a name of God that appears in Jewish Kabbalistic and mainstream literature and it is a sacred phrase that I believe may be recited in any Jewish setting, including formal worship and ordinary conversation.

---

109 *Psalms* 92:6.

110 The teachings contained in the Talmud hail from the Biblical period to 600 C.E. The commentaries that appear around the edges of a traditional page of Talmud were written from the seventh to the sixteenth centuries C.E.

111 After her marriage, Judith Kaplan became Judith Kaplan Eisenstadt. In Judaism, the pulpit—called bimah in Hebrew—refers to the entire area in and around the table where the Torah is read and the table or podium from which worship is led, as well as the place where one stands when speaking to the congregation. In some Christian denominations, the equivalent of the Jewish bimah is called the chancel.

112 *Kol HaNeshama, Shabbat Vehagim* (Wyncote, Pennsylvania: The Reconstructionist Press, 1996) 5.

Chapter 9

Adoshem and Honoring the Third Commandment

When teaching prayers and blessings—as opposed to when one is actually praying—some Orthodox Jews, and some Conservative and other Jews, pronounce the Divine Root Name as Adoshem. Adoshem is a combination of Adonai and HaShem.

The following is an example of using Adoshem when teaching a blessing: Barukh Atah Adoshem Elokaynu Melekh Ha'Olam, HaMotzi Lechem Min Ha'aretz.[113] This is a practice version of the prayer before eating bread. It is not the version recited before one actually eats bread; rather, it is used when one is teaching or discussing the prayer for eating bread.

The actual traditional prayer is: Barukh Atah Adonai Elohaynu Melekh Ha'Olam, HaMotzi Lechem Min Ha'aretz. Reb Zalman's version of the actual prayer is: Barukh Atah YaH[114] Elohaynu Melekh Ha'Olam, HaMotzi Lechem Min Ha'aretz.

The following is an example of using Adoshem when teaching the Shema: Shema Yisrael Adoshem Elokaynu Adoshem Echad.[115] This is the sacred Hebrew declaration of the oneness of God given in the Torah by Moses.[116] As with the prayer for bread above, this version of the Shema is not the one recited during prayer. Rather, it is a version recited during teaching or discussion of the Shema.

The actual pronunciation of Shema during traditional Jewish worship is: Shema Yisrael Adonai Elohaynu Adonai Echad. Reb Zalman's pronunciation is: Shema Yisrael YaH Elohaynu YaH Echad.

In the above teaching versions—or practice versions—of the Shema and the prayer before eating bread, "Adoshem" is the pronunciation of the Divine Root Name, and Elokaynu is the pronunciation for Elohaynu.

Keeping the Third Commandment of the Top Ten

The reason for using Adoshem and Elokaynu instead of Adonai and Elohaynu, is to fulfill the Third of the Ten Commandments. In Hebrew, the Third Commandment is, "Lo Tisa Et Sheym yod hay vav hay Elohecha LaShav, Ki Lo Y'nakeh yod hay vav hay Et Asher Yisa Et Shemo LaShav." There are numerous ways to translate this Third Commandment. The Soncino[117] translation is, "You shall not take the name of the Lord your God in vain; for the Lord will not hold him guiltless who takes His name in vain." The Jewish Publication Society translation of the Third Commandment is, "You shall not swear falsely by the name of the Lord Your God; for the Lord will not clear one who swears falsely by His name." Murshid Sam translated the Third Commandment as, "Repetition of His Name elevates the soul; misuse of His Name deprives the soul of light, and use of any other name is idolatry."

---

113 This practice version of the prayer may be translated as "Blessed are You, L-rd our G-d, Sovereign of the universe, Who brings forth bread from the earth."

114 This prayer may be translated as "Blessed are You, Lord our God, Sovereign of the universe, Who brings forth bread from the earth."

115 This may be translated as "Listen Israel (i.e. "Jewish person" or "G-d wrestler"), the Lord is our G-d, the L-rd is One."

116 *Deuteronomy* 6:4.

117 Soncino is the name of a Jewish publishing company that publishes books as well as searchable texts on CD ROM.

Chapter 10

Vocalizing the Vowel Sounds

Murshid Sam gave the practice of pronouncing the Divine Root Name as a compilation of vowel sounds. I learned this practice from Allaudin Mathieu,[118] who taught us to begin with "ee" and conclude with "ay" as in the word "say." The order of the vowel sounds is "ee" "ah" "o" "u" "eh" "ay" with the shaping of the mouth sliding from one vowel to the next, and with the vocal chords making continuous sound. One may repeat the vowels in this manner numerous times until the musical overtones are heard and experienced.

Murshid Sam's practice of reciting the vowel sounds in order to hear the overtones is on the level of the practices given by the thirteenth century Kabbalist Rabbi Abraham Abulafia and other Kabbalistic masters. The Divine Root Name consists of four consonants and no vowels. Rabbi Abulafia paired the Hebrew vowels with the consonants of the Divine Root Name and chanted them, focusing the sound in the sephirot and various centers of the body. For example, Abulafia chanted ya-ha-va-ha, focusing the sound in tiferet, the heart center. He chanted yu-hu-vu-hu and focused the sound in a different sephirah, and he chanted yi-hi-vi-hi and focused the sound another center. For those interested in learning more about Rabbi Abulafia's teachings and practices, his writings are available in numerous books in a variety of languages.

The sound practices described in this chapter are not to be taken lightly. They are best recited for their own sake, l'sheym shamayim, for the sake of heaven; in other words, without personal motive, without expectation of personal gain, and without trying to show off. Such practices should be undertaken with deep intention, quieting the breath, listening before one begins, and listening after one concludes.

If someone asks, "are you pronouncing the Divine Root Name?" when you intone the vowels in the above practice from Murshid Sam, I would say the answer is no, because the Divine Root Name consists of consonants without vowels, and Murshid Sam's intonation is vowels without consonants. If someone asks, "what is the relationship between the Divine Root Name and the intoning of all the vowels," I would say that the answer is that Shema Yisrael means, "listen Israel," or "listen devotee on the spiritual path," and intoning the vowels from a place of deep quiet and spiritual intention opens within us the ability to hear the overtones that are being intoned by the universe at every moment. Normally, we do not hear these overtones, because we are too busy doing things, or listening to other sounds. When one is completely quiet, and the surrounding atmosphere is in silence, one may hear the sound of the universe without intoning anything. The intoning of the vowels with deep spiritual intention and no personal motive, as given by Murshid Sam and taught to me by Allaudin Mathieu, is a vehicle for opening to the inner sound that is always present, and may be heard even without the aid of this practice.

---

118 Allaudin William Mathieu was a composer and arranger for the Stan Kenton and Duke Ellington Orchestras. He served as Musical Director for Second City Theater in Chicago and the Committee Theater in San Francisco. In the 1970's, he served on the faculties of the San Francisco Conservatory of Music and Mills College. In 1969, he founded the Sufi Choir, which he directed until 1982. In 1974, Reb Zalman invited the Sufi Choir to serve as the High Holy Choir for evening worship on Rosh HaShanah (Jewish New Year) and Yom Kippur (the Day of Atonement) at Glide Memorial Methodist Church as part of the first annual High Holy Days observance of the Aquarian Minyan of Berkeley, which Reb Zalman helped to found. I was a student of Sufism and Theosophy and a founding member of the Aquarian Minyan, and Reb Zalman and Allaudin invited me to coordinate the Sufi Choir's participation. During our preparatory meetings for High Holy Days, Reb Zalman and I began using the techniques and modalities found in many of the practices in this book.

Chapter 11

Sacred Phrases Given By Moses

Moses said to the Israelites, "Shema Yisrael YHWH Elohaynu YHWH Echad,"[119] meaning "Hear, oh Israel, the Lord is our God, the Lord is One," or "Listen Israel, the Divine Root Name is our Elohim, the Divine Root Name is One." "YHWH" is a depiction of the Divine Root Name given by Everett Fox,[120] who uses the English letter "W" in place of the Hebrew letter pronounced "V."

Moses also said to the Israelites, "Atah Har'eyta Lada'at Ki YHWH Hu HaElohim Eyn Od Milvado,"[121] meaning "You have been shown, so that you may know that the Lord is God; there is none else." Or "You have been shown, so that you may know that the Divine Root Name is the Elohim, There is None Else."

And Moses also said, "V'Yadata Hayom V'Hasheyvota El L'vavecha Ki YHWH Hu HaElohim BaShamayim MiMa'al V'Al HaAretz MiTachat Eyn Od,"[122] meaning "And you shall know today, and you shall return to your heart, because the Lord is God in the heavens above and on the earth below; there is none else." Or "And you shall know today, and you shall return to your heart, because the Divine Root Name is Elohim in the heavens above and on the earth below; there is none else."

Alaynu[123] is a prayer of gratitude and hope that is recited toward the end of each Jewish worship service. Alaynu includes the entire sacred phrase that begins "V'Yadata Hayom," and there are a number of prayers that include the sacred sub phrase "YHWH Hu HaElohim."

Shema – As We Recite It During Davvenen

During davvenen (worship), the Shema is recited in two ways. The first way is as a personal practice that we recite during davvenen (worship), both when we davven alone and when we davven in community. During this personal practice, one covers the eyes and then recites or chants the Shema in an audible voice, with deep inward intention. The eyes may be covered by one hand or both hands. If one is wearing glasses, one may remove the glasses and cover the eyes, or one may place the hand over the glasses. I have seen great rabbis recite the Shema both with and without wearing glasses.

---

119 *Deuteronomy* 6:4.
120 *The Schocken Bible: Volume I, The Five Books of Moses,* translator Everett Fox. (New York: Schocken Books, 1986).
121 *Deuteronomy* 4:35.
122 *Deuteronomy* 4:39.
123 Some rabbis and sages attribute the authorship of Alaynu to Joshua the son of Nun. Joshua was the successor to Moses and the one after whom the Biblical Book of Joshua is named. See Rabbi Nosson Scherman, et al., editors. *ArtScroll Transliterated Linear Siddur, Weekday* (New York: Mesorah Heritage Foundation, 1998) 256. Other scholars attribute the authorship of Alaynu to Rav, a Babylonian rabbi of the third century C.E.; while still others believe that Alaynu was composed centuries before Rav and was part of the rituals performed in the Second Holy Temple, which served the Jewish community from late in the sixth century B.C.E to 70 C.E. Some believe that Alaynu was originally composed for the liturgy of Rosh HaShanah, Jewish New Year. Since the middle ages, Alaynu has been part of daily Jewish worship throughout the year. See *Siddur Sim Shalom for Weekdays* (New York: The Rabbinical Assembly; The United Synagogue of Conservative Judaism, 2005) 83.

The second way that Shema is recited during davvenen (worship) is when the Torah is taken out of the ark and before it is unwrapped and read. In this practice, the one who is leading the service chants the Shema in full voice looking at the congregation, and the congregation responds by chanting the Shema in full voice. In some synagogues, particularly in the Reform Movement, the Shema is chanted aloud in full voice both when the Torah is being taken out of the ark, and during the repetition of the Shema as a personal practice.

Shema as a Deep and Elongated Chant

Reb Zalman gives a number of other formulations for chanting the Shema. Before each repetition, be briefly in silence, listen while reciting the Shema, and then be briefly in silence once again.

•Shema (insert your own name) Adonai Elohaynu Adonai Echad. This means "Listen (insert your own name), God is our God, God is One."

•Shema (insert your own name) YaH Elohaynu YaH[90] Echad. This means "Listen (insert your own name), God is our God, God is One."

While performing the two practices above, please keep in mind that Shema means "listen." When you say your own name in these practices, you are asking yourself, or telling yourself, or reminding yourself to listen to the reality that God is our God, God is One.

•Chant Shema Yisrael Adonai Elohaynu Adonai Echad slowly, elongating each word and focusing on the word and the melody.

•Chant Shema Yisrael YaH Elohaynu YaH Echad slowly, elongating each word and focusing on both the word you are pronouncing and the melody you are chanting.

•One Breath One Word - Take a breath, chant the word Shema until you run out of breath. Then breathe and chant Yisrael until you run out of breath. And so on. When doing this practice in a group, one may stop after each word and wait for the rest of the group to begin the next word. Or one may take a breath and begin the next word without waiting for the group. When leading this practice in a group, be sure to let everyone know in advance whether you wish them to wait for one another before beginning the next word, or whether each person should chant at their own pace.

For the "One Breath One Word" practice, one may also chant Shema Yisrael YaH Elohaynu YaH Echad, or Shema Yisrael Adonai Elohaynu Adonai Echad.

Shema as a Zikr

Zikr is a Sufi term meaning remembrance. Shabda Kahn reminds us that the first emotional loss is separation. We have a soul memory of being one with God, and we have human experience of being alone or lonely or bereft or abandoned. A fetus comes into the world from its mother's womb where all of its needs are provided through the placenta, and suddenly the infant has to breathe air instead of fluid, wetness against the infant's skin turns cold, and the infant has to wait to be held, and for hunger to be satisfied. Zikr is the Sufi practice of remembering Oneness, reconnecting with Oneness, reconnecting with the root of our being, and reconnecting with the source of all life and being.

Murshid Sam taught that Zikr and Shema are one.

The Shema may be spoken or chanted as a Zikr, sitting and turning the head from side to side. Begin turning the head to the left and recite Shema, then turn the head to the right and recite Yisrael, then left reciting Adonai, then right reciting Elohaynu, then left reciting Adonai, and then right reciting Echad. Then begin again. The Shema may be repeated as a Zikr so long as each repetition is recited with deep concentration and pure intent.

Hadrat Kodesh

In many synagogues, after reading from the Torah on Shabbat, the Torah is dressed in its cover and ornaments, and the leader of the service carries the Torah around the congregation while everyone sings Psalm 29. The second verse of Psalm 29 says, Havu LAdonai Kavod Va'Ohz, Hishtachavu LAdonai B'hadrat kodesh, which means "Ascribe to God the glory of His name, bow down to God in holy majesty." The last phrase, hadrat kodesh, may be translated as holy majesty, majesty of holiness, holy splendor, or splendor of holiness.

Sheikh Hassan Moumani,[124] of blessed memory, taught Sufi Zikr using what he called hadrat. Hadrat is a series of repetitive movements that involve standing in a circle holding hands, looking up and leaning back slightly while raising the hands, and then looking down and leaning slightly forward while lowering the hands. In Golden Gate Park on Joe Miller's walk,[125] Sheikh Hassan would look at plants and tall grasses that were swaying in the breeze. He would mimic their swaying with his hand and—with eyes twinkling—he would say in Arabic, "See! They are also singing God's praises!" He would also mimic the sprinklers oscillating as they delivered water on the lawns, and he would say, "they are also singing God's praises!" He would then chant "Allah Allah Allah Allah" and sway his hand and arm in the rhythm of the swaying plants, or the oscillating sprinklers, and he would say, "Every thing is praising God!"

---

124 Sheikh Hassan Moumani, also known as Murshid Hassan, was from Saudi Arabia and spent the latter years of his life living in the West Bank. Sheikh Hassan was an initiator in a number of Sufi Orders, including Refai and Bedoui.
125 For decades, Joe and Guin Miller went on a walk in Golden Gate Park in San Francisco on Thursdays. They would begin at the Hall of Flowers, now called the County Fair Building at Ninth Avenue and Lincoln. They would walk through Strybring Arboretum, and then on through the park to the beach. They would stop along the way and Joe would teach and lead the group in song and silence. He would also invite others to lead singing or dancing. Joe would give quarters to the children, and he and Guin bought ice cream for everyone who made it to the beach. For an excellent rendition of the life and teachings of Joe Miller, see Richard Power, *Great Song: Life and Teachings of Joe Miller* (Athens, Georgia: Maypop, 1993).

Circles of people performing hadrat movements look like large human poppy flowers that open to the light, close at dusk, and open again in the morning. Watching hadrat reminds me of the teaching of Rabbi Nachman of Breslov that each letter of our prayers is like a flower. We gather the flowers into bouquets as we recite each sacred word and phrase, and we offer these flowering bouquets to God as we pray.[126]

For these reasons, when using the hadrat movements while reciting Hebrew Zikr and other sacred phrases from the Jewish tradition, I suggest we call it hadrat kodesh, or "movement in the splendor of holiness."

Hadrat Kodesh Movements

To perform the hadrat kodesh, stand in a circle, shoulder to shoulder and hold hands. Lean the head slightly up and to the right and repeat one word. Lean the head down toward the heart and say the next word. Then lean the head up and to the left saying say the next word, and then lead the head down toward the heart and say the next word, and so on.

As you raise the head to the left and right, raise the hands slightly, bend the knees and lean back slightly. As you lower the head toward the heart, lower the hands, and bow forward slightly so that the body is following the head's lead toward the heart. The reason for bending the knees when leaning back is to allow the back to remain straight so one does not get a backache.

It is also possible to begin the hadrat kodesh movement leaning to the left. This would be advisable for a sacred phrase that begins with a negation, such as "Eyn Od," meaning "nothing else" or "Eyn Od Milvado," meaning "nothing but Him." When reciting an Arabic Zikr that begins with a negation, such "La Illaha, Il Allah Hu," meaning "there is no God, but God," one also begins the hadrat by leaning to the left.

Formulations of Shema Zikrs

The following formulations of Shema may be spoken or chanted as a Zikr, either sitting or in hadrat kodesh while standing, as described above.

One may also perform these Zikrs as a breathing practice, thinking "Shema Yisrael … Elohaynu" on the in breath, and "… Echad" on the outbreath. The dots "…" represent the word or words between "Yisrael" and "Elohaynu" in the formulations of the Shema below.

•Shema Yisrael YaH Elohaynu YaH Echad. This means Listen Israel, God is our God, God is One.

•Shema Yisrael YaH Hu Elohaynu YaH Hu Echad. This means Listen Israel, God, He is our God, God He is One.

•Shema Yisrael YaH Hu HaElohaynu YaH Hu HaEchad. This means Listen Israel, God, He is our God, God, He is the One.

---

126 Rabbi Nahman of Breslov, *Sefer Likutey Maharan* (Book of Gleanings of Our Teacher Reb Nahman) (Jerusalem: Publishing Fund of the Chassidim of Breslov, 5738 – 1978). This Reb Nachman teaching is also given in Chapter 4 of this book.

•Shema Yisrael YaH Hi Elohaynu YaH Hi Echad. This means Listen Israel, God, She is our God, She is One.

•Shema Yisrael YaH Hi HaElohaynu YaH Hi HaEchad. This means Listen Israel, God, She is our God, She is the One.

•Shema Yisrael Adonai Elohaynu Adonai Echad, meaning Listen Israel, God is our God, God is One.

•Shema Yisrael HaShem Elokaynu HaShem Echad. This means Listen Israel, God is our God, God is One.

•Shema Yisrael Adoshem Elokaynu Adoshem Echad, meaning Listen Israel, God is our God, God is One.

YaH Hu HaElohim

As part of the teachings of Moses that begin Atah Har'eyta and V'Yadata—which are mentioned at the beginning of this chapter—Moses says to the Israelites, "YHWH Hu HaElohim," meaning "the Divine Root Name is the Elohim," or "God transcendent is God that is both transcendent and in manifestation" or "God the Compassionate is God manifest in all the attributes" or "God the Compassionate is God the Judge.[127] As also mentioned in the beginning of this chapter, the sacred phrase "YHWH Hu HaElohim" appears in the Alaynu and a number of other Jewish prayers. It also appears in the closing sacred phrases chanted on Yom Kippur that are described in Chapter 13.

The sacred phrase YHWH Hu HaElohim may be recited in the following ways:

•YaH Hu HaElohim

•Adonai Hu HaElohim

•HaShem Hu HaElokim

•Adoshem Hu HaElokim

These sacred phrases may be spoken or chanted as a Zikr, sitting and turning the head from side to side.

One may speak or chant these phrases using the following head movements while sitting: Begin lifting the head slightly to the right and recite the first word, then lower the head toward the heart and recite Hu, then lift the head slightly to the left and say HaElo-, then lower the head toward the heart again and say –him (pronounced heem) or kim (pronounced keem). Repeat these sacred phrases with deep concentration and pure intent.

These sacred phrases may also be recited as a Zikr while standing and using the hadrat kodesh movements described earlier in this chapter.

---

127 See the midrash on Elohim in the "Midrash" section of Chapter 7.

Nothing But God

There is a void, an emptiness, a no-thing-ness that is described in the teachings of the Hindus, Buddhists, and Gnostic Christians as well as in the teachings of Rabbi Nachman of Breslov and other rabbis. Since there is nothing but God, and since the Glory of God is at the root of everything, one may find God everywhere, even in the void.

In Deuteronomy 4:35, Moses says eyn od milvado,[128] meaning "There is none but Him." In Deuteronomy 4:39, Moses says eyn od, meaning "There is none else." The teachings from which these phrases derive are given at the beginning of this chapter.

These phrases contain no name of God. They may be recited anywhere any time. And yet, they contain an essential teaching of spiritual reality. How is this possible? How can negation bring one to realization? What separates us from God-realization is our sense of self, our sense that we are separate from God, and our sense that God is this or God is that. God is Mercy, God is Love, God is the Divine Healer, God is the Forgiver of our sins. These are spiritual truths; there is no doubt about it. And these truths are at the basis of both Jewish and Sufi thought and practice. Many would prefer to deny that the opposites are also true; namely, that God is suffering and hatred and disease and condemnation.

Decades ago, Reb Zalman introduced the practice of Kabbalat Shabbat at Lama Foundation in New Mexico. Zalman pronounced Shabbat as "Shabbes,"[129] the Yiddish word for Sabbath.[130] Many of those who learned the practice of Kabbalat Shabbat from Zalman at Lama have come to call it simply "Shabbes." A few years ago, Hakim Sauluddin invited me to lead Shabbes and Hebrew Zikr at a DHO[131] gathering in San Francisco. I was delighted, honored and grateful for the opportunity to lead such an august body of healing devotees on the spiritual path, and it was heavenly to be in the Mentorgarden[132] with old friends. Sauluddin had fortune cookies made with the ninety-nine names of God given in Qur'an. There are numerous modern Sufi books on the ninety-nine names, including *Physicians of the Heart*,[133] *The Sufi Book of Life: 99 Pathways of the Heart for the Modern Dervish*,[134] and *Asm'ul Husna: the 99 Beautiful Names of Allah*.[135] Sauluddin explained that there were two fortune cookies containing each divine name and he invited us to each take a cookie, adding that the divine name in our cookie was to be our homework for the coming year. As a rabbi, I have my own spiritual homework, so I set my intention on translating into Hebrew the Arabic divine name of God that I would receive in my fortune cookie. Perhaps I would find the Hebrew equivalent in the prayers I recite during the week or on Shabbes; or perhaps it would be in scripture or a teaching I would find elsewhere, or one that I already knew. When it was my turn, I closed my eyes, quieted my breath, and took a fortune cookie.

---

128 "Milvado" is pronounced meel-va-doh with the accent on "doh."
129 Normally we see the Yiddish word for Sabbath written as "Shabbos." However, "es" at the end more correctly reflects the pronunciation. Thanks to Rabbi Menachem Creditor for pointing this out.
130 The Lama Foundation Shabbes practice is included in Chapter 24 of this book.
131 DHO stands for Dervish Healing Order, and is the healing branch of the Sufi Ruhaniat International <http://dervish-healing-order.org/>.
132 The Mentorgarden is a house on Precita Avenue in San Francisco that was Murshid Sam's home during the latter years of his life. The Mentorgarden is one of the places where Murshid Sam held classes and meetings and interviews. Khankah SAM is a Sufi center up the street from the Mentorgarden.
133 Wali Ali Meyer, Bilal Hyde, Faisal Muqaddam, and Shabda Kahn, *Physicians of the Heart, a Sufi View of the Ninety-Nine Names of Allah* (San Francisco: Sufi Ruhaniat International, 2011).
134 Neil Douglas-Klotz. *The Sufi Book of Life, 99 Pathways of the Heart for the Modern Dervish*. Penguin Compass, 2005.
135 M.R. Bawa Muhaiyaddeen, *Asm'ul Husna, The 99 Beautiful Names of Allah* (Philadelphia: Fellowship Press, 2002).

I broke open my cookie, removed the paper and held it in my hand. It read Ya Mudhill. There are many ways to understand and translate Ya Mudhill, but in the end—and no matter how I turned it in my mind—I knew that it means the One who causes humiliation, degradation or dishonor; or the One who is humiliation, degradation or dishonor. I immediately attributed my receiving this divine name to having chosen poorly—that is, without sufficient concentration—when reaching into the cookie bowl. A few DHO members were up the street at Khankah SAM cleaning up after our dinner, and Sauluddin asked that someone take up cookies to them. I offered to do it and thought this might give me a chance to choose a second cookie with a more positive divine quality. There were many leftover cookies in the bowl. I took one more cookie than the number of people cleaning the kitchen and went up to Khankah SAM. After everyone took, there was one cookie left, just as I had planned. I said a prayer and opened it. It said "Ya Mudhill."

Over the weeks that followed, I began looking up the divine name Ya Mudhill in Sufi books and papers and I even looked it up on the Internet. I wondered what God was looking to teach me. I found an answer in a teaching of Rabbi Nachman of Breslov in *Lukutei Maharan* where he explains that God's glory is at the root of everything. Every thing—regardless of whether it is inherently good or inherently evil, whether it leads to progress or leads us backward, whether it guides us on our path or causes us to stray from the path, whether it fills us with pride or humility, with holiness or mortification—every thing is God. There is none else.

As the years have unfolded, humiliation has begun to play a different role in my life, and parts of myself that I would not have considered heretofore to be divine are having the crusts broken off and the bandages removed, and the wounds are slowly healing, and although it is not easy to admit—even to myself—divine humiliation has become my teacher.

When all else fails, when nothing seems to be working, remember that that too is God. Eyn Od milvado, Eyn Od. There is nothing but God; there is none else.

Reciting Eyn Od Milvado and Eyn Od

Eyn Od Milvado may be spoken or chanted. Recite Eyn Od Milvado sitting still or shokkelen (defined in the Glossary).

On the breath, breathe out holding the thought Eyn Od, and breathe in thinking Milvado. One may also breathe in holding the thought Eyn Od, and breathe out thinking Milvado. As a walking practice, recite or think Eyn Od as one foot goes down, and Milvado as the other foot goes down. Begin on whichever foot feels right.

Eyn Od may also be spoken or chanted, sitting still or shokkelen (defined in the Glossary).

On the breath, breathe in thinking Eyn Od, breathe out silence, breathe in thinking Eyn Od, breathe out silence, and so on. Or reverse this and breathe out thinking Eyn Od and breathe in silence. Or breathe in Eyn Od and then breathe out Eyn Od.

Chapter 12

Zikrs of Shomer Yisrael

There is a Jewish prayer called Tachanun that is recited during shacharit (the morning service) and mincha (the afternoon service). Tachanun is a forgiveness prayer, during which there is time to pour out one's heart and ask for forgiveness. In many prayer books, Tachanun ends with a piyyut—a spiritual poem—called Shomer Yisrael.[136] Shomer Yisrael means Guardian of Israel. In the Shomer Yisrael prayer, it says, "Guardian of a people, protect the remnant of this people. And do not let this people be lost, who unify Your name: Adonai Elohaynu Adonai Echad."[137]

During the musaf Amidah (silent devotion recited during the additional service) on the Sabbath and festivals, it says in the Kedushah (sanctification), "God will turn in compassion, and grant mercy to the people who unify His name, evening and morning, each day always, reciting 'Shema' with love: 'Shema Yisrael Adonai Elohaynu Adonai Echad."[138]

The following sacred phrases contain the divine name Elohaynu, and the Divine Root Name in the form of YaH, Adonai and HaShem. Each of these sacred phrases may be recited or chanted, and they may be held as a thought on the breath or as a thought in the silence.

•YaH Elohaynu, YaH Echad.

•YaH Hu Elohaynu, YaH Hu Echad.

•YaH Hu HaElohim, YaH Hu HaEchad.

•YaH Hi Elohaynu, YaH Hi Echad.

•YaH Hi HaElohim, YaH Hi HaEchad.

•Adonai Elohaynu Adonai Echad.

•HaShem Elokaynu HaShem Echad. When chanting this phrase, Elohaynu is pronounced Elokaynu, for the reasons explained in Chapter 9.

---

136 Shomer Yisrael is the name of a piyyut (spiritual poem) composed in the middle ages. It was found amid liturgy for the Tenth of Tevet, a fast day commemorating the day on which the Babylonians laid siege to Jerusalem in 586 B.C.E. That siege culminated in the destruction of the First Holy Temple in Jerusalem and the exile of the Judeans to Babylonia. In modern times, Ashkenazi Jews recite Shomer Yisrael as part of Tachanun, the penitential prayers recited during morning and afternoon worship on most ordinary weekdays. Shephardi and Mizrahi Jews recite Shomer Yisrael as part of the High Holy Day liturgy. In Shomer Yisrael, the poet writes: "Guardian of a people, protect the remnant of this people. And do not let this people be lost, who unify Your name, Adonai Elohaynu Adonai Echad." *Siddur Sim Shalom for Weekdays* (New York: The Rabbinical Assembly; The United Synagogue of Conservative Judaism, 2002) 63.
137 Adonai Elohaynu Adonai Echad means "L-rd our G-d, L-rd is One," or "G-d is our G-d, G-d is One."
138 *Siddur Sim Shalom for Shabbat and Festivals* (New York: The Rabbinical Assembly; The United Synagogue of Conservative Judaism, 1998) 157 and 167.

The above sacred phrases are Zikrs. Recite or chant these Zikrs while sitting. Lower the head slightly and place the sound YaH—or Adonai or HaShem—in the heart. Then lift the head and recite the next part of the phrase. Then lower the head and place the second YaH—or Adonai or HaShem—in the heart. Then lift the head as you recite the remainder of the phrase.

One may also recite or chant these Zikrs while standing and using the hadrat kodesh movements described in Chapter 11.

As a breathing practice, breathe in YaH—or Adonai or HaShem—and the next word or two. Then breathe out the second YaH—or Adonai or HaShem—and the rest of the phrase.

YaH Echad

The following are Zikrs that arise from the Shomer Yisrael Zikrs:

Adonai Echad.

YaH Echad.

YaH Hu HaEchad.

They may be spoken or chanted, or held as a thought on the breath or in the mind. When reciting these Zikrs, shokkel while sitting or standing. (Shokkelen is defined in the Glossary.) When reciting Adonai Echad and YaH Echad, lower the head and focus the divine name in the heart. Then raise the head slightly while reciting Echad. For YaH Hu HaEchad, focus YaH Hu in the heart, and then lift the head up and slightly to the right on HaEchad.

Chapter 13

Zikrs of Yom Kippur

Yom Kippur, the Day of Atonement, is the holiest day in the Jewish year. Yom Kippur is considered by some rabbis and sages as a rehearsal for our death.[139] How do we rehearse? By abstaining from working, eating, drinking, washing, using grooming products, having sexual relations, and from wearing leather or other animal products. These abstinence practices are based upon the teaching in Torah given by God that we should "afflict our souls" on Yom Kippur. Abstinence softens the heart and quickens the spirit, making us more desperate, so that our intention might become more intense, and our prayers more fervent.

We end Yom Kippur and our practice of abstinence with the blowing of the shofar, the ram's horn. Shofar blowing is preceded by reciting the Shema once, Barukh Shem Kevod Malkhuto L'Olam Va'ed three times, and Adonai Hu HaElohim seven times. Translations and sources for these phrases are given in the Sources section below.

In Chapter 5, I recounted the story of Papa Ramdas, who tells his disciple that one need recite the Hindu sacred phrase Om Sri Ram Jai Ram Jai Jai Ram[140] only once to achieve enlightenment. Sufis are fond of many repetitions. Jews are fond of reciting a phrase once and moving on to the next phrase, with occasional exceptions such as this next practice. God realization dawns through grace, and in truth, no matter how many times we perform—or fail to perform—a prayer or sacred phrase or mitzvah (divine commandment), God realization will come to us in its own time, and generally when we least expect it.

I recommend reciting these sacred phrases as they are recited at the end of Yom Kippur—the Shema once, Barukh Shem three times and Adonai Hu HaElohim seven times—and also reciting additional repetitions of each sacred phrase to experience them more deeply.

•Traditional Sacred Phrases of Yom Kippur before blowing the shofar:
Shema Yisrael Adonai Elohaynu Adonai Echad (recite or chant once)
Barukh Shem Kevod Malkhuto L'Olam Va'ed (recite or chant three times)
Adonai Hu HaElohim (recite or chant seven times)

•Sacred Phrases of Yom Kippur before blowing the shofar, according to Reb Zalman:
Shema Yisrael YaH Elohaynu YaH Echad (recite or chant once)
Barukh Shem Kevod Malkhuto L'Olam Va'ed (recite or chant three times)
YaH Hu HaElohim (recite or chant seven times)

Sources of the Zikrs of Yom Kippur

Shema - Moses gave the Shema to the Israelites as recorded in the Book of Deuteronomy, chapter 6, verse 4. "Shema Yisrael Adonai Elohaynu Adonai Echad" means "Listen Israel, the Lord our God, the Lord is One." "Israel" refers to the Jewish people, and may also be translated as "God Wrestler" after

---

139 Alan Lew. *This is Real and You Are Completely Unprepared* (Boston: Little, Brown and Company, 2003).
140 Ram is a name of God in the Hindu faith. Om Sri Ram Jai Ram Jai Jai Ram is Sanskrit. It means Hail Holy Ram, Victory to Ram, Victory, Victory to Ram.

Jacob, the third Jewish patriarch whose name was changed from Jacob to Israel after he wrestled with a being. Some believe that being was an angel, while others believe it was a man.

Barukh Shem Kevod Malkhuto L'Olam Va'ed means Blessed is the Name; the Glory of His Kingdom is forever and ever. This sacred phrase is not in the Bible. It is, however, discussed in the Talmud, Deuteronomy Rabbah[141] and the *Zohar*. In these texts, the phrase is alternately attributed to Jacob—the third Hebrew Patriarch—and to Moses and to the angels. Because of these attributions, Barukh Shem Kevod Malkhuto L'Olam Va'ed is recited every day after Shema Yisrael Adonai Elohaynu Adonai Echad, during evening and morning davvenen, and at bedtime. In Orthodox and most Conservative synagogues, the Shema is recited out loud and Barukh Shem is recited quietly or in silence, except on Yom Kippur, when both Shema and Barukh Shem are recited aloud.

The reason for reciting Barukh Shem quietly throughout the year is that when Moses gave the Shema in Deuteronomy, he gave it together with the teaching to love the Lord our God with all our heart and soul and might, but he did not mention Barukh Shem. To honor the midrashim (stories/interpretations) that Jacob, Moses and/or the angels recited, "Barukh Shem Kevod Malkhuto Le'olam Va'ed," it is included in our daily prayers immediately following the Shema. To honor that Moses did not include it in the Torah, Orthodox and many Conservative Jews recite the Barukh Shem quietly, except on Yom Kippur.

Reform Jews tend to recite the Barukh Shem aloud throughout the year. Rabbi Mordecai Kaplan gave the teaching that Jewish law and tradition have a vote, but not a veto. Reb Zalman is fond of quoting this teaching of Rabbi Kaplan, and Zalman gives it as a Jewish Renewal teaching, crediting Rabbi Kaplan as its source. Some Reconstructionist and Renewal Jews also recite Barukh Shem aloud throughout the year, while others recite it quietly, with the exception of Yom Kippur.

On Yom Kippur, in all Jewish congregations, as far as this author knows, Barukh Shem is recited aloud. This is because the Israelites recited it aloud on Yom Kippur in response to the high priest's recitation of the Divine Root Name during his Yom Kippur prayers. According to tradition, every time the high priest recited the Divine Root Name, the people fell on their faces and said Barukh Shem Kevod Malkhuto Le'Olam Va'ed.

This sacred phrase may also be recited after making a mistake when one is reciting a blessing. This explained by Rabbi Eliezer Danzinger of Chabad.[142]

It is permitted to pronounce any of G-d's names when in the context of a prayer, blessing, or when reciting a full passage from the Scriptures—as that is not considered "in vain." If, however, we mention His name inappropriately – for example, if we accidentally recite an incorrect blessing (the formula for every blessing includes His name) – we immediately say, "*Barukh shem kevod malkhuto l'olam va'ed.*" "Blessed is the Name; the glory of His kingdom forever and ever."

---

141 "Devarim Rabbah" is a commentary on the Book of Deuteronomy.
142 Rabbi Eliezer Danzinger, "What should I do if I pronounce G-d's name in vain?" Chabad.org, Ask the Rabbi <http://www.chabad.org/library/article_cdo/aid/608758/jewish/What-should-I-do-if-I-pronounce-Gds-name-in-vain.htm>; also <http://tinyurl.com/6e22sdx>.

Adonai Hu HaElohim and YaH Hu HaElohim[143] mean "God (alone) is the (true) God," or "the Divine Root Name is the God" or "Lord is the God." As mentioned at the beginning of Chapter 11 and discussed elsewhere in that chapter, Adonai Hu HaElohim was given to the Israelites by Moses in Deuteronomy, chapter 4, verses 35 and 39. It also appears in the Biblical books of Kings and Chronicles, and it is discussed in the Talmud, the *Zohar* and numerous other commentaries,[144] Adonai Hu HaElohim or YaH Hu HaElohim, together with the entire verse 39 from chapter 4 of Deuteronomy is included in Alaynu—a prayer attributed either to Joshua ben Nun, after whom the Biblical Book of Joshua is named; or to Rav, a Babylonian rabbi who lived in the third century C.E.

---

143 "YaH" is a placeholder here for the Divine Root Name, defined in Chapter 8.

144 *Deuteronomy* 4:35 and 39; *Kings* I 8:60 and 18:39; *Chronicles* II 33:13. The following are references to the Talmud: Tractate Rosh HaShanah (New Year) 32b; Tractate Gittin (Divorce) 57b; Tractate Sanhedrin (Court) 101b; Tosafot (Additional Commentaries), Tractate Brakhot (Blessings) 34 (appears twice). Bereishit Rabbah (commentary on *Genesis*) 101; VaYikra Rabbah (commentary on *Leviticus*) 30:3; Devarim Rabbah (commentary on *Deuteronomy*) 2:20 and 28; Eicha Rabbah (commentary on Lamentations) 1:50; Kohelet Rabbah (commentary on Ecclesiastes) 10,:2; VaYikra Rabbah Margaliyot (Gems from the commentary on Leviticus (50) 30:4; *Zohar*, 8:1, *Zohar* 8:2 Tosafot (additional commentaries); *Zohar* 8:2 Raya Mehem'na (Faithful Shepherd); *Zohar* 8:3 Tosafot (additional commentaries), *Zohar* 8:3 Raya Mehem'na (Faithful Shepherd).

Chapter 14

Reb Zalman's Four-Part Shema

In this practice, one recites the Shema in four different ways with four different intentions. The four are separate, and yet the four are one. The realization of each repetition is different, as we find our way toward the experience of the One, which Pir-O-Murshid Hazrat Inayat Khan calls "Toward the One." Oneness may be realized at any moment during religious and spiritual practice, as well as during everyday life. May we be graced to glimpse the Oneness and continue to live in this world!

First Repetition

Recite the Shema in the regular way. In other words, recite it in the way you would normally recite the Shema.

If you do not know how to recite the Shema, begin by learning to do so. There is information about reciting the Shema in Chapter 11 of this book, and there are numerous other books and articles that teach the Shema. If you have never heard the Shema pronounced, listen to a recording, such as the ones at http://rebpam.com/, or ask a friend who knows the Shema to teach you how to recite or chant it.

For the First Repetition, Reb Zalman recites the Shema using the following words: "Shema Yisrael YaH Elohaynu YaH Echad." Reb Pam[145] recites it as "Shema Yisrael Adonai Elohaynu Adonai Echad." Both mean "Listen Israel, God is our God, God is One."

The term Israel refers to the Jewish people. As explained in Chapter 11, Moses gave the Shema to the Jewish people, as recorded in the Book of Deuteronomy. Israel also means God wrestler, or one who wrestles with the divine and prevails. The name Israel was given to Jacob, the third patriarch of the Jewish people, after he wrestled with a being and prevailed. The story is recounted in the Book of Genesis.[146] Murshid Sam teaches that "Israel" is a double entendre; it may be translated as the Jewish people, and it may also be translated in the supernal sense of every devotee; we are all God wrestlers as we titrate between the human and the divine.

---

145 Reb Pam is the author of this book.
146 *Genesis* 32:23-33.

Second Repetition

Recite the word "Shema," then insert your own name, then "YaH Elohaynu YaH Echad." This means "Listen (insert your own name), God is our God, God is One." As noted above, Shema means "listen." When you say your own name in this practice, you are asking yourself, or telling yourself, or reminding yourself to listen to the reality that God is our God, God is One.

Many people think of the Shema as a sacred phrase being recited to God. However, when Moses gave the Shema, he gave it to the people. Reciting the Shema brings us to a realizing of God, or aims us toward God realization. On the way to God realization, we may recite the Shema to God, as it were, but in the end, there is no separation between us and God, since God is One and there is none else.

The One Being

The great Sufi Husayn ibn Mansur al-Hallaj, may peace and blessing be upon him, wrote the following prayer in the third century C.E. This translation is from Sidi Muhammad Press of The Tariq Shadhuliyya:

> Is it You or I? That would be two gods in me;
> But far be it from You to manifest as two—
> The He-ness that is Yours is in my One-ness forever;
> My all added to Your All would be a double existence.
> But where is Your Essence, from my place of looking, when I see You?
> Since my essence has become plain, in the place where I am not.
> And where is Your Face, which is the Object of my gaze,
> Whether in my inmost heart, or in the glance of my eye?
> Between You and me there is an I am that battles with me,
> So take away, by Your Grace, this I am from in between.[147]

The second repetition of Reb Zalman's Four Part Shema invites us to move from the impersonal third person calling out to us and those around us, to the first person, our very self calling out to our very self. Every repetition of the Shema invites us to unify God's name by calling on the name pronounced Adonai (or YaH) and Elohaynu in the same phrase. Reb Zalman's second repetition of the Four Part Shema invites us to realize that we are, as it were, a droplet of water in the vast ocean of being. There is no ocean except the ocean of which we are a droplet. As the wave we ride rises and returns to the water's surface, we may lose our droplet consciousness, but we are still part of the one ocean. As the wave we ride washes upon the shore and becomes absorbed in the sand or evaporated into the air, our form may change, but we are still an evaporated or absorbed form of the same one ocean; there is no other. Calling upon God as Adonai and Elohaynu (or YaH and Elohaynu) is analogous to calling upon the ocean as "the great body of water, of which there is no other" and "the great conflation of droplets forming the one ocean." The two names of the same Being point us to the consciousness of that being. By reciting these divine names together with our own name, we are invited to lose individual droplet consciousness in the consciousness of the one ocean.

---

147 This translation of the poem of al-Hallaj, together with a beautiful story about al-Hallaj is available at <http://www.sufimaster.org/husayn.htm> as of May 2012.

After taking the second step described above, Reb Zalman then invites us into the practice of the Third Shema with which we offer the fruits of our realization to the merit of someone of our choosing. This is part of the practice of tikkun olam and tikkun halev. As will be discussed in Chapter 23, tikkun olam means repair of the world, and is a term used to describe the practice of helping to make the world a better place. Another, related practice, is tikkun halev, the practice of repairing the heart and attuning it toward divine realization and divine service. When we focus our prayers on someone else, and when we offer to the merit of someone else the benefit of prayer that has accumulated within us—as Reb Zalman recommends in the third repetition of the Shema given below—we engage in the practice of tikkun halev.

Third Repetition

Recite the Shema with someone's name to whom you wish to send energy, like this:

Shema (insert the person's name) Adonai Elohaynu Adonai Echad.

Or

Shema (insert the person's name) YaH Elohaynu YaH Echad.

Or

Recite the Shema in your own way, inserting someone's name in place of the word "Yisrael."

Or

While reciting the Shema in this manner, send energy—or send the sacred merit of your earlier practice of the First and Second Shema described above; or send the merit of your spiritual state—to the person whose name you recite during this Third Repetition of the Shema.

Fourth Repetition

After the Third Repetition of the Shema, Reb Zalman invites us into the Fourth Repetition in which we practice reciting the Shema in the way we would wish to remember it at the time of our death. During the Fourth Repetition of the Shema, when we imagine leaving our body with the words of the Shema on our lips, and the feeling permeating our dying corpus, we may approach the throne of God—or however we imagine Divine Godliness welcoming us home. As we imagine that moment, Reb Zalman invites us to set aside the "I am" of our individual self, and merge into the "I am" of God. This is not a practice that one completes in this world, but it is precisely in this world—the realm of God's creation—where we may glimpse a moment of what Reb Nachman of Breslov calls the void. In the void, there is no "I am." There is simply IS-ness. I believe that it is this realization toward which Al-Hallaj is pointing in his prophetic words above that describe the ultimate spiritual practice; the practice of losing our self in the One Self of Being.

Recite the Shema in a way that you would like to be able to remember it just before dying. Reb Zalman invites us to use this practice to make a sort of deposit toward the end of our earthly existence in the body that we now inhabit. We may also use this practice to make a deposit toward realization of the teaching of Al-Hallaj given above, because, in the end, the two are one.

Joe Miller used to remind us that we cannot alter the circumstances of our lives, or the challenges that have been placed before us, or the challenges that will be placed before us in the future. We may, however, change our attitude.

May we be graced with the consciousness from which to desire the practice of the Four Shemas given by Reb Zalman. Would that this practice—and indeed, all religious and spiritual practices—may guide us toward the realization of Oneness.

Chapter 15

Halleluyah Zikrs

Hallel means praise. Hallelu means "let us praise" or "you praise" with "you," being in the plural. YaH is a Hebrew name of God discussed in Chapter 8. Thus, halleluyah means "praise God!" or "let us praise God!"

The word "halleluyah" appears in the Biblical Book of Psalms. While some of the psalms contain attributions that identify the person believed to be the author—such as King David, King Solomon, Asaph and the sons of Korach—the psalms that contain the word "halleluyah" do not include attributions.

Murshid Sam gave the practice of reciting halleluyah as a Zikr. This chapter contains three forms of Halleluyah Zikr. Each form uses just one word—halleluyah—but with the emphasis, or accent, on a different syllable. The three Halleluyah Zikrs may be recited or sung or whispered, or held in thought in silence on the breath.

Normally, halleluyah is thought of as an ecstatic expression, and in many settings, of course, it is. However, the recitation of halleluyah as a Zikr is quite subtle, and is best experienced when reciting it in an interior manner rather than with the forcefulness that brings immediate joy. In Sufi terms, one would say that it is best to recite halleluyah in a jemali manner.[148]

I suggest remaining seated while reciting the Halleluyah Zikrs so that one may place one's full concentration on the pronunciation and the aiming of the sound in the centers of the body. After the individual or group has gained some mastery in the recitation of the Zikr, then, if it is desirable, stand up and do one or more of these Zikrs with very slight and gentle head and body movements.

A Word About the Centers in the Body

These Halleluyah Zikr practices focus on three centers: heart, throat and crown. The centers correspond to the sephirot described in the "Sacred Focus" section of Chapter 6, as well as in Appendix D. The heart center is called tiferet, which may be translated as love or harmony or beauty. The throat center and crown center are considered to be part of the same sephirah, which is called ketter. There is a discussion of tiferet and ketter—including information about the relationship between the crown and the throat—in Chapter 6, and in the "Definitions of the Sephirot" section of Appendix D.

Please note that when aiming the sound above the crown, one may feel the vibration of the sound in the actual crown of the head, even though one is aiming above it.

As mentioned earlier, the Halleluyah Zikrs are best recited while pronouncing the words gently, rather than forcefully. This practice may also be done in a whisper.

---

148 A jemali manner is a gentle refined manner.

First Halleluyah Zikr Emphasizing "Ha" and "YaH"

The First Halleluyah Zikr is pronounced **ha**-le-lu-**yah**, with the syllables in bold receiving the emphasis. This Zikr may be performed while moving the energy from the heart to the crown, and from the crown to the heart, as follows:

   Heart to Crown - While sitting, lower the head slightly and say "ha," gently aiming the sound into the heart. Then say "le-lu" as the head comes up. Raise the head a bit more, and say "yah," aiming the sound gently above the crown of the head. Then repeat.

   Crown to Heart - While sitting, raise the head slightly and say "ha," gently aiming the sound above the crown of the head. Then say "le-lu" as the head comes down. Lower the head a bit more, and say "yah," aiming the sound gently into the heart. Then repeat.

This First Halleluyah Zikr may be sung or spoken or whispered. It may also be held as a thought on the breath without head movements.

When singing or reciting this Zikr, remember to emphasize "ha" and "yah." When you complete this Zikr, be sure to be in silence for a few moments.

Second Halleluyah Zikr Emphasizing "Ha"

The Second Halleluyah Zikr is pronounced **ha**-le-lu-yah, with emphasis on "ha." This Zikr may be performed while moving the energy from the heart to the throat, and from the crown to the throat.

   Heart toward Throat - While sitting, lower the head slightly and say "ha," gently aiming the sound into the heart. Then say "le-lu" as the head comes up, and say "yah," aiming the sound in the throat center that is between the back of the physical throat and the back of the neck. Then repeat.

   Crown toward Throat - While sitting, raise the head slightly and say "ha," gently aiming the sound above the crown. Then say "le-lu" as the head comes down, and say "yah," aiming the sound gently into the throat center. Then repeat.

This Second Halleluyah Zikr may be sung or spoken or whispered. It may also be held as a thought on the breath without head movements.

When singing or reciting this Zikr, remember to emphasize "ha." When you complete the Zikr, be sure to be in silence for a few moments.

Third Halleluyah Zikr Emphasizing "Lu"

The Third Halleluyah Zikr is pronounced ha-le-**lu**-yah, with emphasis on "lu." This Zikr focuses the energy in the throat center while moving from heart to throat, or from crown to throat.

Heart to Throat - While sitting, lower the head toward the heart and then raise it until you are looking forward. Then repeat. With head lowered, and as you are beginning to it, say "ha-le." When you are looking forward, say "**lu**-yah," with the emphasis on "lu."

Crown to Throat - While sitting, raise the head until your face is looking slightly upward. Then say "ha-le." As you move your head down, say "**lu**-yah," emphasizing the sound "lu" and aiming the sound toward the back of the throat. Repeat.

This Third Halleluyah Zikr may be sung or spoken or whispered. It may also be held as a thought on the breath without head movements.

When singing or reciting this Zikr, remember to emphasize "lu." When you complete the Zikr, be sure to be in silence for a few moments.

Chapter 16

Zikrs of Balance

The Zikrs in this chapter address the desire among many to experience a balance of the masculine and feminine. See also the Kabbalistic Invocation given in Chapter 25, and the background and practices sections of "L'Sheym Yichud Kudsha Brikh Hu" in Chapter 19.

YaH Hu YaH Hi

YaH Hu YaH Hi is a Zikr that came to me in 1983 while meditating on the bank of the river that runs through the Mendocino Woodlands, during an afternoon break at Sufi Camp where I was teaching a class on Kabbalah.

YaH Hu means God He. YaH Hi means God She. YaH Hu YaH Hi may be recited sitting or standing, it may be spoken or chanted, and it may also be used on the breath or as a thought.

I recite Ya Hu YaH Hi eight times as one repetition. Within the eight times are two series of four. There are samples of this—both spoken and as a chant—on the website listed in the Key to Pronunciation at the beginning of this book.

While sitting, lift the head to the right and recite YaH Hu, aiming the sound into the crown above the head. Lower the head and recite YaH Hi, aiming the sound into the heart. Then repeat.

One may also reverse the direction, lowering the head and reciting YaH Hu, aiming the sound into the heart, and then raising the head to the left, and reciting YaH Hi, aiming the sound into the crown above the head.

YaH Hu YaH Hi may also be recited standing, and using the hadrat kodesh movements described in Chapter 11. Start by lifting the head slightly to the right on YaH Hu and lowering the head, aiming the sound of YaH Hi into the heart. Then lift the head slightly to the left on YaH Hu, and lower the head, aiming the sound of YaH Hi again into the heart. Then repeat. Be sure to take a look at the full instructions for hadrat kodesh movements in Chapter 11, as this paragraph only explains the head movements, and not the bending of the knees.

One may also reverse the hadrat kodesh movements for YaH Hu YaH Hi: Start by lowering the head and aiming YaH Hu into the heart, and raise the head slightly to the right on YaH Hi. Then lower the head on YaH Hu, again aiming the sound into the heart, and raise the head slightly to the left on YaH Hi. Then repeat.

If you count the repetitions of YaH Hu YaH Hi on your prayers beads or on your fingers, count a cycle of eight repetitions of YaH Hu YaH Hi as one bead, or one point on your finger. (Counting is discussed in Chapter 5.) You may experience a change of state after just one repetition, or a few repetitions, or it may take many repetitions to experience this Zikr. I often repeat YaH Hu YaH Hi for a period of time, such as five minutes, rather than for a certain number of repetitions. And sometimes I repeat this Zikr until I feel done without regard to the number of repetitions or amount of time.

If you are going to repeat YaH Hu YaH Hi for a very long time, it may be valuable to stop periodically, watch your breath, and feel your centers before continuing.

Background on Brukha At YaH Shekhinah, Barukh Atah Elohim

Brukha At YaH Shekhinah and Barukh Atah Elohim may both be translated as "Blessed are You God."

Brukha is the feminine form of the verb that means blessed. Barukh is the masculine form of the same verb. At and Atah are the Hebrew feminine and masculine meaning "you." YaH is a name of God. Elohim is also a name of God. These divine names are discussed in Chapters 8, 11 and elsewhere.

Shechina is the feminine divine presence dwelling within all of creation. According to the *Zohar*, the divine name Adonai refers to the Shechina. Thus, in every Jewish blessing, when we recite Barukh Atah Adonai Elohaynu Melekh HaOlam, we are attuning to, and giving thanks to, God in the divine masculine and the divine feminine, as it were. ("As it were" is an expression used here, since, as we know, God is beyond form and gender.)

According to some Jewish sources, the Shechina went into exile when the Holy Temple in Jerusalem was destroyed. She is exiled in this world and is waiting to be able to dwell in the inner planes with God forever. On Shabbes, the Jewish Sabbath, God transcendent and the Shechina enter into divine union. This union is referred to in the Kabbalah, and in the Kabbalistic Invocation, which will be discussed in Chapters 19 and 25.

While Shechina is associated with the feminine, in the Kabbalah, Elohim is associated alternately with the masculine and feminine.

Brukha At YaH Shekhinah, Barukh Atah Elohim as a Zikr

Begin by reciting or chanting the phrase slowly, because it is easier to get the feel of it when repeating it slowly. Then speed it up if you wish.

One may recite or chant this phrase as demonstrated on the website listed in the Key to Pronunciation. When sitting, lower the head toward the heart on Brukha, lift the head to the right on At YaH, lower the head toward the heart on Shekhi-, then lift the head to the left on -inah, with "i" being a continuous sound as the head is raised. Then lower the head to the heart on Barukh, lift the head up to the right again on Atah, lower the head on Elohim, and then lift the head up to the left in silence—or, if your prefer, lift the head to the left while completing the "-im" of Elohim. Then repeat.

When standing, one may recite this Zikr using the hadrat kodesh movements described in Chapter 11.

YaH Hu YaH Hi and Brukha At YaH Shekhinah Barukh Atah Elohim As Counter-Point

The Zikrs YaH Hu YaH Hi and Brukha At YaH Shekhinah Barukh Atah Elohim may be chanted simultaneously in counter-point with groups of worshippers or spiritual practitioners. Both Zikrs may be chanted in four-four time. It takes the time of eight repetitions of YaH Hu YaH Hi to recite Brukha At YaH Shekhinah Barukh Atah Elohim twice.

Divide the group in half, and teach everyone both parts. Then begin with one group chanting YaH Hu YaH Hi, and after eight YaH Hu YaH Hi's, begin Brukha At YaH. This practice may be done sitting or standing. If the group is standing in circles, I suggest separate circles for each phrase, so that one circle is chanting YaH Hu YaH Hi, while the other circle is chanting Brukha At YaH.

The key to spiritual depth and musical success when chanting these two Zikrs as counterpoint is to have one musical instrument to keep the pitch, and another to keep the rhythm. Or have one person standing in the middle and focusing on the pitch, and one standing in the middle and clapping the rhythm.

YaH Hu

Hu is the Hebrew masculine pronoun meaning "he," and is also used as a present tense form of the verb "to be." YaH Hu means God is.[149]

While sitting, shokkel, focusing the sound Hu in the heart. While standing, also shokkel, focusing the sound Hu in the heart. To shokkel is to sway slightly back and forth.

One may also use the hadrat kodesh movements for YaH Hu instead of shokkelen.

One may recite YaH Hu as a Zikr on its own, or as a second form of Zikr that is recited after reciting YaH Hu YaH Hi. One may also recite YaH Hu on its own after reciting YaH Hu YaH Hi with the counter point Brukha At YaH Shechina, Barukh Atah Elohim.

---

149 As mentioned early in Chapter 8, there is no present tense form of the verb "to be" in Hebrew. In general, the present tense form of the verb "to be" is implied from the word order of the sentence or phrase. In some situations, however, pronouns are used to imply the verb "to be." YaH Hu and YaH Hi are examples of this. YaH Hu literally means "God He" and may be understood to mean "God is." Similarly YaH Hi literally means "God She" and may be understood to mean "God is."

YaH Hi

Hi is the Hebrew feminine pronoun meaning "she," and is also used as a present tense form of the verb "to be." YaH Hi means "God is."[150]

While sitting, shokkel, focusing the sound Hi in the area of the forehead. While standing, also shokkel, focusing the sound Hi in the area of the forehead. The forehead is the approximate location in the body of the line between the sephirot of chokhmah, meaning wisdom, and binah, meaning understanding, or what we call in science, the left brain and right brain. Chokhmah and binah are defined in Appendix D.

As mentioned above, to shokkel is to sway slightly back and forth.

One may recite YaH Hi as a Zikr on its own, or as a second form of Zikr that is recited after reciting YaH Hu YaH Hi. One may also recite YaH Hi on its own after reciting YaH Hu YaH Hi with the counter point Brukha At YaH Shekhinah, Barukh Atah Elohim.

---

150 See previous footnote regarding the present tense form of the verb "to be."

Chapter 17

Divine Gratitude

This chapter includes sacred phrases of divine gratitude.

Todah La'EyL

Todah La'Eyl means "Thanks to God," "thank God," or "thank you God." Todah La'Eyl may be used to express gratitude in everyday conversation in modern Hebrew, and it is also a sacred phrase that may be repeated as a spiritual practice. This practice will be welcome in some Jewish settings, but not others. Eyl is a name of God that is replaced by "HaShem" or "Adoshem" in common parlance among the Orthodox, some Conservatives and some others. In such settings, use Barukh HaShem instead, which is a practice given below.

Begin the repetition of Todah La'Eyl by focusing on the sound of each syllable and each word with an intention of gratitude. Then add head movements and focus the sound of each syllable and word in your centers. To do this, move the head forward and then upright. As the head goes down, aim the sound of Todah toward the heart center (tiferet), with the sound "dah" as a gentle tap to open the heart. Let the head rise almost automatically, and say La'Eyl as your head rises, feeling Eyl in the crown center above the head (ketter). When you are able to project the sounds toward your centers, then begin counting the number of repetitions of the phrase if it is your practice to count them. Counting sacred phrases is discussed in Chapter 5.

One of the blessings of Hebrew spiritual practice is that the energy flows in both directions. One may focus the energy in an upward direction or in a downward direction, and use the same sacred phrase to move the energy in both directions. This is discussed in the section entitled "Sacred Focus" in Chapter 6.

After the first 108 repetitions (or more) of Todah La'Eyl described above, switch the focus, raising the head on Todah and lowering the head on La'Eyl, aiming the sound of La'Eyl toward the heart, with Eyl, meaning "God" as a gentle tap to open the heart. Feel Todah in the crown above the head.

After you have mastered the pronunciation, head movements and focusing in your centers with a feeling of gratitude, try alternating between lifting and then lowering the head for a number of repetitions, and then lowering and lifting the head for a number of repetitions, such as 18, 36, 54, 72 or 108 in one direction and the same number of repetitions in the other direction. See what rhythm works best for you and use it in your personal practice.

As a breathing practice, breathe in Todah, and breathe out La'Eyl over and over.

As a thought, think Todah La'Eyl over and over.

As a walking practice, recite or think Todah as you place your right foot down, and La'Eyl as you place your left foot down. Continue to recite or think the words as you walk.

Barukh HaShem

"Shem" means name. HaShem means "the name" and refers to God. Barukh means "blessed." Barukh HaShem means "blessed is the name of God" or "blessed is the Holy Name" and is a common expression of gratitude and appreciation in modern Hebrew, particularly among religious Jews.

Begin by focusing on the sound of each syllable with an intention of gratitude. Then add head movements and focus the sounds in your centers. Lower the head toward the heart on Barukh and feel the sound in the heart. Raise the head on HaShem, feeling Ha in the throat and Shem in the crown.

After 108 repetitions in this manner (or more), reverse the direction of the head movements, raising the head on Barukh and lowering the head on HaShem, feeling Barukh in the crown, Ha in the throat and Shem in the heart.

After you have mastered the pronunciation, head movements, and focusing in your centers with a feeling of gratitude, try alternating between lifting and then lowering the head for a number of repetitions, and then lowering and lifting the head for a number of repetitions, such as 18, 36, 54, 72 or 108 in one direction, and the same number of repetitions in the other direction. See what rhythm works best for you and use it in your personal practice.

As a breathing practice, breathe in Barukh and breathe out HaShem over and over.

As a thought, think Barukh HaShem over and over. See if it fills you with joy.

As a walking practice, recite Barukh as you place your right foot down, and HaShem as you place your left foot down. Or think Barukh as you place your left foot down, and HaShem as you place your right foot down.

Chapter 18

Divine Love

This chapter includes sacred phrases of divine love.

In the practice of Indian raga (sacred spiritual musical compositions), there are evening ragas, morning ragas, and ragas for special occasions as well as for any time. Similarly, different expressions of love are used in Jewish prayer in the morning and in the evening.

Ahavat Olam and Ahavah Rabbah

Ahavat olam is part of ma'ariv, Jewish evening davvenen. I recommend repeating ahavat olam, especially during the evening and at night.

Ahavah rabbah is part of shacharit, Jewish morning davvenen. I recommend repeating ahavah rabbah, especially in the morning and during the day.

Ahavat olam means "eternal love." Ahavah means love. Ahavat means "love of." Olam in modern Hebrew means "world" and "universe," and it also has a connotation of time or timelessness, as in l'olam, which means "forever."[151]

Ahavah rabbah means "great love" or "universal love." Ahavah means love. Rabbah means "great." Ahavah rabbah is a wonderful phrase to repeat aloud, and in silence on the breath, and as a walking practice. When walking, think ahavah as one foot takes a step forward, and rabbah as the other foot takes a step.

Ahavat olam and ahavah rabbah are the opening words to longer prayers that refer to the love of God for Israel, by which is meant the Jewish people. As discussed in the first section in Chapter 14, Murshid Sam translated Yisrael (Israel) in the supernal sense of every devotee, since Yisrael means God-wrestler, and each person on the spiritual path wrestles with the spiritual and material in life, and on the path to God realization.

Ahavat Adonai v'Ahavat Kol Briyat Adonai; and
Ahavat YaH v'Ahavat Kol Briyat YaH

Ahavat Adonai V'ahavat Kol Briyat Adonai means "love of God and love of all of God's creation." Ahavat Adonai means "love of God." Ahavah means "love," and ahavat means "love of." Adon means master or lord (as in lord and lady). The "ai" suffix renders adon as plural and it also includes the first person possessive pronoun ("my"). Thus Adonai is literally "my Lords." This is the same kind of divine plural or as Elohim discussed at the beginning of Chapter 8.

---

151 Love of the world or love of the universe would be ahavat ha'olam.

I believe that "Lord" is a correct translation of "Adonai"—or one of the correct translations—because the divine name "Adonai" relates to the sephirah of Malkhut, which means kingdom, and is centered in the feet. In the *Zohar*, it states that Adonai refers to the Shechina, the feminine indwelling divine presence, as discussed in Chapter 8, and the Shechina is associated with the sephirah of Malkhut. (The sephirot are introduced in the "Sacred Focus" section in Chapter 6 and discussed in Appendix D.)

Ahavat YaH also means "love of God." One may recite the phrase as Ahavat YaH V'ahavat Kol Briyat YaH. These phrases may be recited or chanted aloud, or on the breath, or as a thought. On the breath, breathe in Avahat Adonai, and breathe out V'Ahavat Kol Briyat Adonai. Or breathe in Ahavat YaH, and breathe out V'Ahavat Kol Briyat YaH. And repeat.

The pronunciation for these and other sacred phrases are available at http://rebpam.com/.

Focus and Repetitions

When repeating sacred Hebrew phrases that include Ahavah, which means "love," I focus on love rather than a particular center in the body; but love is naturally associated with the heart, as we know, and there is no harm in focusing these phrases in the area of the physical heart center.

Repeat these phrases invoking divine love a set number of times, or for a set amount of time. Or pepper a few repetitions of these phrases between other spiritual practices. However you do them, and however many times, remember to feel divine love.

You

You is a name of God in every language, when one focuses the expression of "You" toward the divine. Below is a song. The melody is by Michael Baugh. The words are adopted by Michael from a poem in Yiddish by Reb Levi Yitzhak of Berdichev. A recording of the song is available on the website listed in the Key to Pronunciation. Here are the words:

> Where I wander, You. Where I ponder, You. Always You, just You, only You.
> In my gladness, You; in my sadness, You. Always You, You again, only You.
> All the earth is You, and the sky is You; You below and You up above.
> At every end, around every bend, always You, You again, only You.
> Ah You, You, You! Again You, You, You! Again You, You, You!
> Only You!

Nothing!

La Illaha Il Allah Hu is the watchword of Islam, and may be translated as "there is nothing except God." The same message is contained in the Shema given by Moses, which means listen Israel, God is our God, God is One. The same message is also contained in the sacred phrase—also given by Moses—YaH Hu HaElohim, Eyn Od Milvado, meaning "God (alone) is the (true) God, there is none but Him." Paula Markham of Blacksburg, Virginia wrote this song:

There is Nothing, Nothing, Nothing only God

There is nothing nothing nothing, only God, only God!
There is nothing nothing nothing, only God!
There is nothing nothing nothing, only God, only God!
There is nothing nothing nothing, only God!

Remember! Remember! Remember!
Remember! Remember! Remember!

Paula Markham's song is recorded in English, German, Spanish and Russian on the CD entitled, *Echoes of the Heart*.[152] The Hebrew sacred phrase Eyn od milvado was given by Moses and also weaves in nicely with Paula's melody, like this:

Eyn od, eyn od, eyn od, eyn od milvado milvado
Eyn od, eyn od, eyn od, eyn od milvado
Eyn od, eyn od, eyn od, eyn od milvado milvado
Eyn od, eyn od, eyn od, eyn od milvado
Zachor! Zachor! Zachor!
Zachor! Zachor! Zachor!

---

152 *Echoes of the Heart*. CD-ROM, Berlin, Germany: Optimal Media, Röbel, February 2003. Recorded in the Trinitatis Kirche: Tonmeister: Bernd-Ulrich Knothe, Berlin; Text: Scott Sattler; Übersetzung: Barbara Valentin; Gestaltung: Hauke Sturm. I wish to acknowledge and thank Paula Markham for her permission to present her song in this book.

Chapter 19

Divine Unity and Eternity

This chapter includes sacred phrases of divine unity and eternity.

Tamid Echad

Tamid means "always" or "forever." Echad means "one." Tamid Echad means "always one" or "forever one." It is a Zikr, which, to me, means, "Remember, God is always One," and it is a practice that may bring one to ecstasy. Try it and see what it means to you.

One may recite or chant Tamid Echad. When I recite it, I tend to repeat Tamid Echad over and over.

When I chant it, I use a melody that repeats, like this:

Tamid, tamid, tamid, tamid, tamid, tamid echad.
Oy Tamid, tamid, tamid, tamid, tamid, tamid echad.
Echad, echad, echad, echad, tamid, tamid echad.
Echad, echad, echad, echad, tamid, tamid echad.

("Oy" mean "oh.")

The melody for this chant is on the website listed in the Key to Pronunciation toward the beginning of this book.

M'maleh Kol Uhl'min

The following is a sacred chant used in Chabad, a haredi (Ultra Orthodox) Chassidic Jewish sect. It is also chanted in Jewish Renewal and elsewhere in the Jewish world. Although there are a lot of words in this chant that may be unfamiliar, it is worth mastering, as there is much to be gained.

The words are:
M'maleh Kol Uhl'min,
Vesovayv Kol Uhl'min,
Umibaladekha Eyn Shum M'tziyut Klal.

M'maleh kol uhl'min means "fills all worlds." Vesovayv kol uhl'min means "and surrounds all worlds." Umibaladecha eyn shum metziyut klal means, "and without You, there is no reality whatsoever."

The first two lines of the chant arise from teachings in the *Zohar*. The last line arises from teachings in the Tanya, a mystical text by Rabbi Shneur Zalman of Liadi, the founder of the Chabad Chassidism.[153]

---

153 *Zohar* 3:225a. Rabbi Shneur Zalman, *Tanya, Likutei Amarim* (Kehot Publishing Society, 1996).

The pronunciation for the chant is available on the website listed in the Key to Pronunciation. It also includes a melody.

Echad, Yachid U'meyuchad as a Practice

The meaning of Echad Yachid U'meyuchad is "one, unique and special" or "one, unique and interconnected." God is one; there is no second. Reb Zalman feels that the Arabic sacred phrase that parallels Echad Yachid U'meyuchad is Ahad Wahid Wa'Samad. The intention of these phrases is expressed beautifully in Surah Al Ikhlas in the Qur'an.[154]

I learned Echad Yachid U'meyuchad from Reb Zalman, who first heard it being recited by Chabad Chassidim[155] during davvenen. Zalman translates it as "One, Only One, Altogether One." Rabbi David Wolfe-Blank, of blessed memory, translated it as "One, Every Single One, Each One Joined and United In The One." Reb David used to chant it as a Zikr, alternating between Echad Yachid U'meyuchad, and his English translation.

Reb Zalman or I set the Hebrew words Echad Yachid U'meyuchad to Murshid Sam's melodic rendition of Sri Ram Jai Ram Jai Jai Ram. I use it in a dance that I believe was given by Murshid Sam, during which we open our arms and hold hands with the people who are one away from us in the circle. The melody for this chant is also on the website listed in the Key to Pronunciation.

When reciting Echad Yachid U'meyuchad as a spoken practice, move the head slightly from left to right as you repeat the phrase. It may also be done on the breath, breathing in the entire phrase and breathing out the entire phrase. As a walking practice, think Echad as one foot touches, and Yachid as the other foot touches, U'meyu- as the first foot touches again, and -chad as the second foot touches again.

Background on Echad, Yachid U'meyuchad

Rabbi Moshe Hayyim Luzzatto was an Italian Kabbalist who lived from approximately 1707 to 1747. He is known as the Ramchal, an acronym made up of the first letter of each word in his name. Reb Zalman refers to the Ramchal as a chakham—a sage—the highest Jewish post-Biblical title reflecting spiritual capacity.[156]

In the article in Appendix F, Reb Zalman and Murshid Mu'in-ad'Din Netanel note that Echad, Yachid, U'meyuchad first appeared in the Ramchal's writings. The phrase appears to have had earlier roots as discussed below; however, the exact wording seems to be attributed to the Ramchal.

---

154 "In the name of God, Most Gracious, Most Merciful. Say: He is Allah, the One and Only! Allah, the Eternal, Absolute; He begetteth not nor is He begotten. And there is none like unto Him." "Surah Al Ikhlas," *Holy Qur'an*, translator Abdullah Yusuf Ali, < http://wahiduddin.net/quran/ikhlas.htm>.

155 As mentioned elsewhere, Chabad is an Ultra Orthodox Chassidic Jewish sect of those who are followers of Rabbi Shneur Zalman of Liadi. Rabbi Zalman Schachter-Shalomi was trained and ordained as a rabbi at Yeshivas Tomchei Temimim, a Chabad Yeshiva (seminary).

156 The Ramchal's most famous work is a highly regarded text on musar (Jewish spiritual ethics). Rabbi Mordecai Kaplan, founder of the Reconstructionist Movement prepared an excellent rendition of the text in Hebrew and English. Moshe Hayyim Luzzatto, *The Path of the Upright, Mesillat Yesharim*, translator Mordecai M. Kaplan. (Northvale, New Jersey: Jason Aronson, Inc., 1995).

The twentieth century professor and scholar Gershom Gerhard Scholem states in a footnote, in his book Origins of the Kabbalah[157] that the earliest source of the teaching—if not the exact wording—of Echad Yachid U'meyuchad, dates back to Saadya Gaon in the ninth and tenth century of the Common Era, and Nachmanides[158] in the thirteenth century.[159] Professor Scholem also states in the same footnote that he found a similar Arabic formula in the writings of a Sufi mystic in the fourteenth century, which Scholem assumes is from a much older Arabic source. In the article in Appendix F, Reb Zalman and Mu'in-ad'Din refer to the Arabic phrase as Aḥad Waḥid waSamad.

Background on L'sheym Yichud Kudsha Brikh Hu U'Shekhintay

There are many sections in this book that will be esoteric to some readers and transparent to others. Spiritual seekers whose primary path is outside Judaism may find the explanations in this section to be overly esoteric. On the other hand, students of Jewish and Christian Kabbalah may find the explanations to be valuable, and I include them for that reason.

L'sheym Yichud Kudsha Brikh Hu U'Shekhintay is Aramaic. The phrase literally means "in the name of [the] unity of the Holy One, Blessed Be He, and the Shechina." Kudsha is holiness or holy one, and refers to God. Shechina is the indwelling presence of God, that is to say, God within all manifestation. There are those who define Shechina as the divine presence in all Jews, and that is also correct, and traditional Jewish mystical sources express it that way. However, there are ample expressions of the universal understanding in words and in print from throughout the Jewish world in recent decades, that the Shechina is the indwelling presence in all of creation.

I asked Reb Zalman how he would define the source of L'sheym Yichud Kudsha Brikh Hu U'Shekhintay. He said that it is a phrase that finds its roots in the *Zohar*, and its directive in the teachings of Rabbi Isaac Luria. The *Zohar* is a mystical commentary on the Bible. No one knows when the *Zohar* was written. On the one hand, the *Zohar* is attributed to Rabbi Shimon bar Yochai, who lived in the second century of the Common Era. The evidence for this view is that Rabbi Shimon bar Yochai, a disciple of Rabbi Akiva, is quoted in the *Zohar*, together with many other luminaries of his time. On the other hand, the *Zohar* first appeared in print in Spain in the thirteenth century. Historians generally believe that the *Zohar* was written around the thirteenth century, and that references to Rabbi Shimon bar Yochai and the other luminaries of the second century were due to mystics writing in the name of those luminaries, or—so to speak—channeling them.

---

157 Gershom Gerhard Scholem, *Origins of the Kabbalah,* editor R. J. Zwi Werblowsky, translator Allan Arkush (New York: Jewish Publication Society, 1987) 342, footnote 284.
158 Nachmanides is referred to as Ramban in Hebrew. Ramban consists of the first letter of each of the words in his name—Rabbi Moshe ben Nachman.
159 In a footnote in *Origins of the Kabbalah,* Gershom Scholem writes, "The formula, whose origin is not clear to me, to the effect that G-d is 'ehad yahid u'meyuhad, reappears in many of the 'Iyyun writings, as well as in Azriel. In the fourteen century, we find a very similar though undoubtedly much older Arabic formula in a Sufi mystic; cf: R. Nicholson, *Studies in Islamic Mysticism Cambridge*, 1921), 104. I found this formula also in piyyutim of the period after Saadya (for the first time) as well as in the spurious gaonic responsum Sefer Sha'are Teshubah, Section 26, and in good manuscripts of the mystical commentary of Nahmanides on Genesis 1:1 (See Kiryat Sefer 6:3 [1929]: 415-416. Cf. also chap. 2, n. 27, herein.)" *Origins of the Kabbalah.*

Rabbi Isaac Luria is known as the Ari HaKodesh, the Holy Lion. For short, we call him the "Arizal," written as Ari, z"l. Z"l is an acronym for zichrono livracha, "may his memory be a blessing," or "may he be remembered for blessing." The Ari z"l studied with Rabbi Moshe Cordevero, a Kabbalist who introduced the teachings on the transmigration of souls, which we call reincarnation. The earliest Jewish written teachings on the transmigration of souls are in Sefer HaBahir, the Book of Illumination, attributed to Reb Nehunia ben HaKana in the first century C.E., as well as in the *Zohar* described above. Rabbi Moshe Cordevero's book on the subject is called *Pardes Rimonim*, An Orchard of Pomegranates.[160] The pomegranate is considered to be as a soul, and the seeds are its lifetimes. The love poetry that is part of the Friday evening Jewish Sabbath liturgy is attributed to the mystics who lived around the time of Cordovero and the Ari z"l. On the Sabbath, the Holy One and the Shechina are said to have yichud, union. This union may occur and be experienced at any time, but is especially accessible on Shabbat. There is no way to explain or define this union, or to prove it, but when one experiences the yichud of Kudsha Brich Hu and Shechina, then it is real.

L'Sheym Yichud Kudsha Brikh Hu U'Shekhintay As a Practice

Recite L'sheym Yichud Kudsha Brikh Hu U'Shekhintay softly with an attunement to the interior feeling. It also works well on the breath. Breathe in the entire phrase and breathe out the entire phrase.

There is also a Jewish Renewal chant with these words:
L'Sheym Yichud Kudsha Brikh Hu U'Shekhintay
Yod Hay Vav Hay, Yod Hay Vav Hay

A recording of this chant is on the website listed in the Key to Pronunciation.

This Renewal chant may also be recited without singing, and it may be recited in silence on the breath or held in the mind.

This Renewal chant is a summary, or essence teaching, of the following Kabbalistic Invocation:

L'Sheym Yichud Kudsha Brikh Hu U'Shekhintay
Bi'Dchilu UR'chimu, UR'chimu U'Dchilu
L'Yachda Shem Ot Yod V'Ot Hay B'Ot Vav V'Ot Hay
BeYichuda Shlim B'Shem Kol Yisrael.

In the name of unity of the Holy One and the Shechina,
In reverence and compassion, and in compassion and reverence
For the unity of the name of letter yod and letter hay with letter vav and letter hay
In complete unity in the name of Israel."

---

160 Moshe Cordevero, *Pardes Rimonim, Orchard of Pomegranates, Parts 1-4,* Mul Edition (Providence University, 2007).

The opening section of Chapter 12 and the "The One Being" section of Chapter 14 include discussions about uniting the Divine Root Name and the divine name Elohim. We participate in this unification when we recite the sacred phrases "Shema Yisrael Adonai Elohaynu Adonai Echad," "Adonai Elohaynu Adonai Echad," "Adonai Hu HaElohim," and similar phrases. In other words, when we recite a form of the Divine Root Name (defined in Chapter 8) and a form of the name Elohim (discussed in Chapter 8) in the same sacred phrase, we are participating, God willing, in the practice of unifying God's name. To be sure, there are many other names for God in scripture and other Jewish sacred texts, but according to the Kabbalah there is something that is particularly valuable about uniting the Divine Root Name and Elohim together.

Similarly, it is considered to be of great spiritual value to recite the letters of the Divine Root Name, and such recitation takes place in numerous ways among Kabbalists and mystics. For example, Rabbi Abulafia combines the consonants of the Divine Root Name with vowels such that each consonant is repeated with the same vowel, such as Ya-Ha-Va-Ha, Yu-Hu-Vu-Hu, and so forth. This is discussed in Chapter 10. Another example is the pairing of the letters of the Divine Root Name with the months of the Jewish calendar, which is discussed in Appendix E.

In the *Zohar*, a mystical commentary on the Torah discussed in Chapter 2, it states that Adonai is one of the names of the Shechina, the feminine indwelling presence of God, or God in manifestation. The unification of God in creation and God beyond creation is considered to be the goal—or a goal—of creation. According to the Kabbalah, the Holy One, blessed be He, and the Shechina have yichud, divine union on Shabbat, the Jewish Sabbath. The mitzvah of making love with one's earthly beloved is considered to be a double mitzvah on Shabbat.

The Kabbalistic invocation above condenses into a few Aramaic words the intention to unify the Holy One, blessed be He and the Shechina, blessed be She in reverence and compassion—and in compassion and in reverence—with the unification of the letters of the Divine Root Name, which is the name of the Holy One, blessed be He. Thus, the Kabbalistic invocation is, to the mind, a going in circles. One may explain it, or attempt to explain it, but like so many spiritual principles and cosmic realities, it is beyond the mind and cannot be contained sufficiently in words to be explained to the mind's satisfaction.

Because it is impossible to explain God, or to define God in a way that responds to all of our inquiries, and because spiritual practice has power that can be misused, and often has been misused for inappropriate and unsavory purposes, mystics of various faiths kept spiritual teachings secret in order to avoid confusion and misuse. In this day and age, there is a sense that sharing deep spiritual teachings may be preferable to hiding them away.

Chapter 20

Divine Strength and Courage

This chapter includes sacred phrases of divine strength and courage.

Atah Hu Gibbor

Atah Hu Gibbor means "You are All Powerful." "You" in this sacred phrase refers to God.

I whisper this sacred phrase over and over and over. I do not count the repetitions; rather, I recite Atah Hu Gibbor until I feel comforted or strengthened or protected. I shokkel as I do this practice. (To shokkel is defined in Chapter 6 and the Glossary. Literally, it means to "shake," and refers to the practice of swaying forward and back slightly.)

As a breathing practice, breathe in Atah Hu Gibbor, and breathe out Atah Hu Gibbor.

As a thought, think Atah Hu Gibbor.

As a walking practice, recite Atah Hu as you place your right foot down, and Gibbor as you place your left foot down. Or think Atah Hu as your place your right foot down, and Gibbor as you place your left foot down.

Additional Note: I am sure that the sacred phrase Atah Hu Gibbor may be recited with full voice and without conjuring up a violent image from the other end of the continuum, but I am not yet able to do that, so I whisper Atah Hu Gibbor instead.

YaH Hu HaGibbor

YaH Hu HaGibbor means "God is strength" or "God is the strength" or "God is power" or "God is the power."

Recite or chant YaH Hu HaGibbor softly. I shokkel, leaning forward on YaH Hu, and straightening on HaGibbor.

As a breathing practice, breathe in YaH Hu HaGibbor, and breathe out YaH Hu HaGibbor.

As a thought, think YaH Hu HaGibbor over and over.

As a walking practice, recite YaH Hu as you place your right foot down, and HaGibbor as you place your left foot down. Or think YaH Hu as your place your right foot down, and HaGibbor as you place your left foot down.

Chapter 20 – Divine Strength and Courage

Background on Atah Hu Gibbor

In 1974, the Sufi Choir, under the direction of Allaudin Mathieu, sang during evening worship at Glide Memorial Methodist Church in San Francisco on the evenings of Rosh HaShanah, Jewish New Year, and Yom Kippur, the Day of Atonement. Prior to these worship services, Reb Zalman, Allaudin and I collaborated on what the Sufi Choir would sing, and how their music would be integrated into the innovative Jewish service that Zalman would lead. I was the go-between during a meeting or two, explaining Jewish liturgy to Allaudin, and Sufi practice to Zalman.

There was a part in one of the services where Reb Zalman wanted a song with the energy of gevurah. Gevurah is one the ten sephirot, the emanations or qualities with which—according to the Kabbalah—God created the universe. (See the Introduction to the Ten Sephirot in Appendix D.) Gevurah is the sephirah of strength and boundaries on the positive end of its continuum, and severity and cruelty on the negative end. As I explained the intention of gevurah to Allaudin, he suggested an original musical piece that used the Arabic sacred phrase Allaho Akbar. I explained Allaho Akbar to Zalman, and after we contemplated it, both as a spiritual practice and a call to war to exclaim that God is on our side, Zalman taught us the sacred Hebrew phrase Atah Hu Gibbor, meaning "You are Mighty" or "You are Powerful." It has the intention of "You" being directed to God, as in the sacred phrase at the beginning of the second blessing of the Amidah (silent devotion) which says, Atah Gibbor L'Olam Adonai, meaning "You are forever powerful, God," or "Your might, God, is boundless."

Allaudin set the phrase Atah Hu Gibbor to the music of his Allaho Akbar composition, and the Sufi Choir sang it to punctuate a moment in our journey through the High Holy Day worship services; These High Holy Day services led to the creation of the Aquarian Minyan of Berkeley, the first Jewish Renewal congregation in Northern California.

Chapter 21

Trust, Surrender and Divine Holiness

This chapter includes a sacred phrase of trust in the divine, surrender to the divine, and divine holiness.

Bayh Ana Rachaytz

Bayh Ana Rachaytz, pronounced like "beyana rachaytz," is a phrase from a meditation in Aramaic recited on the Sabbath while standing before the open ark in the synagogue. After the meditation is completed, the Torah is removed and read.

Bayh Ana Rachaytz is Aramaic and means "I trust in God," although literally, it means "I trust in Him." The full sentence—which is part of a longer paragraph—is Bayh Ana Rachaytz, V'Lishmay Kadisha Yakira Ana Ehmar Tush'bechan, meaning "I trust in God, and to God's Glorious and Holy Name do I declare praises."

Start by reciting Bayh Ana Rachaytz while sitting or standing and shokkelen (swaying and forth). It may also be sung. One may recite the entire sentence, of course, and sing it as well, as we do each Sabbath in many synagogues. The longer and shorter phrases may also be recited in silence on the breath.

You will find the pronunciation of this meditative phrase and the others in this chapter on the website listed in the Key to Pronunciation toward the front of this book. This is also a recording of it on website listed in the Key to Pronunciation.

Ana Avda D'Kudsha Brikh Hu

Ana Avda D'Kudsha Brikh Hu is also Aramaic, and means "I am a servant of the Holy One, Blessed be the Holy One," although literally, it means, "I am a servant of the Holy One, Blessed be He."

This phrase is part of the same Aramaic prayer—and comes slightly earlier in the paragraph—as Bayh Ana Rachaytz. One may recite the phrase aloud, or sing the phrase, or recite it on the breath. The intention is humility and love. In the author's experience, reciting the entire phrase may bring one to ecstasy.

Kadosh Kadosh Kadosh Adonai Tzeva'ot, Melo Khol Ha'Aretz Kevodo

Kadosh Kadosh Kadosh Adonai Tzeva'ot, Melo Khol Ha'Aretz Kevodo means "Holy, holy, holy is the Lord of Hosts. The whole world is filled with God's Glory." In the Book of Isaiah, the prophet describes a vision of God seated on a high and lofty throne, attended by seraphim. Each seraph has six wings. With two wings, the angel would cover its face, with two, it would cover its legs, and with two, it would fly. [161] One seraph would call to another: "Kadosh Kadosh Kadosh Adonai Tzeva'ot, Melo Khol Ha'Aretz Kevodo." This sacred angelic Hebrew phrase is recited every morning during the shacharit service. In addition, when the Amidah (silent devotion) is repeated aloud in the morning and afternoon, this sacred phrase is also recited.[162]

I introduced this sacred phrase into Sufi practice decades ago, Reb Zalman gave it with the movements set forth below, and Saadi Shakur Chisti[163] set it to a Dance of Universal Peace.

It may also be recited or chanted while sitting or standing. It feels like a different practice when recited or chanted in full voice than in a whisper.

To recite in a whisper, sit comfortably, practice reciting in a whisper, and then try it with the six head movements described in the Index and Guide to Sacred Phrases.

As a walking practice, start on the left foot and whisper or think the words
>   Left – Kadosh
>   Right – Kadosh
>   Left – Kadosh
>   Right – Adonai
>   Left – Tzeva'ot
>   Right – Melo Khol
>   Left – Ha'Aretz
>   Right – Kevodo
>
>   Or in English:
>   Left – Holy
>   Right – Holy
>   Left – Holy
>   Right – God
>   Left – of Hosts
>   Right – the whole world
>   Left – is filled with
>   Right – God's glory

Reb Zalman's Kadosh Kadosh Kadosh

These are movements and intentions that accompany the sacred phrase Kadosh, Kadosh, Kadosh Adonai Tzeva'ot, Melo Khol Ha'Aretz Kevodo given on the previous page:

As a standing practice, hold the hands over the heart and chant Kadosh. Then hold the hands in front of the head and chant Kadosh a second time. Then lift the hands high and chant Kadosh a third time. Then, as you chant Melo Khol Ha'Aretz Kevodo, sweep the hands as if over the horizon before you.

---

161 *Isaiah* 6:1-3.
162 The evening Amidah is not repeated aloud, and therefore, does not contain the full Kedushah (holiness section) that appears in the morning and afternoon Amidah.
163 Saadi Shakur Chisti is also known as Neil Douglas-Klotz.

The intention that goes with these movements is:[164]

> Kadosh – how the body feels Holy
> Kadosh – how the mind understands Holy
> Kadosh – there is more to "Holy" than the reasoning mind can understand
> Melo Khol Ha'Aretz Kevodo – the whole world is filled with God's glory

These same movements may be done while walking and chanting Kadosh Kadosh Kadosh Adonai Tzeva'ot, Melo Khol Ha'Aretz Kevodo. One may also use these movements as a dance.

---

164 The movements for this Kadosh, Kadosh Kadosh practice, as well as the intentions set forth next to each Hebrew word were given by Reb Zalman.

Chapter 22

Divine Healing

Music as Healer

Singing often lifts the spirit and helps to heal a broken heart. The singing of a niggun[165] with or without words, the chanting of a sacred phrase, or the singing of a religious or spiritual song, or a folk song, rock song, rap song, or any kind of song may do this. One who plays an instrument may benefit greatly by playing, and those who listen may benefit as well. In "Jewish Shamanism and the Power of Chant," by Rabbi Miriam Maron writes:

I learned about the efficacy of what I had done by following intuition while in that room at the hospital [visiting a woman in a fatal coma]; that chanting has the power to "lift up souls from out of the fertile void," and that "the benefit of chant is without end and is the most potent form of healing" (18th-century Rabbi Nachmon of Breslav in *Likkutei HaMaHaRaN*, Ch. 60, No. 4, and in *See'chot Ha'Ran*, No. 273); and that chant was the very fabric that held together all of Creation: "If not for the songs and chants that you sing every day," God says, "I would not have created my world" (*Midrash O'tiyo't D'Rebbe Akiva Ha'Sha'leym, Nusach Alef [beginning]*).[166]

Debbie Friedman's Healing Mishebeyrakh

Mishebeyrakh means "the one who blessed" or "may the one who blessed." A healing mishebeyrakh is a prayer for healing. Debbie Friedman, of blessed memory, wrote a healing mishebeyrakh in the form of a song that is sung in many synagogues and other settings around the world. Some rabbis, cantors and other leaders invite the congregation to call out the names of those in need of healing and then they lead Debbie's Healing Mishebeyrakh. Others lead the Debbie's Healing Mishebeyrakh and invite people to call out the names while the song is being sung.

If there is a need for confidentiality about someone's condition, it is best to not call the name out loud when using Debbie's healing prayer or any other; instead hold the name in your heart and mind.

The words and melody for Debbie Friedman's Healing Mishebeyrakh are found on her CD entitled, *And You Shall Be a Blessing.*[167]

---

165 Niggun literally means melody in both Hebrew and Yiddish. In Hebrew, it is pronounced with emphasis on the last syllable, whereas, in Yiddish, it is pronounced with emphasis on the first syllable. To be a niggun, a song must have two distinct musical parts; some niggun have three distinct parts. When one sings a chant that has just a single musical part, one may continue to sing while spacing out, but with a niggun, one needs to pay attention when the melody changes; this helps to bring our wandering mind back into focus.
166 Rabbi Miriam Maron, R.N., M.A., "Jewish Shamanism and the Power of Chant."
<http://www.miriamscyberwell.com/articles-by-miriam.htm>. I have preserved Rabbi Maron's spelling of Reb Nachman's name and other references in the quotation.
167 Friedman, Debbie, *And You Shall Be a Blessing*, CD-ROM, 1997.

Prayer After Relieving Ourselves

The following is a prayer that is recited by the observant after relieving oneself and then washing one's hands:

Praised are You, Adonai, our God, Sovereign of the universe, fashioning the human body in wisdom, creating openings, arteries, glands, and organs, marvelous in structure, intricate in design. Should but one of them fail to function by being blocked or open, it would be impossible to survive and to serve You. Praised are You Adonai, healer of all flesh, sustaining our bodies in wondrous ways.[168]

This prayer that acknowledges the inner workings of the body and its mysteries—together with its chatimah (seal) for the healing of all—may be recited every day of the year.

Daily Prayer For Our Healing

Three times a day on ordinary days—that is, days that are not Shabbat or a festival—Jews are invited—and by Orthodox halakhic[169] standards, we are required—to recite the Amidah, the silent devotion that includes nineteen separate blessings. The following is the traditional healing blessing recited during the evening, morning and afternoon Amidah:

Heal us, Adonai, and we shall be healed. Save us and we shall be saved, for You are our glory. Grant perfect healing for all our afflictions, for You are the faithful and merciful God of healing. Praised are You, Adonai, Healer of the sick among Your people Israel.[170]

Reb Zalman's version of the healing blessing recited during the Amidah on ordinary days borrows the chatimah (seal/closing blessing) of the prayer recited after relieving ourselves. It goes like this:

Heal us, YaH, and we shall be healed. Save us and we shall be saved, for You are our glory. Grant perfect healing for all our afflictions, for You are the faithful and merciful God of healing. Praised are You, YaH, Healer of all flesh, and Doer of wonders.[171]

It is noteworthy that the previous blessing for healing that appears in the weekday Amidah is recited every day by people who are well! Like healthy food, vitamins and exercise, this healing blessing is spiritual and religious preventative medicine. Of course, one may also recite it when one does not feel well.

---

168 Adapted from *Siddur Sim Shalom for Weekdays* (New York: The Rabbinical Assembly; The United Synagogue of Conservative Judaism, 2002) 4.
169 "Halakhah" is a Hebrew word that comes from the same root as "holeykh," which means walking. Halakhah refers to the body of Jewish law that set of parameters for walking the Jewish path.
170 This English translation is rendered by the author, based upon the traditional Hebrew found in *Siddur Sim Shalom for Weekdays* (New York: The Rabbinical Assembly; The United Synagogue of Conservative Judaism, 2002) 38.
171 The last sentence of the prayer is known as the chatimah (seal). Reb Zalman uses the chatimah from the prayer after relieving oneself as the chatimah for the healing prayer during the weekday Amidah.

When Praying For the Healing of Others, Who May Pray and For Whom?

The Talmud teaches that before engaging in acts of healing others, one must obtain permission from the person who is ill.[172] Before praying for someone's healing, one ought to obtain permission from that person. The Sufis teach this same principle.[173] If a person is not conscious, or not able to communicate permission—such as an infant—then it might be appropriate to consult with a caregiver who is empowered to make decisions on behalf of the person who is ill, in order to obtain permission.

Daily Prayer For Our Healing With Insert For Those Who Are Ill

In the middle of the Daily Prayer for Our Healing described above, additional words may be added to pray for those who are in need of healing. When one gets to the blank line, that is the time to think of the names of those in need of healing, or to recite the names. Below is Reb Zalman's translation of this addition to the daily healing prayer:

Heal us, YaH, and we shall be healed. Save us and we shall be saved, for You are our glory. Grant perfect healing for all our afflictions, and may it be Your will, YaH our God and God of our ancestors to send complete healing, of body and soul, to _____, along with all others who are stricken, and strengthen those who tend to them, for You are the faithful and merciful God of healing. Praised are You, YaH, Healer of all flesh, and doer of wonders.

Giving Tzedakah (Charity) on Behalf of Those in Need of Healing

In some prayer books, the above prayer includes a phrase such as "I will offer such and such amount to charity on behalf of" the one(s) in need of healing. Reb Zalman keeps a charity box in the area where he davvens during the week, and he places money in the box when he prays for healing, and at certain other times. Periodically, he gives away the contents of the box, and then begins to fill it again. Over the years, when Reb Zalman has been ill and I have mentioned to him that I am keeping him in my prayers for healing, he always says thank you, and "remember to give tzedakah (charity)." This prayer of giving charity during davvenen is kept by many individuals and congregations. I have davvened in Orthodox congregations where a push'keh (charity box) is kept in a conspicuous and accessible place during weekday davvenen and individuals come up to insert coins and paper money during the service.

Healing Continues on the Sabbath and Festivals

On the Sabbath and festivals, we take a break from reciting penitential prayers, including the thirteen central blessings of the total nineteen blessings contained in the Amidah (silent devotion). This includes taking a break from reciting the Daily Prayer for Our Healing, together with the Insert For Those Who Are Ill, which also includes a prayer for caregivers ("those who tend to them"). However, one continues to recite the prayer after relieving oneself even on the Sabbath and festivals.

---

172 *Brachot* 5a. [Babylonian Talmud, Tractate Brachot (Blessings), page 5, side a.]
173 I learned this teaching from Hakim Sauluddin.

Notwithstanding the abeyance of penitential prayers described above, because the healing of the sick is so central and so important, we recite a special blessing in community called the mishebeyrakh for healing on the Sabbath and festivals. The mishebeyrakh for healing is recited during the Torah service. This prayer has a place where the leader of the prayer may stop, and everyone who is praying for the healing of others may add the names, and then the blessing is concluded:

My God who blessed our ancestors, Abraham, Isaac and Jacob, Sarah, Rebecca, Rachel and Leah, bring blessing and healing to _____, and all those who suffer illness within our congregational family. May the Holy One mercifully restore them to health and vigor, granting them physical and spiritual wellbeing, together with all the others who are ill. And although Shabbat [or Yom Tov[174]] is a time to refrain from petitions, we yet hope and pray that healing is at hand. And let us say: Amen. [175]

Caregivers

It is important to remember to pray for caregivers. On the Sabbath and festivals, observant Jews take a break from doing so, but during the other six days of the week, the healing prayer that includes caregivers is recited three times: evening, morning and afternoon. And notwithstanding the abeyance from prayers for caregivers on the Sabbath and festivals, if a person is ill or wounded and needs care, or if a woman is giving birth, or there is a similar need, then it is incumbent upon one to help in the care giving even if it is on the Sabbath or a festival.

Moses Praying for Miriam

In the Book of Numbers, there is a story about Miriam becoming ill with a skin disease. Her brother Aaron, the High Priest, asks their brother Moses to pray for Miriam. Moses recites the following words: "El Nah Refa Nah Lah," which means God, please heal her.[176]

This sacred phrase is part of Yedid Nefesh, a chant to the Beloved recited on Friday as a prelude to welcoming the Sabbath. However, the phrase is not used in traditional communal Jewish healing prayers for weekdays, or for Sabbath and festivals. Rabbi Yaacov gave the teaching in the name of Rabbi Hisda that if one is praying for healing for someone who is close to us—such as Moses praying for his sister Miriam—then one does not need to say the person's name.[177] Since one may be praying for a person who is not close, or even for a person one does know if one is asked to pray for him or her, traditional communal healing prayers provide an opportunity for names to be called in the middle of the prayer.

The sacred phrase of Moses may be used nevertheless as a healing chant alone or in community. There are a number of Jewish Renewal communities, and other Jewish communities, that use the sacred phrase of Moses, and provide an opportunity for the calling of names either before the chanting, or during the chant.

---

174 Yom Tov literally means "good day" and is the Hebrew expression meaning festival.
175 *Siddur Sim Shalom for Shabbat and Festivals* (New York: The Rabbinical Assembly; The United Synagogue of Conservative Judaism, 2005) 144.
176 *Numbers* 12:13.
177 *Brachot* 34a. [Babylonian Talmud, Tractate Brachot (Blessings), page 34, side a.]

El Nah Refa Nah Lah Is A Prayer For Healing

El Nah Refa Nah Lah means "God, please heal (please) her." One may recite it thus for a male or female since the soul, called neshama in Hebrew, is considered, according to Kabbalah, to be feminine.

Call to mind the person or persons for whom you wish to pray, or call the person's name out loud. Holding a name in one's consciousness rather than calling it out loud is particularly helpful when praying for someone whose condition is best kept confidential.

After calling out the name(s), or keeping the name(s) in mind, chant or recite El Nah Refa Nah Lah.

El Nah Refa Nah Lanu

El Nah Refa Nah Lanu means God please heal (please) us. This is a slight variation on the words of Moses, which concludes with the pronoun "her" since Moses was praying for his sister.

One may also chant El Nah Refa Nah Lo, meaning God please heal (please) him.

The instructions in the section above for El Nah Refa Nah Lah also apply to El Nah Refa Nah Lanu and El Nah Refa Nah Lo.

Chapter 23

Repairing Our Broken World

Tikkun Olam

Tikkun is a noun meaning a repair or a fix. Olam means world or universe. Tikkun olam is a Hebrew expression meaning "repair of the world to help make it a better place."

Toward the end of every Jewish worship service, we recite Alaynu, a prayer of gratitude and hope. The traditional Alaynu is attributed either to Joshua ben Nun, successor to Moses, and the one after whom the Biblical book of Joshua was named; or to Rav, a Babylonian rabbi who lived in the third century C.E..[178] The second paragraph of Alaynu asks God for many things, including, "L'Takeyn Olam B'Malkhut Shaddai," which means "to perfect the world through the Almighty's sovereignty" or "to repair the world in the Kingdom of God," or "to perfect the universe[179] through the sovereignty of the Divine Mother."[180]

The Torah tells us in its very first chapter that all human beings are created in the image of God.[181] Not only do we pray for the repair of the world in the Alaynu, but we are also expected to be partners with God in helping to repair the world.

Rabbi Tarfon was a kohen (a member of a priestly family) on both his father and his mother's side. He lived during the first century of the Common Era in Lydda, which was between Jerusalem and Yavneh. Rabbi Tarfon participated in priestly ritual service in the Holy Temple in Jerusalem, and he occasionally visited Yavneh, a city along the Mediterranean where he would join in discussions with members of the Sandrehin, the Jewish high court. Rabbi Tarfon was a wealthy man. Once, his disciple and colleague, the great Rabbi Akiva, met Rabbi Tarfon and said to him: "Would you like me to buy you some durable goods?" Rabbi Tarfon immediately gave Rabbi Akiva four thousand golden coins. Rabbi Akiva took the money and gave it away to poor Torah scholars.

When Rabbi Tarfon met Rabbi Akiva later, he asked Rabbi Akiva, "so where are the properties that you have purchased for me?" Rabbi Akiva took Rabbi Tarfon by the hand to the Beth HaMidrash—house of study. He took out a book of Psalms, and began reciting the psalms out loud from the beginning until he came to a verse that spoke about giving to the poor. "These are the everlasting possessions that I purchased for you," said Rabbi Akiva, referring to the fact that the sages teach that charity is a mitzvah (commandment) from which we derive great spiritual benefit. Upon hearing Rabbi

---

178 On the first page of Chapter 11, there is a footnote with citations regarding the origin of the Alaynu prayer.

179 As noted above, the Hebrew word olam means both world and universe.

180 The Hebrew word shad means breast. Shaddai means my breasts and it is also a name of G-d. Shaddai is traditionally translated as Almighty. I believe that it has a feminine meaning as well, because of its literal translation.

181 Genesis 1:26 (chapter 1, verse 26) includes the following teaching: "And God said, 'Let us make Adam in our image, after our likeness….'" Verse 27 continues: "And God created Adam in His image, in the image of God He created him; male and female He created them." Thus, the Bible tells us that human beings were created male and female from the beginning. The story of Eve being created from Adam's rib is in the second chapter of Genesis. There are many ideas and commentaries about why two creation stories are side by side in the Bible. The preceding quotations are from *JPS Hebrew-English Tanakh, the Traditional Hebrew Text and the New JPS Translation*, second edition. (Philadelphia: The Jewish Publication Society, 1999).

Akiva's words, Rabbi Tarfon arose and kissed Rabbi Akiva on his head and exclaimed, "My teacher and leader; my teacher in wisdom and my leader in conduct."[182]

The following teaching of Rabbi Tarfon is cited in the Mishna, "The day is short, the work is great, and the laborers are lazy, and the reward is great, and the Master of the house[183] is urging us on. It is not upon you to complete the task, and neither are you free to abstain from it."[184] According to Rabbi Tarfon, we do not need to complete the task of helping others, but neither are we free to walk away; it is incumbent upon us to help make the world a better place so long as we are here in it. Reb Zalman is fond of reminding us that repairing the world is not like repairing a watch; no matter how much repair we are able to accomplish, the world is still in constant need of repair, because as karma unfolds, there is always someone suffering, someone hungry, someone in need. When we help human beings, animals, plant life or minerals or the elements—anything in God's creation—we are participating in tikkun olam. Recycling, conserving resources, reversing pollution, preventing soil erosion, rescuing pets that do not have a home may not seem as obvious as feeding the hungry or clothing the naked, but they too are forms of tikkun olam.

L'Takeyn Olam B'Malkhut Shaddai

As explained earlier in this chapter, "L'Takeyn Olam B'Malkhut Shaddai" means "to repair the world in the kingdom of the Almighty" or "to repair the world in the queendom of the Divine Mother."

The spiritual practice of tikkun olam involves actually helping those in need. Chanting this sacred phrase or holding it on our breath is a valuable spiritual practice, but it must also be accompanied by action.

Synagogue Practice – When the Alaynu is recited in silence—or when the remainder of the Alaynu is recited silently after the first section is chanted aloud—lift your voice when you get to the words "L'Takeyn Olam B'Malkhut Shaddai," so that the phrase becomes audible. No need to shout; just say or chant the words in a sincere request.[185]

Chanting Practice - One may chant L'Takeyn Olam B'Malkhut Shaddai, or speak it, or hold the thought of it on the breath, or while walking.

There is a chant on the website that goes like this: Takeyn olam, takeyn olam, takeyn olam b'malkhut Shaddai.

Which is the Best Path to God?

We each believe that our path is the best path; if we do not think our path is the best, then we are wasting our time.

182 Chabad.org *Jewish History* Nov 9 2009, August 2011
<http://www.chabad.org/library/article_cdo/aid/112314/jewish/Rabbi-Tarfon.htm>.
183 The "Master of the house" is G-d.
184 *Pirkei Avot* 2:15. [Babylonian Talmud, Pirkei Avot (Ethics of the Fathers), chapter 2, verse 15.]
185 I learned this practice from Rabbi Lavey Derby.

Neem Karoli Baba was a famous spiritual teacher who lived in India during the twentieth century, and was known to his students as Babaji. Babaji's disciples included Ram Dass—the author of *Be Here Now;*[186] Jaffar Michael Baugh—a psychotherapist and spiritual teacher;[187] and Larry Brilliant—a physician and epidemiologist, who led the World Health Organization effort to eradicate smallpox.[188] **Babaji taught that the best way to serve God is every way.[189]**

In the 1980's, a delegation of rabbis and other Jewish leaders traveled to Dharamsala, India to meet with the Dalai Lama. The journey is chronicled in *The Jew in the Lotus* by Rodger Kamenetz.[190] When I heard about the trip, my first thought was, what could rabbis teach the Dalai Lama? I have heard from trip participants that Blu Greenberg recommended creating and running Buddhist summer camps to expose children to Tibetan culture and living Buddhism.[191] Years later, I drove to pick up my son from a Jewish summer camp, and a Tibetan monk in red and saffron robes greeted me. As we spoke, I discovered that he was at camp to learn how the Jewish people have preserved the "Jewish Dharma" in exile. Over the years, I saw other Tibetan monks and lamas touring Jewish settings. I am silenced by the depth of Blu's faith and insight that the Jewish path is one from which others steeped in their own practice may learn methodologies for preserving their faith and practice in exile from their natural cultural setting.[192]

Reb Zalman suggested adding a festive meal to the celebration of Buddha's birthday with symbolic foods such as Jewish people set out on their table for the Passover Seder. "What if there were wilted lettuce on a plate with other rituals foods," Zalman mused, "and it would be held up when telling the story of how Gautama's father tried to prevent Gautama from viewing suffering and death, and how that prevention backfired when Gautama went out into the countryside and saw plants dying and people infirmed." Zalman drew an analogy to dipping greens in salt water at the Passover Seder to remind ourselves that the Israelites were freed from bondage in the spring, and that the slaves cried out through their tears for freedom from servitude."

During a private moment in the presence of the Dalai Lamai and a translator, Reb Zalman had the privilege of asking a question and receiving an answer. Together with the answer to his question, Reb Zalman also received the following teaching from the Dalai Lama: "Before, I thought that Buddhism was the best path to enlightenment. Now I realize that every path is the best path to enlightenment."

Zalman was delighted to receive this teaching from the Dalai Lama, because Zalman had had the same realization in relation to Judaism. As a younger man, Reb Zalman was reading *Autobiography of a Yogi* by Paramahansa Yogananda. At one point, Zalman realized that Yogananda's teacher had the same level of spiritual realization that Zalman's Rebbe had. It dawned on Zalman that Yogananda's teacher had attained that level of realization without the benefit of the Jewish body of spiritual teachings; as Zalman contemplated that reality, he realized that all true paths lead to the Oneness.

---

186 Baba Ram Dass, *Be Here Now* (San Cristobal, New Mexico: Lama Foundation, 1971).

187 A brief biography of Michael Baugh, L.C.S.W. is available at <http://dbtsf.com/?page_id=2> May 2012.

188 A brief biography of Dr. Lawrence Brilliant is available at <http://www.skollfoundation.org/staff/larry-brilliant/> May 6, 2012.

189 Ram Dass, *The Miracle of Love* (Hanuman Foundation, 1995).

190 Rodger Kamenetz, *The Jew in the Lotus* (Harper One, 1995, 2007).

191 With gratitude to Rabbi Jonathan Omer-Man for transmitting this story to the author.

192 Blu Greenberg is a courageous forward thinking Orthodox Jewish woman and writer. Her books include *On Women and Judaism, a View from Tradition.* (Philadelphia: The Jewish Publication Society, 1998) and *How to Run a Traditional Jewish Household* (Touchstone, 1985).

Believing that our particular path is the best—whether it be Jewish or Muslim, Hindu or Christian, Buddhist or Tao, age old or newly formed—is part of the faith needed to succeed in fulfilling our purpose in life. Pir-O-Murshid Hazrat Inayat Khan tells the story of a Sufi mureed (disciple) who is told that his teacher is a false teacher. The disciple is not swayed, however, and instead tells the doubter that, although his teacher may be a false teacher, his faith in his teacher is not false.

While believing in our own particular path, it is important to also remember—and abide by the reality—that the best way to serve G-d is every way, and that all true paths lead to the Oneness; the Great Spirit. In 2011, a right wing murderer slaughtered scores of teenagers attending a summer camp with a political theme in Norway. In a follow up news article, Rabbi Shaul Wilhelm, who runs the Chabad-Lubavitch center in Oslo, was quoted as saying, "What we should try to learn from all this is that multiculturalism isn't just a thesis and a concept… That would be the greatest revenge against this murderer and against people of his ilk: that we can actually practice tolerance in a very real way."[193]

In the midst of suffering, it is important to find ways to maintain faith, and this is, of course, easier said than done. Chapter 3 includes a quote from Rabbi David Weiss Halivni, a Holocaust survivor who recommends changes in the focus of Jewish liturgy in light of the suffering of the Holocaust.

Rabbi Levi Yitzhak of Berdichev lived in the eighteenth century in an area where Jewish people experienced a great deal of suffering due to persecution. There is a story about Rabbi Levi Yitzhak putting God on trial. The Jewish people were suffering mightily from persecution and many were suffering from poverty. The trial started early in the day and lasted into the afternoon, much testimony was taken, and then the Beit Din—the tribunal of those qualified to make religious decisions--made its determination: They found God guilty for failing to protect and provide for the Jewish people as God had promised. When the trial was over, Reb Levi Yitzhak's disciples turned to him and asked, "What do we do now?" "Now," said Reb Levi Yitzhak, "we recite the afternoon prayers."[194]

Elie Wiesel tells a story of concentration camp inmates putting God on trial, finding God guilty, and then going into a corner hidden from view and worshipping. The author's cousin, Zelik Stanley Frydman, entered his first concentration camp in 1942 at the age of fifteen. By the end of the war, he had been interned in six camps, including Bautzen, to which he was forced to travel as a human beast of burden, along with other inmates, pulling wagons full of ammunitions to the German front in Poland. Stanley says that he too heard about putting God on trial. I asked Stanley if the prisoners davvened mincha (the afternoon service) at the end of the trial. "Mincha and ma'ariv,"[195] said Stanley.[196]

---

193 Alex Weisler, "Norway's Jews Hope Attack Won't Spur Even More Anti-Zionist Sentiment," *J, The Jewish News Weekly of Northern California*, July 28, 2011, May 6, 2012 <http://www.jweekly.com/article/full/62408/norways-jews-hope-attack-wont-spur-even-more-anti-zionist-sentiment/>.
194 Mincha is the Jewish afternoon service described in Chapter 1 of this book.
195 Mincha is the Jewish afternoon service, and ma'ariv is the evening service. Also see Chapter 1 of this book.
196 Excerpts from Zelik Stanley Frydman's story will appear in a book by Pamela Frydman containing stories of the Holocaust, slated for release in approximately 2013. Part of Zelik's story is included in Rabbi Pamela Frydman Baugh, "Her Brother's Sandals," *Poetica Magazine*, August 2009.

Chapter 24

Shabbes

Shabbes on Tuesday

There is a story about two Chassidic masters, Rabbi Elimelekh of Lizhensk and Rabbi Zusia of Anypol. Reb Zusia and Reb Elimelekh loved Shabbes, the Jewish Sabbath, when they would enjoy a respite from the difficulties, challenges and responsibilities of everyday life. As Shabbes began, they felt the presence of the neshama y'tayrah—the additional soul that God bestows upon those who observe Shabbes—entering them. They soared in spiritual ecstasy and plumbed the depths of divine union. Shabbes was heaven on earth for Reb Zusia and Reb Elimelekh—a true taste of the world to come.

Over time, they began to doubt themselves, however, wondering if they were conjuring up the phenomena that they were experiencing. Was their observance of Shabbes real? Were they really experiencing states of divine union, or had their abilities to conjure phenomena allowed them to delude themselves? Was their ecstasy real divine ecstasy or was it similar to the intoxication of the ordinary tavern? They also wondered if their experiences were tied to the day of the week. Was Shabbes an experience that could only begin on Friday before sunset and end with the appearance of three stars in the sky on Saturday night?

Reb Zusia and Reb Elimelekh took their questions to their Rebbe, the Maggid of Mezrich,[197] and with the Maggid's blessing, they made a plan to observe Shabbes beginning on a Tuesday at sundown and concluding when they saw three stars in the sky on Wednesday evening.

On Tuesday, they made purchases, prepared delicious food, and got everything ready. Just before sundown, they lit and blessed the candles. They recited their prayers, and then made Kiddush, washed hands, recited hamotzi,[198] and ate a delicious meal. They sang zemirot (songs) to God, and in the morning they continued with the celebration of Shabbes all day until it was dark. They had experienced the neshama y'tayrah (additional soul) entering them on Tuesday as they welcomed the unusually timed Shabbes, and Wednesday evening, when they made Havdallah—the ceremony of separation between Shabbes and the ordinary days of the week—they felt the neshama y'tayrah depart and their everyday consciousness return.

Delighted and befuddled, they went to see the Maggid on Thursday. "So how was it?" the Maggid asked his disciples. "It was Shabbes! It was really Shabbes!" exclaimed Reb Zusia and Reb Elimelekh. They went on to explain that they had made their usual preparations, they had recited the prayers they always recite on Shabbes, they had made Kiddush (sanctification of wine) and enjoyed challah; they sang zemirot and learned and talked and walked and napped; they had done all of their Shabbes rituals, and it really felt like Shabbes.

---

197 The Maggid of Mezrich was a direct disciple of the Baal Shem Tov, the father of modern Chassidism. Reb Zusia and Reb Elimelekh were disciples of the Maggid of Mezrich, as were Reb Levi Yitzhak of Berdichev and Reb Shneur Zalman of Liadi and numerous other Chassidic luminaries. Reb Nachman of Breslov was the great-grandson of the Baal Shem Tov.
198 "Hamotzi" refers to the Jewish prayer recited before eating a meal. Traditionally, hamotzi is recited over bread, and its recitation includes all food eaten at the same meal where bread is served. Today, many Jews recite hamotzi over a meal even when they are not eating bread.

"How is this possible?" they asked the Maggid. "Where do you think the Shabbes goes during the week?" the Maggid asked them, and he explained that Shabbes goes up—back to God, as it were—at the end of Shabbes to wait for the following week. Shabbes is always available, but to experience it, we must enter into the state of Shabbes.

"Then why celebrate Shabbes from Friday evening until Saturday night?" Reb Zusia and Reb Elimelekh asked the Maggid. "Why not celebrate it on Tuesday evening until Wednesday night, like we did? Or on another day?"

The Maggid pointed out that Shabbes is a communal practice. We observe Shabbes in community, coming together at the synagogue with others who celebrate Shabbes, praying together, singing together, sharing meals, walks, learning, relaxing, enjoying. Shabbes is available at every moment, explained the Maggid. We can call it down and experience and enjoy it whenever we are ready, but for the sake of community, those who observe Shabbes religiously enter into Shabbes at the same time every week.[199]

Shabbes at Lama with Reb Zalman

In the 1970's, Reb Zalman began to spend time with the Sufis. In addition to deep and abiding friendships, there has been a great deal of spiritual collaboration between Zalman and a number of Sufi teachers and communities. During visits to the Lama Foundation in New Mexico, Reb Zalman taught the Friday evening practice that he called "Making Shabbes." Making Shabbes means to bring Shabbes into the world. Zalman explained that Shabbes continues from late on Friday afternoon until three stars appear in the sky on Saturday, but what stuck with Lama residents was the joy and music and rituals that Reb Zalman shared, and not the teachings about how Jewish communities and individual Jews celebrate Shabbes for twenty-five hours or more each week. Indeed, there are many Jews who learned how to make Shabbes this way from their families or in a congregation and they do the same—lighting and blessing the candles, singing joyous songs, making Kiddush over wine or grape juice, blessing and eating challah and enjoying a delicious meal—without keeping Shabbes for a full twenty-five hours.

If Shabbes may be brought down to this world from the world to come on a Tuesday, as illustrated in the story of Reb Zusia and Reb Elimelekh, then it may also be brought down at any time, including for a short time, such as on a Friday evening without continuing through Saturday night. One may see the evidence of this in the Shabbes glance that shines in the eyes of Lama residents and former residents when they talk about Shabbes with Reb Zalman.

---

199 Zalman Schachter, *Fragments of a Future Scroll* (Leaves of Grass, 1975) 45-48. With appreciation to Rabbi Raachel Jurovics for this source.

Preparing for Shabbes

This prayer encapsulates the attitude of Shabbes preparation and the observance of Shabbes. It may be read before or after lighting candles, or at any other time.

Catching Our Breath[200]

Tonight is a time to catch our breath.
Whatever we have been doing, making, working, or creating…
Tonight is a time to catch our breath.

No matter how necessary our work, how important to the world, how urgent that we continue it;
No matter how joyful our work, how urgent that we set it right;
No matter our how hard we have worked to gather
Our modest fame, our honorable livelihood, our reasonable power;

Tonight we pause to catch our breath.
Tonight we pause to share whatever we have gathered.

Remembering the Earth on Shabbes

The following prayer was part of the United Nations Environmental Shabbat Program in the 1980's.[201]

Earth Prayer

We join with the earth and with each other
To bring new life into the land,
To restore the waters,
To refresh the air.

We join with the earth and with each other
To renew the forests,
To care for the plants,
To protect the creatures.

We join with the earth and with each other
To recreate the human community,
To promote justice and peace,
To remember our children.

We join with the earth and with each other.
We join together as many and diverse expressions
Of one loving mystery
For the healing of the earth and the renewal of all life.

---

200 I received this prayer as one for which the author is presently unknown.
201 Thanks to Susan Rothstein who gave me a copy of this prayer on a handout in the early 1990's.

What the Candles Symbolize

One may use any white candles for Shabbat. White is the color that includes all colors of the rainbow, and that is why white represents purity in religious settings. White is not a skin color, even though we use the word "white" to describe some skin tones in English. Every color of skin is sacred, and every color of hair and fur. There is a morning prayer that is recited every day of the year—whether weekday or Sabbath or holy day—that begins "Elohai Neshama SheNatata Bi Tehorah Hi," which means "The soul that You have placed in me is pure."

The wax represents life in this world. The flame represents the soul. The wick represents the spirit. So long as there is wax, the flame may continue to burn. When there is no wax on the wick, the wick burns up quickly and the flame is soon extinguished. A candle needs one additional element in order to burn after being lit, and that is air. Air represents God. When air is removed from the surroundings, the presence of wax and wick are not sufficient to sustain the flame. There is nothing but God. Nothing exists in the absence of God.

If I have five dollars in my pocket and I give it away, my pocket is empty. If I have a lighted candle, and I use it to light your candle, then you have light and I have light. The flame of the Shabbat candles may be viewed as the soul. The soul who cares for others, who loves others, who has compassion upon others, who goes out of the way for others is a bright light in God's world. The soul who thinks only of itself is like the man who gives away all the dollars in his pocket.

Wine and Juice as Symbols

Grapes grow on a vine. It is traditional to make Kiddush over wine or juice that comes from grapes. However, one may also make Kiddush over challah.[202] Kiddush is from the word kadosh, meaning holy. Kiddush is the sanctification of the wine or juice so that when we drink it, we receive the benefit of the delicious liquid, and the blessing with which it has been imbued.

In order for the grape to become wine, it loses its stem, skin and seeds. The remaining pulp is then crushed and a delicious juice emerges. The juice must ferment in order to become wine.[203] So it is with life. We are born fine; imperfect in our fleshy existence, but fine nevertheless. Then we grow and we begin to define, so we find a teacher and our teacher teaches us to refine.[204]

Another way to understand the journey of the grape is that we are born pure, and the trials and challenges and suffering of life remove from us our stem, skin and seeds, as it were. Joe and Guin Miller were fond of reminding us that in order for a seed to grow, it has to ferment and break out of its shell. "And you know what that means," Joe would say, "It has to rot! And then it grows into something living and worthwhile." This is analogous to certain periods of one's life when something wonderful is about to bloom, but it looks as though it is falling apart in the meantime. Like the intense darkness right before dawn, it takes tremendous faith to believe that light will come when we cannot see even a glimmer in the darkness.

---

202 Challah is a Hebrew word that describes the special bread eaten on the Sabbath and Jewish holy days. Grocery stores that go out of their way to sell kosher food, such as those that have a kosher food section, tend to carry challah either all the time, or on Thursday and Fridays for purchase before the Jewish Sabbath. Some grocery stores sell challah all the time even though they do not stock a kosher food section. Challah makes especially good French toast.
203 I heard the seeds of this teaching from a story attributed to Hazrat Inayat Khan.
204 I learned this from Swami Satchidananda.

We sanctify wine or juice on Shabbes and festivals by reciting Kiddush, and its blessing enters us when we drink. Hopefully, the blessing has the capacity to carry us higher and higher into communion with the One Being.

The Symbol of the Challah

Reb Zalman once told a story at Lama Foundation that I had heard from my rabbi while growing up. I did not hear Zalman tell it, so I am going to share my version here, which is based on the version I learned from Rabbi Aaron J. Tofield, of blessed memory:[205] Once there was a tragic plane crash; everyone on the flight perished. When they arrived at the gates of the world to come, the angel on duty explained that heaven was full just then and rooms had to be arranged for them, because the plane accident happened "at the last minute" and heaven didn't have a chance to prepare. "So go down to the other place," instructed the angel, "and in a while when we are ready for you, we will call for you."

The souls of the passengers from the tragic flight made their way to the nether world. There they found beings that looked very much like the ones they had seen as they peered over the angel's shoulder into the world to come. But unlike the heavenly beings, the beings in the nether world were miserable. There were delights of every kind to be consumed—drinks, food, and other sources of pleasure—but these were all tethered to a ceiling that was like the top of a sukkah—the hut that Jews build in their backyard or elsewhere to sit in during the autumn festival of Sukkot, when they remember the forty years of wandering in the wilderness. The souls interned in the nether world are, by definition, selfish self-centered, interested only in themselves, and giving little thought to helping others. It is these qualities that got them into trouble in this world and caused them to be selected for the nether world after their death.

The passengers from the flight made the best of it. At first, they reached up to the delights that were strung from the ceiling, but alas, rigor mortis, the condition of flesh after death, had settled in to their souls bodies and they could not bend their elbows to feed themselves. That was also the condition of the long-term residents of the nether world, who had long since given up trying.

The next day, there was space in heaven and an angel came and fetched the passengers of the doomed airplane flight and brought them up. They entered through the gates into the world to come, and to their shock, they saw that the delights of this world were also tethered to the ceiling in the world to come, and rigor mortis had also set in on the elbows of the soul beings in heaven so that they could not feed themselves or provide drink or other pleasures for themselves. The defining difference between the beings in the world to come and the beings in the nether world, however, was that those in the world to come had been caregivers. They had spent their lives caring not only for themselves and their families and their communities and the poor and the disenfranchised, but when faced with the challenge of rigor mortis on their elbows, these holy beings reached up to the ceiling and chose the choicest delights that were pleasing to those near and they each fed their neighbor.

---

205 Rabbi Aaron J. Tofield, of blessed memory, served as spiritual leader of Temple Beth Emet in Anaheim, California from the 1950's to the 1990's.

Feeding One Another

Reb Zalman told his version of this story at Lama Foundation, and in many communities throughout the world as he taught people to hold the challot—the festive breads of Shabbat. He invited everyone to touch the challot, or to touch someone touching the challot, and while connected, to sing hamotzi[206] together. After singing the prayer together, those with their hands on the challot would break off pieces and pass them back into the crowd so that there were chunks of challah in every cluster of people, and each person could break off a small piece and feed his or her neighbor. Now that's Shabbes! And one may bring down that part of Shabbes late on a Friday afternoon, or on Shabbat midday, or any other time—even Tuesday.

Traditional Candle Blessings

This is the traditional blessing over the Shabbes candles. There are lovely alternative blessings in *Kol HaNeshama*, the Sabbath and Festivals Prayer Book of the Reconstructionist Movement, and in a variety of Jewish Renewal prayer books. One may also find lovely readings to share before and after candle lighting in Ultra Orthodox, Orthodox, Conservative, Reform, Reconstructionist and Renewal prayer books.

Barukh Atah Adonai Elohaynu Melekh HaOlam Asher Kid'shanu B'mitzvotav V'tzivanu L'hadlik Ner Shel Shabbat.

Blessed are You, Lord our God, All Pervading Spirit of the Universe, Who sanctifies us with Your Mitzvot and gives us the mitzvah of lighting the Sabbath candles.

Reb Zalman's Candle Blessings

This blessing has the same translation as the traditional blessing over the candles given above:

Barukh Atah YaH Elohaynu Melekh HaOlam Asher Kid'shanu Bemitzvotav Vetzivanu Lehadlik Ner Shel Shabbat.

Blessing Over Wine

Those who wish to recite the full Kiddush from Friday evening or Shabbat day are invited to consult a Jewish prayer book or a rabbi or cantor or observant Jewish friend. The following is the blessing over wine that is recited as part of the full Kiddush. This is the blessing Reb Zalman taught at Lama to render the ritual of Kiddush accessible to everyone.

Traditional version:
Barukh Atah Adonai Elohaynu Melekh HaOlam Borey Pri HaGafen.

Reb Zalman's version:
Barukh Atah YaH Elohaynu Melekh HaOlam Borey Pri HaGafen.

---

206 Hamotzi is the Jewish blessing over breads and matzo. (Matzo is a large cracker made quickly of flour and water. Matzo is the staple of Passover when traditional Jews do not eat anything containing leaven, such as yeast.)

Both versions may be translated in a number of ways, including this one:

Blessed are You, Lord our God, All Pervading Spirit of the Universe, Creator of the fruit of the vine.

Blessing Over Challah

The following is the blessing over challah, which may be recited over all bread; and indeed, some Jews recite this blessing over a meal regardless of whether it includes bread.

Traditional version:
Barukh Atah Adonai Elohaynu Melekh HaOlam HaMotzi Lechem Min HaAretz.

Reb Zalman's version:
Barukh Atah YaH Elohaynu Melekh HaOlam HaMotzi Lechem Min HaAretz.

Both versions may be translated in a number of ways, including this one:
Blessed are You, Lord our God, All Pervading Spirit of the Universe, Who brings forth bread from the earth.

Hand Washing and Grace After Meals

Traditionally, one washes hands, recites a blessing over hand washing, blesses the challah and then enjoys it. In addition, at the end of the meal, one traditionally recites a prayer of thanksgiving for the food and drink that one has consumed, and hopefully enjoyed. Those wishing to learn the traditional hand washing and accompanying blessing, as well as the grace after meals, are invited to consult a Jewish prayer book that includes the blessings before and after eating, or to consult a rabbi or cantor or observant Jewish friend.

Welcoming the Angels

There are many faiths that harbor a belief in angels, although some faiths call them by other names. According to Judaism, we each have two guardian angels, one leading us toward goodness, and one leading us away from goodness. During the repetition aloud of the Amidah—the silent devotion— recited in the synagogue in the morning and afternoon, there is a section known as Kedushah from the word kadosh, meaning holy. During the Kedushah, we remember the teachings of the prophets that the angels on high call one to another, saying "Holy, Holy, Holy is the Lord of Hosts; the whole world is full of God's Glory." When we recite the words "one to another," we turn to the left and right to acknowledge the angels who accompany us through life.

On Shabbes, there are additional angels, called ministering angels, or service angels—malachey hashareyt—whom we welcome and invite to bless us before or after Kiddush. Shalom Aleichem is the traditional prayer that goes with this custom.

Shalom Aleichem

Shalom Aleichem Malakhey HaShareyt Malakhey Elyon
Mi Melekh Malakhey HaM'lakhim HaKadosh Barukh Hu

Bo'akhem L'Shalom Malakhey HaShalom Malakhey Elyon
Mi Melekh Malakhey HaM'lakhim HaKadosh Barukh Hu

Barkhuni L'Shalom Malakhey HaShalom Malakhey Elyon
Mi Melekh Malakhey HaM'lakhim HaKadosh Barukh Hu

Tzeytkhem L'Shalom Malakhey HaShalom Malakhey Elyon
Mi Melekh Malakhey HaM'lakhim HaKadosh Barukh Hu

These verses mean:

Peace to you, ministering angels, angels on high.
Which king is the king of the angels? The Holy One, blessed be He.

Come in peace, angels of peace, angels on high.
Which king is the king of the angels? The Holy One, blessed be He.

Bless us with peace, angels of peace, angels on high.
Which king is the king of the angels? The Holy One, blessed be He.

Go in peace, angels of peace, angels on high.
Which king is the king of the angels? The Holy One, blessed be He.

Other Shabbat Customs

In keeping with the traditions embodied in "Catching Our Breath" presented earlier in this chapter, we are invited to take a break from creating and accomplishing on Shabbat in order to relax, enjoy and return refreshed, at the end of Shabbat, to our everyday lives. Relaxing with friends and family has always been part of the traditional Shabbat experience, together with going for walks, playing with the children, learning together, singing together, praying and communing with God, and enjoying intimacy with our earthly beloved.

Gutt Shabbes![207] Shabbat Shalom![208]

---

207 Gutt Shabbes is Yiddish, meaning "Good Sabbath," and is a traditional Shabbat greeting.
208 Shabbat Shalom is Hebrew, meaning "Sabbath peace," and is a traditional Shabbat greeting.

Chapter 25

Invocations

Sufi Invocation

This Sufi Invocation was given in English by Pir-O-Murshid Hazrat Inayat Khan:

Toward the One, The Perfection of Love, Harmony and Beauty,
The Only Being, United with All the Illuminated Souls,
Who Form the Embodiment of the Master, The Spirit of Guidance.

The Sufi Invocation is recited to begin a variety of intentions and activities. We begin spiritual gatherings, rehearsals and meetings with the Sufi Invocation. We may recite it when beginning a new task at home or at work, or when going on a journey. The power of the Sufi Invocation is transformative: it transforms us, the place in which we recite it, the objects in the vicinity, and the tasks at hand. This is illustrated in the following story:

A person once asked Pir-O-Murshid Hazrat Inayat Khan what to do when we find ourselves in a situation where we need to eat food that does not have a good vibration.[209] Hazrat Inayat Khan recommended reciting the Sufi Invocation over the food. "And if the food still does not have a good vibration?" the person asked. "Recite the invocation again," was Inayat Khan's answer. "And if the food continues to not have a good vibration?" "Recite the invocation a third time," was the answer.

Islamic Invocation

The Islamic Invocation is Bismillah ErRahman ErRahim. Almost every Surah[210] of Qur'an begins Bismillah ErRahman ErRahim. When Muslims begin a task, or begin discussing a topic, or begin to address a group, they recite the Bismillah. And when Muslims eat, they begin by reciting the Bismillah.

Although the Bismillah is not part of the Sufi Invocation, many Inayati Sufis recite Bismillah ErRahman ErRahim immediately following the Sufi Invocation. Inayati Sufis often recite the Bismillah in Arabic and then translate it into English as, "We begin in the name of Allah, Who is Mercy and Compassion," or "We begin in the name of Allah, Most Merciful and Compassionate."

These English translations approximate the literal Arabic, which is, "In the name of Allah, the Merciful, the Compassionate."

---

209 In other words, food that does not have a good vibration. This does not refer to food that is spoiled.
210 A Surah is a chapter, or section, of the *Holy Qur'an*.

Kabbalistic Invocation

The following Kabbalistic Invocation is in Aramaic, and is found and used among Kabbalists and modern Chassidim:

L'Sheym Yichud Kudsha Brikh Hu U'Shekhintay
BiDchilu Ur'chimu, Ur'chimu U'Dchilu
L'Yachda Shem Ot Yod V'Ot Hay
B'Ot Vav V'Ot Hay
BeYichuda Shlim B'Shem Kol Yisrael.

The literal translation is:

In the name of unity of the Holy One and the Shechina,
in reverence and compassion, and in compassion and reverence
for the unity of the name of letter yod and letter hay
with letter vav and letter hay
in complete unity in the name of Israel.

This Kabbalistic Invocation is also presented toward the end of Chapter 19.

Blessing of God's Goodness

Decades ago, Ruhaniat Sufis asked Reb Zalman and myself—along with other rabbis and other Jews—to translate the Sufi Invocation into Hebrew, just as it is being translated into many other languages. I soon realized that translating the Sufi Invocation into Hebrew would not have the same spiritual capacity as the Sufi Invocation in English; or as Reb Zalman expresses it in the article in Appendix F, a translation into Hebrew would not convey "the message" the way the Sufi Invocation in English does. Translating the Sufi Invocation into Hebrew has value nevertheless, and I have included Reb Zalman's translation on the first page of the "Openings" section, and in Appendix F. I believe that others have translated the Sufi Invocation into Hebrew as well.

Decades ago, I asked Reb Zalman for a practice to begin the process of finding an invocation in Hebrew that had the capacity and intention of the Sufi Invocation, rather than a translation of it. Zalman pointed me toward two resources: One is the Kabbalistic Invocation in Aramaic above, and the other is the Blessing of God's Goodness. This blessing may be recited in the six ways set forth on the next page. There are, no doubt, many other formulations in which this blessing may also be recited.

For purposes of translating this blessing, I have coined the word "engooden." Its root is "good." The Hebrew word "maytiv" means what I imagine the word "engooden" would mean if it already existed in our English vocabulary. For example, we have the words "power" and "empower," "light" and "enlighten," "garden" and "gardener." Similarly, for purposes of the translations on the next page, we have the words "good" and "engooden."

Barukh Atah Adonai Elohaynu Melekh HaOlam, HaTov V'Hamaytiv.
Blessed are You, Lord our God, Sovereign of the universe, the Good and the Engoodener.

or

Barukh Atah YaH Elohaynu Melekh HaOlam, HaTov V'Hamaytiv.
Blessed are You, God our God, Sovereign of the universe, the Good and the Engoodener.

or

Barukh Atah Adonai Elohaynu Melekh HaOlam, HaTov V'Hamaytiv LaKol.
Blessed are You, Lord our God, Sovereign of the universe, the Good and the Engoodener of all.

or

Barukh Atah YaH Elohaynu Melekh HaOlam, HaTov V'Hamaytiv LaKol.
Blessed are You, God our God, Sovereign of the universe, the Good and the Engoodener of all.

or

Nevareykh et Eyn HaChayyim, Ruach Chay HaOlamim, HaTov V'Hamaytiv.
We bless the Source of Life, Spirit, Life of the worlds, the Good and the Engoodener.

or

Nevareykh et Eyn HaChayyim, Ruach Chay HaOlamim, HaTov V'Hamaytiv LaKol.
We bless the Source of Life, Spirit, Life of the worlds, the Good and the Engoodener of all.

Rabbi Nachman of Breslov,[211] Rabbi Levi Yitzhak of Berdichev,[212] and other Chassidic masters express the belief that everything is "tov" at its root. Tov is the Hebrew for "good," as mentioned above. God is at the root of everything, and the root of everything is God. The root of everything has goodness and is goodness. By "goodness," we do not mean pleasantness or peacefulness or niceness. Rather, we mean something along the lines of "true essence" or "returning to the source from which all things manifest."

The Chassidic masters go to great lengths to give examples of suffering that is, at its root, divine goodness or divine glory. If we could only see the source and purpose of our suffering, if we could experience the divine plan in relation to our suffering, then our suffering would be over. The Chassidic masters also tell us that when there is yichud (Aramaic and Hebrew meaning "union") between Kudsha Brikh Hu and Shekhintay, there is no more suffering. Kudsha Brikh Hu is Aramaic for Holy One, Blessed be He. Shekhintay is Aramaic for Shechina, the feminine indwelling presence of God, or the presence of God in creation. When there is yichud between Kudsha Brikh Hu and Shekhintay, there is no more suffering; there may still be pain, but it is no longer suffering.

---

211 Rabbi Nachman ben Simcha of Breslov, *Likutey Maharan*, section 65.
212 Rabbi Levi Yitzhak of Berdichev, *Kedushat Levi.*

Martin Buber tells the following stories in his book, entitled *Tales of the Hasidim*:

> When Rabbi Shmelke [of Nikolsburg] and his brother [Rabbi Pinchas] visited the [M]aggid of Mezritch, they asked him about the following. "Our sages said certain words which leave us no peace because we do not understand them. They are that men should praise and thank God for suffering just as much as for well-being, and receive it with the same joy. Will you tell us how we are to understand this, rabbi?" The [M]aggid replied: "Go to the House of Study. There you will find Zusya smoking his pipe. He will give you the explanation." They went to the House of Study and put their question to Rabbi Zusya. He laughed. "You certainly have come to the right man! Better go to someone else rather than to me, for I have never experienced suffering." But the two knew that from the day he was born to this day, Rabbi Zusya's life had been a web of need and anguish. Then they knew what it was: to accept suffering with love.[213]

The Blessing of Goodness at Its Root given in the six formulations above is an expression of gratitude for everything, together with an acknowledgement that everything is goodness at its root. This is similar to the Sufi grace given by Pir-O-Murshid Hazrat Inayat Khan, and recited by many Inayati Sufis before meals:

Oh Thou, the Sustainer of our bodies, hearts and souls,
Bless all that we receive in thankfulness. Amin.[214]

Thanking God for all that we receive is an acknowledgement that everything is to be appreciated. One way to understand this is through the assumption that everything is goodness at its root, as explained above.

New Jewish Invocation

For years, I recited the Blessing of God's Goodness. Then I began to recite L'sheym Yichud Kudsha Brikh Hu U'Shekhintay, and over time, the following emerged:

> L'sheym Yichud Kudsha Brikh Hu U'Shekhintay,
> HaM'kadeshet Otanu U'M'varekhet Otanu
> B'Shalva V'Hashket Va'Vetach.
> Barukh Atah Adonai,
> HaTov Shimkha U'Lekha Na'eh L'Hodot.

> In the name of the unity of the Holy One and the Shechina,
> Who sanctifies us and blesses us
> With equanimity, quietude and assurance.
> Blessed are You, O God,
> Whose Name is Goodness and to Whom it is pleasant to give thanks.

---

213 Martin Buber, *Tales of the Hasidim, Volume I: The Early Masters* (Schocken Books, Inc., 1970) 237-238.
214 "Amin" is the Islamic equivalent of the Hebrew "Amen." The IslamicDictionary.com defines "Amin" as a dua (supplication) meaning "O Allah, respond to (or answer) what we have said." <http://www.islamic-dictionary.com/index.php?word=ameen> May 2012.

L'sheym Yichud Kudsha Brikh Hu U'Shekhintay is the opening phrase of the Kabbalist Invocation given earlier in this chapter, and may be translated as, "in the name of unity of the Holy One and the Shechina."

B'Shalva, v'hashkeyt va'vetach is a sacred phrase that appears in the central prayer of the Amidah (silent devotion) recited during the mincha[215] service on Shabbat afternoon. The prayer begins, "You are One and Your Name is One." In the middle of the prayer, it speaks about rest, which is the goal of Shabbat, namely, to rest from the ordinary tasks we perform during the week. When we chant sacred phrases, the deepest part of the practice may be the moment of breathing in silence at the end. That moment of silence is a Shabbat moment. Among the central lines of this central prayer is menuchat shalom v'shalva v'hashkeyt vavetach, which may be translated as "peaceful rest and tranquility and quietude and contentment." These are qualities that are attained, God willing, through the practice of Shabbat and spiritual retreat, and other opportunities in life that provide us with a respite from the ordinary challenges and difficulties of everyday life. The last three words of this sacred phrase are contained in the third line of the New Jewish Invocation given above.[216]

The chatimah (seal) of the central prayer of the Shabbat afternoon Amidah is Barukh Atah Adonai, Mekadesh HaShabbat, which means Blessed are You O God, Who sanctifies the Sabbath. M'qadesh is a verb meaning "sanctifies," and it appears in numerous places in the Shabbat liturgy. M'qadesh is in its masculine form in the Shabbat afternoon Amidah, and in its feminine form in the New Jewish Invocation above.

The chatimah (seal), or closing blessing, of the New Jewish Invocation given above comes from the chatimah of the blessing of thanksgiving that is recited toward the end of every Amidah, including on weekdays, Shabbat, holy days and fast days.

I recite the New Jewish Invocation from time to time throughout the day when I begin a new activity, or when I lose my concentration on the activity in which I am engaged. I do not recite the invocation before washing dishes or doing housework, but one could. I do not recite the invocation over food and drink; instead I recite traditional blessings over food and drink. I might recite the invocation when going on a journey, along with the traditional Jewish travel prayer. I might recite the invocation when beginning my work day, and when beginning a new work related task, when I am about to read an email that I know will be difficult to countenance or understand, or when responding to such an email, or when taking a phone call that I suspect may be challenging, or when beginning a creative task. When I need to find strength, when I have lost my way, when I am joyous or ecstatic or grateful, I might talk to God or recite a different prayer. On the other hand, when preparing to take action to garner strength or to help find my way or to reach out to someone to appreciate them, I might say the invocation. When I am angry or frustrated and unable to locate my patience and forbearance, I recite the invocation with the intention of finding a way to act constructively.

I do not share these as a prescription. Rather, I share them as ideas of how this person uses the New Jewish Invocation. If the invocation speaks to you, find your way with it. Perhaps begin by repeating it for its own sake, without motive, and without a task that will follow it, and see how it feels.

---

215 Mincha is the name of the afternoon worship service discussed in Chapter 1 of this book.
216 "V'shalva" means "and equanimity." "B'shalva" means "in equanimity." The former appears in the Shabbat afternoon Amidah, and the latter appears in the New Jewish Invocation given above.

Chapter 26

Sacred Merit

These days I am gardening, and one of my tasks is weeding. When I reach into the soil to pull out the root of a stubborn weed growing near one of my plants, I have to decide how deep to dig with my fingers or a tool. If I do not remove the weed root, that weed will likely grow back more quickly with a stronger thicker root to better sap the nutrients from the plants I have intended for the garden. If I am not careful, I might accidentally dig up the roots of the plants that beautify my garden. Yet, on the other hand, if I do everything perfectly, the weeds will be gone and my precious plants will be happy; but only for a few days or a week until new weeds begin to sprout, and the cycle of weeding begins all over again.

There is a discussion in Chapter 23 about tikkun olam, the process of helping to make the world a better place. As mentioned in that chapter, Reb Zalman teaches that repairing the world is not like repairing a watch. No matter how much we repair the world, the world will still be in need of repair. Similarly, no matter how much we tend the garden of our hearts, and no matter how much attention we bring to the cleansing and purifying of our thoughts, there is always more to do. And as long as we are alive in these bodies, there are weeds to pull up from our inner garden, just as there is always work to be done to help make the world a better place. One important goal of faith that manifests in the form of religion and spirituality is to help us remember that it is always worth helping others even if there is no end to the cycle of the needy requiring our help; and it is always worth tending the garden of our hearts and purifying our thoughts even if our inner weeds seem to appear endlessly, along with the joys and challenges of life.

When my father, of blessed memory, was dying, and his medical condition left no alternative but palliative care, my mother, of blessed memory, and I were with him every day in the hospital. As Mom left Dad's bedside the night before he died to go home for a bit of sleep, she asked him if there was anything he wanted her to bring him in the morning. Dad looked at Mom with a look I had seen a thousand times, but this time, there was no smile, no hope, no romance, just love. I can see my Dad's face even now, twenty-four years later. With his look of love, with no smile and no frills, Dad pointed his index finger toward Mom. Neither of them said a word; there was no need.

As the years went by, Mom relocated from the United States to Israel. A while later, after a visit to the United States, Mom's health deteriorated and her Israeli physician advised us that she was no longer well enough to travel back and forth between the United States and Israel. My brother explained the situation to our mother, and she said that was fine so long as we promised that when she died, we would bury her next to Dad, and that otherwise she was not going to stay in Israel. With the help and advice of rabbis and morticians, arrangements were made, and my father's remains were reburied outside Jerusalem. Mom's next wish was to visit his grave; and once she did, she was content and never breathed another word about leaving Israel until she left this world twelve and a half years after Dad.

Whether one believes in reincarnation,[217] or resurrection,[218] or heaven and hell, or that this world is "all there is" and life ends with the death of the body, we all have a sense that love keeps going when someone we love passes from this world. [219] In the Song of Songs attributed to King Solomon, the author writes:

> Simayni khachotam al libekha,
> Kachotam al zro'echa,
> Ki aza khamavet ahavah
> Kashah khish'ol kin'ah,
> R'shafehah rishpay aysh shalhevet'yah,
>
> Place me as a seal upon your heart,
> As a seal upon your arm,
> For love is as strong as death;
> Passion is as strong as she'ol[220]
> Its darts are darts of fire,
> A blazing flame."[221]

The Song of Songs is seen as a series of love sonnets depicting human love, or as a metaphor for the love between God and Israel (in other words, the Jewish people), or as a metaphor for the love between God and all people. Sacred phrases of divine love may also be found in Chapter 18 of this book.

When my mother was dying, she spent some days in intensive care and was then moved to another ward in the hospital. While she was in intensive care, my brother and I took turns at her bedside. We had been told that her emergency surgery had failed, and that she would never regain consciousness. We knew that this was through no fault of her physicians, and that even her survival beyond the one-last-chance surgery was a miracle. I continued to pray for Mom, but I no longer prayed for her to get well. Amid my prayers, I recited birkat kohanim, the priestly blessings with which Jewish people have blessed—and been blessed—since the Torah was given three thousand and some years ago. The priestly blessings are in bold in the following quote from the book of Numbers:

---

217 Reincarnation, commonly called transmigration of souls in Judaism, is mentioned in numerous Jewish sources, including the following: *Sefer HaBahir, The Book of Illuminations* attributed to Rabbi Nehunia ben HaKana, Part One, paragraphs 184 to195; the *Zohar* (commentaries on Parashat Mishpatim, *Exodus* 21:1-11); *Shaar HaGilgulim, Book of the Transmigrations* attributed to Rabbi Hayyim Vital recording the teachings of his teacher, Rabbi Isaac Luria; and references in the texts of many Chassidic rabbis.
218 The notion of resurrection appears in the Biblical Book of *Daniel* (12:2).
219 Simcha Raphael, Ph.D. has created an excellent text and extensive resource surveying Jewish views of the afterlife over the four thousand years of Jewish history. Anne Brener also touches upon important views of the afterlife in her text. Simcha Paull Raphael, *Jewish Views of the Afterlife* (Rowman & Littlefield Publishers, 2009). Anne Brener, *Mourning and Mitzvah: A Guided Journal for Walking the Mourner's Path Through Grief to Healing* (Woodstock, Vermont: Jewish Lights Publishing, First Edition, Sixth Printing 2000).
220 Heaven is called "shamayim," which also means sky. "She'ol" refers to a lower world, or netherworld, and is mentioned in a multitude of verses in scripture, including: *Genesis* 37:35, 44:29 and 31, *Deuteronomy* 32:22, *Samuel* II 22:6 ("… the Lord kills, and returns to life, he brings down to Sheol and brings up…"), *Isaiah* 14: 15, and *Psalms* 55:16.
221 *Song of Songs* 8:6.

The Lord spoke to Moses, saying:
"Speak to Aaron and to his sons, and say
'Thus shall you bless the children of Israel. Say to them:
The Lord bless you and protect you.
The Lord shine His face upon you and be gracious unto you.
The Lord lift his face to you and grant you peace.'
And place My name upon the children of Israel, and I will bless them."[222]

In the intensive care unit in which my Mom was being treated, there were many patients in one large room, and staff would move from bed to bed as they checked on patients and treated them. I stood by my Mom looking at her, holding her limp hand, remembering, praying, crying as she lay in a semi-comatose state. There were always others around, including patients, visitors and staff. Occasionally the curtains would be drawn around a bed for a procedure, but otherwise, we were all in one large room together. As the hours passed, I gained courage and began to sing to Mom in a low voice, and to recite prayers slightly audibly, instead of in silence. One afternoon, a haredi (Ultra Orthodox) man was visiting a patient near my Mom. I didn't know the man's relationship to the patient; I didn't know anything about the man, except that by his side locks[223] and his clothing, I knew he was haredi. I don't know what he knew about me, because we never spoke, but it was clear that he was visiting someone and staying for a long time, and so was I.

I lifted my hands and closed my eyes and recited the priestly blessings for Mom as I had been doing from time to time. Suddenly, there was so much energy. An amazing amount of energy. I didn't know what was happening. Suddenly this prayer that I had recited so many times in the synagogue as a pulpit rabbi was pouring out my hands with more energy and magnetism than I had ever felt while reciting it. I was grateful. I hoped my prayer would make a difference. I didn't know what difference was needed to help my Mom through her ordeal, but I had chosen the priestly blessings, because I had a sense that perhaps what Mom needed was peace.

I finished the prayer and opened my eyes, and as I did, I saw that the haredi man was looking at me. He was holding his hands in the exact same position that I was holding my hands; only the palms of my hands opened toward Mom, and the palms of his hands opened toward me. This man whom I had not met, and never did meet, was adding his magnetism to my prayer. I smiled and nodded. He smiled and looked away. That was it. Until a half hour or so passed, and again I lifted my hands and prayed, and again there was so much magnetism, and again I opened my eyes and he was praying with me.

That was the last time I saw the man. I was sorry afterward that I did not try to speak with him to thank him properly. I just wasn't sure how to speak with him, and how to bridge the gap between myself—a woman rabbi from North America visiting a hospital in Jerusalem where my mother lay dying—and him—a haredi man from who-knows-where, visiting a woman who lay next to my mother.

The next day, my mother was moved to a regular ward, and it was there that she died ten days later, with my brother and me by her side just a few hours after visits from her grandchildren. I had

---

222 *Numbers* 6:22-27.
223 Ultra Orthodox Jewish men generally have payyot, side locks that either grow without being cut—or are trimmed, or that are cut from time to time, but not cut short like the rest of the hair on their head or beard. Growing payyot adheres to the mitzvah given in the Torah that states, "You shall not round the corners of your heads; nor shall you mar the corners of your beard." *Leviticus* 19:27.

befriended the visitors of Mom's roommates in this new room, because I didn't want to find myself again with a deep connection to someone and unable to speak in a powerfully potent moment. In the bed cattycorner from Mom was a twenty-eight year old Palestinian woman with young children at home, who had just had a shunt placed in her brain to drain fluid from a difficult stubborn condition. I knew about this from speaking with members of her family who traveled more than two hours each way to take turns at her bedside.

One day, I was sitting in the large waiting room down the hall from Mom's hospital room. I had brought a watermelon and was slicing it. The waiting room was filled with Arabs sitting in chairs and on the floor, gathered around food and eating and talking. I walked over to the woman whose daughter was being treated in the bed cattycorner from my mother, and offered her some watermelon. She smiled, took a slice and thanked me. A younger Arab woman whispered sharply in Arabic, "don't eat it!" "Why?" asked the older woman. The young woman darted a glance at me and then looked back at the older woman and exclaimed in a whisper, "She's a Jew!"

"She *is* a Jew, and she brought us watermelon." The older woman responded. I stood frozen. Should I put each person in the position of having to choose between the two women, I wondered. Or should I impolitely serve only the older woman? As I stood thinking, the older woman motioned with her hand. "To everyone!" she said. I followed her instruction, and offered everyone, even the young woman whom I knew would refuse, which she did very politely.

On the night my mother died, the Palestinian mother was with her daughter who lay cattycorner across the room. Mom died just after midnight. My brother and I stayed with Mom for a long time after she died. Then my brother left to inform family members and make funeral arrangements. I asked the nurses for a bit more time with Mom and they agreed. After holding her limp hand that was now beginning to turn cool, I sat and sat and then the tears came. Not just a few, but the endless sobbing that sometimes takes a while to come forward. As I sobbed, I heard a voice calling me in Arabic. It was the mother of the young woman. I looked, and through my tears, I saw her beckoning to me with her hand and arm.

"Come, my daughter, come," she said. I let go of my mother's hand and walked across the dark room that lacked even moonlight. I was too sad to think. I was on "automatic." I didn't ask myself what this woman wanted. I just walked to her as if I had always known her. She was holding her daughter's hand, and when I came over to her, she let go of her daughter's hand, and she reached up and put her arms around me and held me while I sobbed. "I know what it is to have a mother like this," she said. I looked at her. Her eyes were kind and she was nodding her head gently. She held me more until my sobbing finally subsided.

I thanked the woman for her kindness, and she thanked me for watching over a fan, some dishes and utensils that her family had left in my care when there was a break in their comings and goings from Nablus in the Northern West Bank. Then I went back over to my Mom, and held her and kissed her and said good-bye.

The Hebrew word chesed means loving-kindness. According to the Kabbalah, chesed is one of the ten sephirot—emanations or qualities—with which God created and sustains the universe. This is discussed in Appendix D. My Dad pointing to his beloved—my Mom—the night before he died was an act of love, and it was also an act of chesed, loving-kindness. My brother arranging to have my Dad's remains exhumed and reburied in Israel was an act of chesed. The haredi man who joined his energy with my prayers for my Mom in intensive care was also engaging in an act of chesed. The Palestinian woman from Nablus was also engaging in acts of chesed when she held and comforted me the night my Mom died, and when she joined me in reaching across a cultural divide as we ate watermelon. I prayed for that woman and her daughter who lay, barely conscious, cattycorner from my Mom eleven years ago. I hope they are alive and well and safe and enjoying their children and grandchildren.

Chesed, loving-kindness, is a gift that we can offer to anyone, rich or poor, old or young, far away or near at hand, known or unknown. There are countless ways to offer chesed, and they are collectively known as Gemilut chassadim,[224] deeds of loving-kindness. One form of chesed is offering sacred merit on behalf of others. In Reb Zalman's Four Part Shema given in Chapter 14, the third repetition involves replacing the word "Yisrael" with the name of someone to whom we wish to send sacred merit. In other words, we repeat the Shema in the first two ways described in Chapter 14. Then, while repeating the Shema a third time, we insert the name of a person to whom we wish to send sacred merit, and with our intention, we send the merit before, during and/or after this third repetition of the Shema.

Over the years, when I am preparing to go on spiritual retreat, Reb Zalman always recommends that I conclude the retreat with the practice of bestowing sacred merit. "When you finish, take the energy and send it to those who need it," Reb Zalman would say. "Send it to your loved ones, your community, those with whom you struggle, and those whom you do not know."

Joe Miller was a spiritual teacher who gave teachings and practices from Theosophy, Vedanta, Christianity and Mahayana Buddhism. Joe was also a spiritual uncle to Inayati Sufis who were part of the Sufi Order International and Sufi Ruhaniat International. Reb Zalman and Joe used to love to converse on a variety of spiritual topics, and when I was a rabbinic student, Zalman arranged for me to study Christian Kabbalah with Joe. At the end of meetings and classes at the Theosophical Society in San Francisco, and during walks in Golden Gate Park, Joe would ask us to hold hands and sing:

> May all beings be well;
> May all beings be happy;
> Peace, peace, peace.

This chant is a Buddhist form of sending sacred merit. The melody that Joe used for the chant is on the website listed in the Key to Pronunciation at the front of this book.

---

224 Chesed is a Hebrew singular noun. Chassadim is plural.

Joe would invite Sufi leaders and leaders-in-training to lead a chant or dance or other spiritual practice on the Thursday walk. For years, Joe would ask me every week to lead "May the Blessings of God Rest Upon You," which is a blessing given by Pir-O-Murshid Hazrat Inayat Khan that goes like this:

> May the blessings of God rest upon you.
> May God's peace abide with you.
> May God's presence illuminate your heart now and forever more.[225]

As mentioned in Chapter 6, Pir-O-Murshid Hazrat Inayat Khan brought a universal form of Sufism to the West in 1910. "May the Blessings of God Rest Upon You" is one of the many gifts we have received from Hazrat Inayat Khan that has a ring and relevance with Judaism. It feels to me that Hazrat Inayat Khan has given a twentieth century interpretive—or as we say in Judaism, midrashic—translation of birkat kohanim, the priestly blessings, given by God to Aaron, the first high priest, through Moses, his brother. The priestly blessings form the prayer given above that I recited for my mother when she was in intensive care. Traditionally, the priestly blessings are recited twice each day in the synagogue to bless the congregation during the repetition of the Amidah (silent devotion). In some synagogues, the priestly blessings are recited at the end of worship, and they are also recited at weddings to bless the newly weds.

The priestly blessings are also found in the liturgy of some Christian denominations. Christians sometimes refer to the priestly blessings as the Aaronic blessings, after Aaron the high priest.[226]

Each week on Joe's walk for months on end, I would lead Hazrat Inayat Khan's version of the priestly blessings as a Sufi dance, except on weeks when a number of Sufi leaders were present. Then Joe would come up and whisper in my ear that a certain very important Sufi leader would be leading a practice during my time and then he would say, "but next week, it's yours."

I looked forward to leading a dance on Joe's walk because it was so filled with magnetism. Occasionally Wali Ali invited me to lead a dance during his Monday Night meeting at the Women's Building in San Francisco. My leading went fine, and Wali Ali had certified me as a dance leader, but something bothered me. When I led a dance in the park in the open air where the energy could dissipate easily, the dance was strong; that is to say, it felt as though there was a great deal of magnetism and spiritual presence. Yet when I led a dance at Monday Night meeting where we were in a large hall and the sound and energy was contained within the room, I didn't feel as much magnetism.

---

225 This blessing given by Pir O Murshid Hazrat Inayat Khan is recorded and remembered in slightly different versions. Hazrat Inayat Khan had four children. His older daughter Noor-un-Nisa was killed during the Holocaust (see Chapter 3). His younger daughter Khair-un-Nisa, known as Claire Ray Harper, died in 2011. Claire co authored, with David Ray Harper, *We Rubies Four; the Memoirs of Claire Ray Harper* (Omega Publications, 2011). His older son was Pir O Murshid Vilayat Inayat Khan who served as head of the Sufi Order International and died in 2004. His younger son is Murshid Hidayat Inayat-Khan, who is in his nineties as of this writing and is the former Pir of the Sufi Movement International. Hidayat remembers his father giving the blessing as "May the blessings of God rest upon you; May His peace abide with you; May his presence illuminate your heart now and forever more." I studied with Pir Vilayat and I remember him reciting the blessing in the way that Hidayat remembers. I also remember Pir Vilayat discussing the intentions of reciting it with "heart" and "hearts." In the manual entitled, Universal Worship (Sufi Movement, Geneva, 1936) the blessing is given as, "May the Blessing of God rest upon you; may His peace abide with you; and may His presence illuminate your hearts; now and for evermore. Amen." This blessing is recited with "blessing" or "blessings" and with "heart" or "hearts." In light of changing gender sensitivities, some also change "His" to "God" and I recite it thus.
226 *Numbers* 6:22-27

One week, in the park near the duck pond, someone else was giving instructions for a dance. I sidled up to Joe and began chatting. Suddenly he stopped and said we would finish talking later. He stood with eyes closed and I could feel his spiritual presence. Afterward I asked him what he was doing. "Sending juice!" he exclaimed. "Juice?" I asked. "Yeah!" he said. "Energy, magnetism, you know!" I knew what Joe was talking about, but I suddenly also knew that it wasn't me who was "juicing" my dance leading in the park. It was Joe. He was sending sacred merit, and in my case, he began to do so when I was giving instructions for newcomers as well as while we were dancing. Go figure! This Buddhist Dharma Master and Christian minister[227] whom Reb Zalman would later ask to teach me Christian Kabbalah during my rabbinic studies was now helping me along from spiritual infancy into adulthood by quietly adding his energy without an agenda. Joe's transmission was so smooth and selfless that I didn't even realize that the energy was not coming to me straight from on high.

Around the time that I began to understand Joe's method of spiritual empowerment, he stopped inviting me to lead "May the Blessings of God Rest Upon You" on the Thursday walk, and he stopped inviting me to lead dances weekly, and instead, I took my turn along with the many dance leaders who frequented the Thursday walk. Joe introduced "May the Blessings of God Rest Upon You" at the Theosophical Society as a song without the dance. Joe would have us sing it through twice. The first time we would send the energy of the song to those in the room and others with whom we felt very close; and the second time we would send the energy to the whole world or to all beings everywhere. We would also sing:

> May all being be well;
> May all beings be happy;
> Peace, peace, peace.

This Buddhist sacred phrase is given earlier in this chapter. At the end of singing both Pir-O-Murshid Hazrat Inayat Khan's midrashic (interpretive) version of the priestly blessings and this Buddhist phrase, Joe would say, "and now we turn to the phone company!" and he would sing a ditty that played on television commercials for the telephone company that had a monopoly in our area at that time. The ditty went like this: "Reach out, reach out and touch someone! Reach out, reach out and just say hi!" We would then drop hands and hug people around us. No one left without a hug unless they went out of their way to do so.

Shortly after I was ordained as a rabbi, I was invited to cover for the rabbi and cantor at Congregation Beth Israel-Judea in San Francisco by leading services during their respective vacations. Rabbi Herb Morris, of blessed memory, asked me to attend services before the summer vacation cycle began so I could get a feel for their style of services before leading them. On Friday evening, Rabbi Morris and Cantor Henry Greenberg, of blessed memory, led a Reform style service, and on Saturday morning, they led a Conservative style service. As the Friday evening service came to an end, Rabbi Morris asked everyone to rise from their seats in the pews and join together holding hands. Cantor Greenberg then sang the priestly blessings in Hebrew, and then Rabbi Morris said, "and now let's sing it in English," and the congregation proceeded to sing Hazrat Inayat Khan's version of the priestly blessings.

---

227 Joe and Guin Miller were both ordained as ministers in the United Church of Christ.

I asked Rabbi Morris where he got the idea of holding hands during the priestly blessings and where he learned the translation. He said he didn't remember. I spent weeks afterward contemplating how Rabbi Morris might have learned it. Was it from someone who learned it at the Aquarian Minyan of Berkeley, a Jewish Renewal congregation where I used to lead it? Was it from someone who attended the classes and holiday gatherings I was leading for unaffiliated families? Was there a member of Beth Israel-Judea who attended Sufi events? Or Joe's Miller's walk? Or meetings at the Theosophical Society? Finally, I realized that I wanted to solve the riddle because I wanted to know if I could take credit for the fact that this congregation that was affiliated with both the Reform and Conservative Movements was singing the midrashic (interpretive) translation of the priestly blessings given by a great Sufi.

I thought of the Ashkenazi[228] melody most commonly used for Eyn Keloheynu, a piyyut—spiritual poem—recited at the end of musaf (the additional service) on Shabbat and major Jewish holidays. The cantor of my teenage years, Philip Moddel, of blessed memory, was born and raised in Germany. I had an interest in the origins of the melodies we sang in synagogue and Cantor Moddel taught me that this melody for Eyn Keloheynu was borrowed from a drinking song sung in German pubs. Now a newly minted rabbi, I began to wonder if non-Jewish Germans had ever stood outside synagogues wondering what words were being paired with their drinking song.

Then I remembered Joe standing in the park and "juicing" dances and Zikrs that were being led by Sufi leaders and leaders-in-training. I remembered Zalman telling me to send the energy at the end of my retreats in seclusion to those I knew and those I didn't know. That was when I decided to borrow from Rabbi Morris his style of singing Pir-O-Murshid Hazrat Inayat Khan's English version of the priestly blessings with no explanation of the source of the English translation.

I wish to offer the sacred merit of this book, if any there be, to the memory and teachings of Hazrat Inayat Khan and Samuel L. Lewis, and to the living legacy of Zalman Schachter-Shalomi and Wali Ali, and to all the rabbis and cantors and educators who participated, and continue to participate, in my Jewish education, and to all the universal Sufis and Buddhists, Hindus, Muslims, Zoroastrians, Christians, Theosophists and Vedantists who have nourished my curiosity and longing during my explorations beyond the mehitza—divider—that divides the faiths and spiritual paths from one another and allows us to enjoy the illusion that our path is best in order that we might fulfill it, and be fulfilled within it, and teach it to future generations, so that some day God will be known as One and God's name will be One even as it is sung in all the languages by all the faiths of all the beings in all the realms where there is life.[229]

> May we all be blessed
> In all that we do,
> In all that we feel,
> In all that we think and ponder, and
> In all that we are,
> Both now and always.
> And let us say,
> Amen.

---

228 Ashkenaz is Yiddish for Germany. Ashkenazi is defined in the Glossary of Terms.

229 This is a midrash (interpretation) of the closing lines of Alaynu, a prayer described in the text and/or footnotes in Chapters 11, (toward the end of) 13 and 23 of this book.

Appendices

Appendix A

Glossary of Terms

Adab – Arabic. Noun. Adab is translated in the Islamic Dictionary (http://www.islamic-dictionary.com/) as "Islamic manners." Adab is derived from the sunnah, which is the ways and teachings and activities of Prophet Muhammad, peace and blessings be upon him. "Muslims should emulate the sunnah of the Prophet to be good Muslims," says the Islamic Dictionary. Among Inayati Sufis, Adab is understood to mean respect or good practice. One learns adab from one's teacher. One practices adab by respecting the sensibilities and practices of the teacher, the order and the lineage, as well as for fellow human beings, and indeed, for all of God's creation. Inayati Sufis may also practice adab by adhering to the teachings of scriptures, religious and spiritual law, and religious and spiritual customs and practices of all faiths.

Adon – Hebrew. Noun. Adon means "lord" or "mister." "Adon" is found in the Biblical Books of Joshua (3:11 and 13), Jeremiah (22:18, 34:5), Zechariah (4:14, 6:5), Psalms (12:5, 97:5, 105:21, 114:7), and Nehemiah (7:61). These are references to God and may be properly translated as "Lord." "Adoni" means "sir" and is used in modern Hebrew. For example, a waiter in a restaurant in Israel might say to a customer, "Shalom Adoni," meaning "Hello Sir."

Adonai – Hebrew. Noun. Adonai is pronounced "a-doh-na-ee" with the accent on "na-ee." Adonai means "my Lord" or "my God." "Adonai" is found in numerous places in the Hebrew Bible. In addition, the pronunciation "Adonai" is used to pronounce the Divine Root Name, which is found all over the Torah, and in all the others Books of the Bible except Esther and Song of Songs. (See the beginning of Chapter 2 and Appendix B.) The word "Adonai" is often written in place of the Divine Root Name in English translations of the Torah and other Books of the Bible, as well as in prayer books. "Lord" is also often used in English translations of these sacred texts.

Adoshem – Hebrew. Noun. Adoshem is a combination of Adonai and HaShem and may be translated as the Lord Name. In certain settings, it is appropriate to say Adoshem as a placeholder or reference for the Divine Root Name.

Ahavah – Hebrew. Noun. Ahavah means love.

Ahavah Rabbah – Hebrew. Ahavah Rabbah means great love.

Ahavat Olam – Hebrew. Ahavat Olam means eternal love.

Alaynu – Hebrew. Alaynu means "it is upon us" or "it is incumbent upon us" and refers to a prayer traditionally recited toward the end of each Jewish worship service. There are alternative Alaynu prayers that may be found in Jewish Reform, Reconstructionist and Renewal prayer books. In this book, however, all references to Alaynu are to the traditional Alaynu prayer. The traditional Alaynu is believed to have been given to the Jewish either by Joshua ben Nun, successor to Moses, or by Rav, a rabbi who lived in Babylonia in the third century Before the Common Era.

Appendix A – Glossary of Terms

Amidah – Hebrew. Noun. Amidah literal means "standing." In Jewish worship, Amidah refers to a lengthy prayer consisting of multiple blessings that is recited quietly on one's own regardless of whether one is worshipping alone or in community. The Amidah is traditionally recited three times a day during evening (ma'ariv), morning (shacharit) and afternoon (mincha) worship. On the Sabbath, festivals and fast days, there is an additional service called musaf, consisting primarily of an Amidah. On Yom Kippur, there is yet another service at the end of the day, called ne'ilah. Ne'ilah also includes an Amidah. When praying in community, the Amidah is repeated out loud in the morning and afternoon, during the additional (musaf) service and during ne'ilah.

Aramaic – (pronounced a-rah-may-'k) Noun. Aramaic is a Semitic Language that was spoken in a number of locales in the Middle East during ancient times. Some forms of Aramaic are still in use today. As discussed in Chapter 4, the Aramaic used in this book is often called Jewish Aramaic. Jewish Aramaic was a common language studied and spoken by Jews over many centuries, including during the time of Jesus (approximately 3 to 36 C.E.) and the period during which the Gemara was being compiled (200 to 600 C.E.). The Jerusalem Gemara and the Babylonian Gemara are in Aramaic interspersed with Hebrew. A great deal of other rabbinic literature is also in Aramaic either in whole or in part.

Aron Kodesh – Hebrew. Noun. Means "Holy Ark." **Aron Ko**desh refers to the Holy Ark containing the Ten Commandments that was part of the portable Tabernacle that accompanied the Israelites during their wandering in the wilderness after slavery; as well as the Holy Ark in the Temple in Jerusalem that first contained the Ten Commandments, and later contained the Torah; as well as the modern Holy Ark that contains the Torah scrolls in modern synagogues and temples.

Aron Ha Kodesh – Hebrew. Noun. Means "the Holy Ark." (Also see **Aron Ko**desh.)

Ashkenazi – The Hebrew word for Germany is **Ash**kenaz. Ashke**na**zi (pronounced "ash-keh-na-zee") means "German" in Hebrew, and refers to Jewish people whose ancestors lived, at a certain point in time, in the lands in and around modern Germany. Ashke**na**zi Jews tended to be the ones who spoke Yiddish, and some still do. Yiddish is a hybrid language consisting primarily of German and Hebrew, with additions from the local language where it is spoken. The Ashke**na**zi pronunciation of Hebrew and the Ashke**na**zi pronunciation of Jewish Aramaic is quite different from the standard pronunciation of Hebrew in the modern State of Israel. Among the most prominent differences are: The vowel "o" as in "vote," in Israeli Hebrew is pronounced "oi" as in "voice" in Ashke**na**zi Hebrew. The letter tav is pronounced "t" in Israeli Hebrew; in Ashke**na**zi Hebrew, it is generally pronounced "t" if it contains a dagesh (dot within the letter), and it is always pronounced "s" if it does not contain a dagesh.

Atzay Chayyim – Hebrew. Eytz means tree. Eytzim means trees (plural). Atzay means "trees of." Chayyim means life. Atzay chayyim literally means "trees of life" and refers to the two woods handles on which the Torah scroll is rolled and kept.

Atah – Hebrew. Pronoun. Atah is the masculine second person singular pronoun, meaning "you."

Atah Hu Gibbor – Hebrew. Atah Hu Gibbor means, "You are strong" or "You are strength" with "You" referring to God.

118

Bar – Aramaic. Noun. Bar means son in Aramaic. "Bar" was used in ancient times as part of a male's Jewish name. For example, Shimon bar Yochai (Simon son of Yochai), Yohanan ben Zakai (Johanan son of Zakai), Bar Kamsa (son of Kamsa), and so on.

Bar Mitzvah – Aramaic. "Bar mitzvah" means "son of the commandment" in Aramaic, and it is an expression that has been adopted into Hebrew, English and many other languages. According to the Talmud, a male attains religious and legal responsibility as of the age of bar mitzvah, which is defined as thirteen and one day. *Encyclopedia Judaica* (Jerusalem: Encyclopedia Judaica, 1996) pages 243-247. The celebration of the bar mitzvah in the synagogue was introduced centuries after the Jerusalem and Babylonian Talmuds were completed.

Barrai**tah** – Aramaic. Noun. Barraitah is a singular word; the plural is barraitot. Barraitot were traditions that the rabbis learned and collected that were not in the codified Mishna. In the Gemara, the rabbis comment on Mishnayot (plural of Mishna) and Barraitot.

B'raitot – Plural of Barraitah.

Barukh Ha**Shem** – Hebrew. Barukh HaShem means thank G-d or blessed is G-d or praise G-d. ("God" is written as "G-d" because "Barukh hashem" expresses gratitude to the divine without using a divine name that is considered to be so sacred that we only use it during prayer, or when reading scripture in a sacred setting.)

Barukh Shem – Hebrew. Barukh Shem means blessed is the name. The expression "barukh shem" refers to the sacred phrase "Barukh Shem Kevod Malkhuto L'Olam Va'ed" that is discussed in Chapter 13 and defined below.

Barukh Shem Kevod Malkhuto L'Olam Va'ed – Hebrew. Barukh Shem Kevod Malkhuto L'Olam Va'ed means, Blessed is the name of the glory of His Kingdom forever and ever.

Bat – Hebrew and Aramaic. Noun. Bat means "daughter."

Bat Mitzvah – Aramaic and Hebrew. "Bat mitzvah" means "daughter of the commandment" in both Aramaic and Hebrew, and it is an expression that has been adopted into English and many other languages. According to the Talmud, a female attains religious and legal responsibility as of the age of bat mitzvah, which is defined as twelve and one day. *Encyclopedia Judaica* (Jerusalem: Encyclopedia Judaica, 1996) pages 243-247. The celebration of bat mitzvah in the synagogue was introduced by Rabbi Mordecai Kaplan in 1922 when he invited his daughter Judith to stand on the bimah "a respectable distance" from the table on which the Torah scroll lay open after having been read by men during the service. Judith became bat mitzvah as she recited the prayers for being called to the Torah. She read the text of her Torah portion from a book rather than the Torah scroll itself.

Bayh Ana Rachaytz – Aramaic. Bayh Ana Rachaytz is pronounced with the emphasis on "Ana" and "chaytz" and it means "I place my trust in You," with "You" referring to God.

B.C.E. – B.C.E. is an abbreviation that stands for "Before the Common Era." B.C.E. is used by Jews, Hindus and others who do not count time from the birth of Jesus.

Ben – Hebrew. Noun. Ben means son.

Bible – English. Noun. "Bible" is used by both Jews and Christians to refer to their respective holy scriptures. (See Appendix B.) While there is overlap, the Hebrew Bible and the Christian Bible are not identical. The Hebrew Bible refers to the twenty-five books, including the Torah, Prophets and Writings. The Christian Bible refers to the Old Testament and the New Testament. The New Testament contains the Gospels and other writings, which transmit stories and teachings relating to Jesus and his disciples. The Old Testament is the same as the Hebrew Bible, except that Jewish scholars divide the Hebrew Bible into twenty-five books, and Christian scholars divide the Old Testament into thirty-nine books. The difference in the number of books is due to the fact that, on the one hand, Samuel I and II, Kings I and II, and Chronicles I and II are each considered to be one book by Jews, and two books by Christians. On the other hand, Jewish scholars refer to the twelve short books of prophecy as one volume, called the "Tray Asar," meaning "twelve in Aramaic; whereas Christian scholars refer to each of these twelve books of prophecy as separate volumes.

Binah – Hebrew. Noun. **Bi**nah is one of the ten sephirot. **Bi**nah is defined in the Introduction to the Ten Sephirot in Appendix D.

C.E. – C.E. is an abbreviation that stands for "Common Era." C.E. is used by Jews, Hindus and others who do not count time from the birth of Jesus.

Cha**BaD** is the name of a Chassidic Jewish sect and it is an acronym for the three sephirot known in Hebrew as chokhmah, binah, and da'at; and in English as wisdom, understanding and knowledge. "Ch" stands for the letter chet at the beginning of chokhmah; "B" stands for the letter beyt at the beginning of binah: and "D" stands for the letter dalet at the beginning of da'at. Cha**bad** is further defined in the Introduction to the Ten Sephirot in Appendix D. Also see Appendix H for further information on the Hebrew alphabet. (See also the footnote regarding Rabbi Shneur Zalman in Appendix D.)

Cha**gas** – See Chagat.

Chagat (is also pronounced Cha**gas**) is an acronym for the three sephirot known in Hebrew as chesed, gevurah and tiferet; and in English as loving-kindness, severity (or boundaries) and beauty (or harmony). Chagat is further defined in the Introduction to the Ten Sephirot in Appendix D.

Challah – Hebrew and Yiddish. Noun. Challah is bread baked specially for the Sabbath and holy days. Challah comes in a variety of shapes and sizes. Braided challah symbolizes the braids of the Shechina, the feminine divine presence, which is said to have union with the Holy One, blessed be He on Shabbat. During the Days of Awe (Yamim Nora'im in Hebrew and High Holy Days in common English), we eat challah made in a round spiral that is either plain or contains raisins or bits of glazed fruit. The roundness signifies our wish for a smooth year and the spiral signifies our desire to rise higher and higher in our spiritual life. Supermarkets that carry kosher foods often carry challah either all the time or on Thursdays and Fridays in anticipation of the Jewish Sabbath. Some markets carry cinnamon challah[230] all year 'round, which is sweet and sticky. Some supermarkets also carry round challah for the High Holy Days. Braided, round, raisin filled, glazed fruit filled and cinnamon challah make great French toast.

---

230 Some bakeries also make challah with raisins or candied fruit. Generally such challot (plural of challah) are available around the Jewish high holy days of Rosh HaShanah and Yom Kippur, but some bakeries may carry them all year 'round.

Challah (continued) During the wandering in the wilderness following slavery in Egypt, God caused manna to fall on the ground each morning. People could take as much as they needed, but not more, because leftovers would rot overnight. This helped avoid greed and hoarding by some, which would have left others hungry. On Fridays, God caused a double portion of manna to fall on the ground and the Israelites were allowed to take and prepare a double portion so they did not need to gather and prepare it on Shabbat. To remember this miracle, we place two loaves of challah on our Sabbath table.

Chasid – Hebrew. Noun. Cha**sid** refers to a type of Jew. The ancient Chassidim are mentioned in the Talmud. Modern Chassi**dim** are Ultra Orthodox. It is the intention of a Cha**sid** to focus upon loving-kindness.

Chassidim – Hebrew. Noun. Plural of Chasid.

Chassidus – Yiddish. Noun. Means Chassidism, or the movement or teachings of the Chassidim.

Chasi**dut** – Hebrew. Noun. Means Chassidism, or the movement or teachings of the Chassidim.

Chesed – Hebrew. Noun. **Che**sed is one of the ten sephirot. **Che**sed represents loving-kindness, and is discussed in the Introduction to the Ten Sephirot in Appendix D.

Chokhmah – Hebrew. Noun. **Chokh**mah is one of the ten sephirot. **Chokh**mah is defined in the Introduction to The Ten Sephirot in Appendix D.

Da'at – Hebrew. Noun. **Da**'at is an aspect of ketter. Da'at is located in the throat and ketter is just above the crown of the head. This is discussed in the Introduction to The Ten Sephirot in Appendix D.

Darshan – Hebrew. Noun. A darshan is one who creates and gives over (i.e. teaches), insights and interpretations based upon Written Torah and Oral Torah as defined at the beginning of Chapter 2.

Darsha**nit** – Hebrew Noun. Darshanit is the feminine of darshan.

Davven – Yiddish. Verb. Literally means "pray" or "worship," and refers to Jewish prayer. Includes both formal prayer alone or in community from a prayer book or prayer guide, as well as informal prayer from the heart and speaking with God. One may say, "I **da**vven every day," or "I **da**vven when I feel like it," or "we're going to **da**vven mincha (the afternoon service) at 5:00 pm."

Davvenen – Yiddish. Verb. Plural and infinitive of **da**vven. Literally means "pray" or "worship," One may say, "We are **da**vvenen together," or "we will be **da**vvenen shacharit (the morning service) at 9:00 am," or "where will you be **da**vvenen for Rosh HaShanah (Jewish New Year)?" or "I enjoyed your **da**vvenen," (which could mean watching you **da**vven or could mean watching you lead the **da**vvenen).

Derech Eretz – Hebrew. Derech eretz means respect or the way of the land or the custom of the place or good breeding. Derech eretz means respect in the ordinary use of that word in English. It also refers to religious and spiritual respect as demonstrated in the following quote from the Mishna: "Rabbi Eliezer ben Azariah said, 'where there is no Torah, there is no derech eretz. Where there is no derech eretz, there is no Torah." (Avot 3:17)

Divine Root Name – English. Divine Root Name refers to the ineffable name of God that is spelled with the Hebrew letters yod and hay and vav and hay. "Divine Root Name" is discussed in Chapter 8.

E**chad** – Hebrew. Noun. Echad means one.

El **Nah** Refa Nah **Lah** – Hebrew. El Nah Refa Nah Lah means God please heal her. Moses cried out to God with these words when his brother Aaron pleaded with him to pray for the healing of their sister Miriam. Numbers 12:13.

Elo**hay**nu – Hebrew. Noun. Elohaynu means our God.

Elo**him** – Hebrew. Noun. Elohim is a name of God discussed at the beginning of Chapter 8.

Eyl – Hebrew. Noun. Eyl is a name of God.

Eyn HaChayyim – Hebrew. Eyn HaChayyim literally means "nothing of the life" or "nothingness of life," and is understood to mean "source of life." Eyn HaChayyim is a term used in Reconstructionist and Renewal Judaism to refer to the Oneness without anthropomorphizing. Anthropomorphizing means using human imagery or creation worthy imagery to describe divinity, such as speaking about the hand of God when God has no hands, nor any form whatsoever, or speaking about God the Father or God the Mother, when God is beyond gender. "Eyn HaChayyim" is sometimes used among atheists and secular humanists to refer to the Oneness without meaning God.

Eyn **Od** – Hebrew. Eyn od means none else or nothing else.

Eyn **Od** Milva**do** – Hebrew. Eyn Od Milvado means there is nothing but him. Moses said "Eyn Od Milvado," meaning there is nothing but God. (Deuteronomy 4:35)

Eyn **Od** Milva**da** – Hebrew. Eyn Od Milvada means there is nothing but her. This is a feminine form of Eyn Od Milvado, which means there is nothing but him. "Eyn Od Milvada" may be used to state that there is nothing but God, with "da" at the end of Milvada being understood as "Her," i.e. God.

Ge**ma**ra – Aramaic. Noun. The Gemara is a voluminous commentary on the Mishna. The Mishna is a brief compilation in Hebrew consisting of teachings, commentaries, stories and laws, based upon the Hebrew Bible and Jewish life of the times. The Gemara—written in Aramaic with Hebrew—captures within its page the fruits of in-depth study of topics covered in the Mishna and in Barraitot, as well as many other topics. The Gemara includes analysis, dialectics and critical thinking. A key feature of the Gemara is that divergent and seemingly opposite opinions are given side by side. Sometimes they are reconciled by another opinion and sometimes not.

There are, in fact, two Gemaras, both of which are written primarily in Jewish Aramaic. The Babylonian Gemara was compiled in Babylonia, primarily in the Academies of Sura and Pumpedita. It was completed in the sixth century of the common era. The Jerusalem Gemara, also called the Palestinian Gemara, was compiled primarily in the Academies in Tiberias and was redacted in the fourth century. The Jerusalem Gemara was never completed, due to the difficult conditions for Jews under Roman rule. This is discussed in Chapter 2. Both the Babylonian Gemara and the Jerusalem Gemara are voluminous.

Gemara (continued) In some settings, the "Talmud" refers to the Gemara, and in other settings, it refers to the Mishna and Gemara together with additional commentaries in the margins. (See "The Talmud" section in Chapter 2. See also "Barraitah," "Mishna" and "Talmud" in this glossary.)

Gematria – Hebrew. Noun. Gematria means numerology, and is discussed in Chapter 5 and Appendix H.

G'vurah – Hebrew. Noun. Gevurah is one of the ten sephirot. Gevurah is defined in the Introduction to the Ten Sephirot in Appendix D.

Hadar – Hebrew. Noun. Glory or splendor.

Hadrat Kodesh – Hebrew. Hadrat means "splendor of" or "majesty of." Kodesh means holy. Hadrat kodesh is a sacred phrase that appears in verse 2 of Psalm 29. Hadrat kodesh is also the name of a set of movements performed while standing and reciting Zikr or other sacred phrases. One might define "Hadrat kodesh movements" as "movements in the splendor of holiness." See the "Hadrat Kodesh" and "Hadrat Kodesh Movement" section of Chapter 11.

Hamotzi – Hebrew. Literally means "who brings forth" or "who brings out" and refers to the Jewish prayer recited before eating a meal. Technically, hamotzi is recited over bread, and its recitation includes all food eaten at the same meal where bread is served. The Talmud gives other prayers for eating meals and snacks that do not include bread, and these are used by many Jews today. However, there was a time when the word "lechem" (meaning "bread" in modern Hebrew) referred to other food as well, and some Jews recite hamotzi over all food regardless of whether bread is served.

Haredi – Hebrew. With utmost respect, I use the terms "haredi" and "Ultra Orthodox" to refer to those Jews who live in such a fashion and with such standards of faith and practice as to be on the "ultra" side of Orthodoxy. My teachers, Rabbi Zalman Schachter-Shalomi and Rabbi David Wolfe-Blank, of blessed memory, were both ordained as rabbis at Yeshivos Tom'khey Temimim, a Chabad yeshiva (seminary) in New York. Yeshivos Tom'khey Temimim is one of the many Ultra Orthodox yeshivot (seminaries) in North America.

HaShem – Hebrew. Noun. Literally "the Name," HaShem is a Hebrew name for God that is appropriate to use in all settings, both sacred and ordinary, as a placeholder or reference to the Divine Root Name.

Hay – Hebrew. Noun. Hay is the fifth letter of the Hebrew alphabet and the second and fourth letter of the Divine Root Name discussed in Chapter 11. The Divine Root Name is spelled with the Hebrew letters yod and hay and vav and hay.

Hebrew – English. Noun. Hebrew is a Semitic language in which the Hebrew Bible is written, except for some of the chapters in the Book of Daniel. Like all languages, Hebrew evolves over time and distance. The Hebrew of the Torah is more ancient, and a bit different, than the Hebrew of the later books of the Hebrew Bible. The Hebrew of the Mishna is different from Biblical Hebrew, and the Hebrew of rabbinic literature throughout the centuries is different. Modern Hebrew spoken in the State of Israel, and by Hebrew speakers in the other parts of the world is different still, and is continuing to evolve, as are all spoken languages.

Hod – Hebrew. Noun. Hod is one of the ten sephirot. Hod is defined in the Introduction to the Ten Sephirot in Appendix D.

Jnana – Sanskrit. **Jna**na means wisdom or discernment and is used among Hindus and in Vedanta to refer to divine wisdom and omnipotence.

Kadosh – Hebrew. Noun. Kadosh means holy.

Kabbalah (also pronounced Ka**bba**lah) – Hebrew. Noun. Kabbalah means receptivity and refers to the study of certain texts and understandings and practices of mystical Judaism.

Kiddush – Hebrew. Noun. "Kiddush" derives from the same linguistic root as "kadosh." Kiddush means sanctification, and is used to refer to the blessing of wine or grape juice on the Sabbath and festivals.

Kavannah – Hebrew. Noun. Kavannah means intention.

Ketter – Hebrew. Noun. Ketter is one of the ten sephirot. It is located just above the crown of the human head, and defined briefly in the Introduction to the Ten Sephirot in Appendix D.

Kodesh – Hebrew. Adjective. Literally means "holy."

Korban – Hebrew. Noun. Literally means "sacrifice," including animals, grains and other items offered to God in ancient times.

Lashon – Hebrew. Noun. Literally means "tongue." It refers to "language," such as "the Hebrew tongue," or "the Sanskrit tongue. And it also refers to the part of the body that is in one's mouth.

Leshon **Ko**desh – Hebrew. Literally means "holy tongue," and refers to a holy language—usually Hebrew. (The Hebrew lashon becomes leshon when paired with kodesh to form leshon kodesh.)

Ma'ariv – Hebrew. Noun. **Ma**'ariv is the daily evening worship service. **Ma**'ariv is related to the Hebrew word erev, meaning evening. See additional information in Chapter 1.

Mah Gad**lu** is the name of a sacred phrase found in Psalm 92, verse 6 that says, Mah Gad**lu** Ma'asekha YaH, Me'od Am**ku** Mach'shevo**te**kha. This means "How vast are your works, oh YaH, your thoughts are very deep," or "How grand are your deeds, oh YaH, your designs are beyond our grasp."

Malkhut – Hebrew. Noun. Mal**khut** is one of the ten sephirot. It is associated with the area of the feet in the human body, and is defined briefly in the Introduction to the Ten Sephirot in Appendix D.

Midrash – Hebrew. Noun. Midrash is parsing and interpreting Written Torah and Oral Torah as defined at the beginning of Chapter 2.

Midra**shim** – Hebrew. Plural of Midrash.

Mincha – Hebrew. Noun. **Min**cha means gift and refers to the daily afternoon worship service. See additional information in Chapter 1.

Mishebeyrakh – Hebrew. Mishebeyrakh means "the one who blessed" or "may the one who blessed," and refers to prayers of blessing. A Mishebeyrakh is recited to bless those who have been called to the Torah for an aliyah (the honor of reciting the blessing and standing next to the scroll while it is read). A mishebeyrakh may also be recited for those in need of healing and their caregivers, or to bless an infant and bestow a name upon the infant, or to bless a bar mitzvah or bat mitzvah, or on the occasion of someone's birthday, or when a couple are about to get married or are celebrating an anniversary, as well as for many other occasions.

Mishna – Hebrew. Noun. The Mishna is a compilation of brief Jewish teachings, commentaries, stories and laws based upon the Hebrew Bible and Jewish life of the times. The Mishna was compiled by Yehudah HaNasi in approximately 200 C.E. and was written in Hebrew. The Mishna is divided into short teachings and stories. Each one is called a Mishna, and the entire work is also called the Mishna. When referring to two or more such short teachings or stories found in the Mishna, we call them Mishnayot. See "The Talmud" in Chapter 2, and also "Gemara" and "Talmud" in this glossary.

Mishna**yot** – Plural of Mishna.

Mitzvah – Hebrew. Noun. (Plural is mitz**vot**.) Commandment, good deed, deed that helps to make the world a better place, religious precept.

Mitz**vot** – Plural of Mitzvah.

Miz**ra**hi – The Hebrew word for east is miz**rach**, which can also be written mizrah. Miz**ra**hi means eastern, and refers to the Jewish people whose ancestors lived, at a certain point in time, in the lands to the east of modern Israel, including such places as India, China, Afghanistan, Iran, Iraq, Kurdistan and Yemen, as well as the Jews of North Africa who lived in places such as Egypt, Libya, Tunisia, Algeria and Morocco. The Miz**ra**hi pronunciation of Hebrew is similar to Sephardi—and thus to the official pronunciation of Hebrew in the State of Israel—but there are some differences.

Musaf – Hebrew. Adjective. Musaf means additional, and refers to the additional sacrifices made in the Holy Temple on the Sabbath and festivals in ancient times. In modern times, musaf refers to the additional worship service that followings shacharit (the morning service) on the Sabbath, festivals and fast days.

Netzach – Hebrew. Noun. Netzach is one of the ten sephirot. **Ne**tzach is defined briefly in the Introduction to the Ten Sephirot in Appendix D.

Niggun and **N'**gguhn - literally means melody in both Hebrew and Yiddish. In Hebrew, it is pronounced "niggun" with the emphasis on the last syllable. In Yiddish, it is pronounced "n'gguhn" with the emphasis on the first syllable. To be a niggun, a song must have two distinct musical parts. When one sings a niggun, one needs to pay attention to the melody changing from one part to the other, and this helps us to bring our wandering minds back into focus. While most niggunim (plural of niggun) have two distinct musical parts, some niggunim have three.

Nusach – Hebrew. Noun. Nusach means formula and refers to the formulation of chants and melodies used during worship and the recitation of prayers and blessings in the home and synagogue on ordinary days, Sabbath, festivals, fast days, and days of celebration and mourning.

Pesach – Hebrew. Noun. Pronounced "**pay**-sach" with the emphasis on the first syllable, and also "**peh**-sach" with the emphasis on the first syllable. Pesach is the Hebrew name for the festival of Passover when Jewish people celebrate freedom from slavery in Egypt. The story of Egyptian slavery, freedom from slavery and the festival of Passover are described in the Biblical Book of Exodus.

Piyyut – Hebrew. Noun. A piyyut is a spiritual poem. The plural is piyyutim. Many piyyutim are included in Jewish worship.

Piyyu**tim** – Hebrew. Noun. Plural of Piyyut.

Purim – Hebrew. Noun. "Pur" mean "lot" in the sense of drawing lots or drawing straws. Purim is the plural of "pur" and mean "lots." Purim is also the name of a Jewish holiday that occurs in late winter during the Hebrew month of Adar. Purim is mentioned in chapter 9 of the Book of Esther and is further defined in the Talmud and later rabbinic literature. On Purim, Jewish people read the Book of Esther and celebrate by dressing in costume, having carnivals, eating, drinking and carousing, as well as giving gifts of food or drink to their friends, and charity to those in need. There is a teaching that says that on other days, if someone asks us for charity, we may decide if the person or cause is worthy, and we may decide whether to give charity. However, if a person asks us for charity on Purim, we must give something without any evaluation of the worthiness of the person or cause.

Se**phi**rah– Hebrew. Noun. Pronounced "sfeerah" with the emphasis on the first syllable. Sephirah comes from the root meaning to count. A sephirah is an energy, an attribute, an emanation. According the Kabbalah, God created the universe with ten sephirot, which are named and defined in the Introduction to the Ten Sephirot in Appendix D.

Sephi**rot** – Hebrew. Noun. Pronounced "sfee-rote" with the emphasis on the last syllable. Sephirot is the plural of sephirah.

Sephardi – The Hebrew word for Spain is Spharad. Sephardi means Spanish and refers to the Jewish people whose ancestors lived, at a certain point in time, in the vicinity of modern Spain. Sephardi Jews tended to speak Ladino, and some still do. Ladino is a hybrid language consisting primarily of Spanish and Hebrew, with additions from the local language or dialect where it is spoken. The official pronunciation of Hebrew in the State of Israel is the Sephardi pronunciation. However, the guttural sounds, particularly of the letter ayin, as in the word "olam," meaning world, or "ayin," meaning eye, tend to be pronounced by those of Sephardi origin, and not by native-born Israelis, or those of Ashkenazi extraction.

Shabbat – Hebrew. Noun. Shabbat is the Hebrew word for Sabbath, which is discussed in Chapter 24. In Genesis (2:1-4), it says, "The heavens and the earth were finished, and all their array. On the seventh day God finished the work that God had been doing, and God ceased from the work. And God blessed the seventh day and declared it holy, because on it God ceased from all the work of creation."

Shabbes – Yiddish. Noun. Shabbes is the Yiddish word for Sabbath. Shabbes may also be spelled "shabbos."

Shacharit – Hebrew. Noun. Literally means dawn, and refers to the daily morning worship service. See additional information in Chapter 1.

Sha**vu**'ah – Hebrew. Noun. Shavu'ah means week.

Sha**vu**'ot – Hebrew. Noun. Shavu'ot is the plural of week. It is also the name of a Jewish holiday, which is called in English the "Feast of Weeks." Shavu'ot is described in the Torah, though not by name. On Shavu'ot, we celebrate receiving the Ten Commandments and the Torah at Mount Sinai. Jewish people count forty-nine days from the second day of Passover, and celebrate Shavu'ot beginning on the fiftieth day. In recent times, Shavu'ot is observed in many communities with all night study and celebration in preparation for receiving one's "personal Torah" or personal teachings and insights on Shavu'ot morning.

She**chi**na – English. (See also Shekhinah.) Shechina refers to the feminine indwelling presence of G-d; that is the presence of God dwelling within creation.

Shekhi**nah** – Hebrew. (See also Shechina.) Shekhinah refers to the feminine indwelling presence of G-d; in other words, the presence of God dwelling within creation. Reb Zalman has recommended that the Hebrew letters chet and kaf be represented differently in the transliterations in this book, as discussed in the entries for "Shechina and Shekhinah" in the Key to Pronunciation. To honor Zalman's request, I have transliterated the Hebrew as "Shekhinah" with "kh" representing the letter kaf. On the other hand, "Shechina" is a popular spelling of the word in English and I have therefore used it as well.

Shem – Hebrew. Noun. Shem means name.

Shem HaMefo**rash** – Hebrew. Literally means "Root Name" and refers to the Divine Root Name spelled with the Hebrew letters yod and hay and vav and hay.

Shem Hava**yah** – Hebrew. Literally means "Havayah Name" and refers to the Divine Root Name spelled with the Hebrew letters yod and hay and vav and hay.

Sho**far** – A shofar is a ram's horn that has been carved on the inside so that a hole runs from its narrow end into its wide-open end. The shofar is blown like a musical instrument in order to make a series of sounds to awaken both joy and sadness during the Jewish season of repentance that begins during the Hebrew month of Elul and continues through Rosh HaShanah (Jewish New Year) and Yom Kippur (Day of Atonement). During the month of Elul, the shofar is traditionally blown at the end of morning worship. The shofar is traditionally blown one hundred times during services on Rosh HaShanah, and it is blown one final time at the very end of Yom Kippur. (The Hebrew months are discussed in Appendix E.)

Shokkel – Yiddish. Verb. (See also Shokkelen) Literally means "shake," and refers to the practice of swaying during davvenen (worship). One may say, "I shokkel when I davven," or "he shokkeled while leading that practice." One also says, "I am shokkelen while I davven," or "s/he is shokkelen while doing that practice." Shokkelen is the practice of swaying forward and back during davvenen. When sitting, one may shokkel by moving the head just a bit together with the upper body. When standing, shokkel by bending forward from the waist just a bit. One shokkels when leading davvenen, or when participating in davvenen, both in community and on one's own, and when praying in full voice, quietly or silence. See additional teachings in the "Shokkelen" section of Chapter 6.

Shokkelen – Yiddish. Noun and verb. Literally means "shaking," and refers to the practice of swaying during davvenen (worship). One may say, "I am shokkelen while I davven," or "There is a lot shokkelen during davvenen, especially when one is praying silently."

Appendix A – Glossary of Terms

Shulchan **A**rukh – Hebrew. Shulchan Arukh means "Set Table" and refers to volumes compiled by Rabbi Joseph Caro in the fifteenth century C.E. The Shulchan Arukh is a compendium or encyclopedia of Jewish law that draws on previous sources from the Written Torah forward, and is considered to this day to be a standard in the codification of Jewish Law.

Siferes – See Tiferet.

Simcha – Hebrew and Yiddish. Noun. Simcha means joyous occasion. It is pronounced **sim**cha in Yiddish, and sim**cha** in Hebrew.

Simchas – Yiddish. Noun. Simchas means joyous occasions, and is the plural of simcha in Yiddish.

Sma**chot** – Hebrew. Noun. Smachot means joyous occasions, and is the plural of simcha in Hebrew.

Tacha**nun** – Hebrew. Noun. Tachanun refers to a series of prayers recited in the morning and afternoon on most ordinary days of the year (i.e. on days that are not Sabbath, festival, fast day or other special occasion or special season). Tachanun is a confessional forgiveness prayer during which there is an opportunity to place our head on our forearm and pour out our heart.

Talmud – Hebrew. Noun. The word Talmud means teaching, and refers to a compilation of teachings, stories and laws that consists of two distinct parts, each compiled in different centuries and different languages. The Mishna is written in Hebrew. It was compiled by Yehudah HaNasi in approximately 200 C.E. in Judea—which was the name of the Jewish kingdom in the time of the Roman occupation. There are two Gemaras, both of which are written primarily in Jewish Aramaic. The Babylonian Gemara was compiled in Babylonia, and was completed in the sixth century The Jerusalem Gemara was compiled in Judea in the fourth century; it was never completed, however, due to the unrelenting ferocity of the Roman occupation and its focus on eradicating Judaism.

Sometimes, the word "Talmud" is used to refer to the Gemara alone. However, "Talmud" generally refers to the standard published set of Mishna and Gemara, together with a number of commentaries written and compiled in later centuries.

When the word "Talmud" appears on its own in rabbinic texts and footnotes, it generally refers to the Babylonian Talmud. "Yerushalmi," which means "Jerusalemite," generally refers to the Jerusalem Talmud. (Also, see "The Talmud" in Chapter 2 and "Mishna" and "Gemara" in this glossary.)

Ta**mid** – Hebrew. Tamid means always.

Ta**mid** E**chad** – Hebrew. Tamid echad means always one. When recited as a sacred phrase, tamid echad refers to God as one throughout time, or for all time.

Ta**nakh** – Hebrew. Tanakh is the Hebrew Bible or the Jewish Bible. Tanakh is an acronym for Torah (the spiritual teachings of the Divine Parent), Nevi'im (Prophets) and Ketuvim (Spiritual Writings). Tanakh is discussed in Chapter 3. A summary of each of the Book of the Tanakh may be found in Appendix B.

Tiferet – Hebrew. Noun. Tiferet is one of the ten sephirot. Tiferet is the spiritual heart and is defined briefly in the Introduction to the Ten Sephirot in Appendix D.

Tikk**un** – Hebrew. Noun. Tikkun means repair.

Tikk**un Olam** – Hebrew. Tikkun Olam means repair of the world or repair of the universe and refers to the practice of helping to make the world a better place.

Tikk**un HaLev** – Hebrew. Tikkun HaLev means repair of the heart and refers to the practice of repairing the wounds of the spiritual heart and cleansing and polishing and opening the spiritual heart.

Todah – Hebrew. Todah means thanks or thank you.

Todah La'**Eyl** – Hebrew. Todah La'Eyl means thanks to God or thank God.

Torah – (pronounced **tow**-rah with "tow" as in "to tow the line") – Hebrew. Noun. (The following definition is also contained in footnote 11.) The Torah is the first five books of the Hebrew Bible, which are described in brief in Appendix B, entitled "Guide to the Books of the Hebrew Bible." In summary, the Torah contains stories about the creation of the world, the founding fathers and mothers of the Jewish people and numerous other peoples, Israelite slavery in Egypt, freedom from slavery and forty years of wandering in the wilderness. The Torah contains many stories that took place during the forty years of wandering, including receiving the Ten Commandments at Mount Sinai, learning how to build a portable Tabernacle (sanctuary) that was assembled when the Israelites camped, and disassembled and carried when the Israelites were moving from place to place in the wilderness. At the end of the Torah, the Israelites are camped on the shore of the Jordan River, prepared to enter the Land of Israel. Moses speaks to the Israelites for thirty-seven days and then he passes from this world. In addition to these stories, the Torah contains 613 mitzvot—commandments that are the basis of traditional Jewish life. (See also the discussion about Sacred Texts at the beginning of Chapter 2, and the Guide to the Books of the Bible in Appendix B.)

Tzeda**kah** – Hebrew. Noun. Tzedakah means charity. The word comes from the root meaning justice. Charity is understood in Judaism as helping to level the playing field or doing what is just.

Vav – Hebrew. Noun. Vav is the sixth letter of the Hebrew alphabet and the third letter of the Divine Root Name discussed in Chapter 11. The Divine Root Name is spelled with the Hebrew letters yod and hay and vav and hay.

YaH **Hi** – Hebrew. YaH Hi means "God is" or "It is God" or "God is She."

Yah **Hu** – Hebrew. YaH Hu means "God is" or "It is God" or "God is He."

Ye**shi**vah – Hebrew. Noun. Yeshivah comes from the Hebrew root meaning to sit or to dwell, and refers to a seminary or school for Jewish religious studies.

Ye**sod** – Hebrew. Noun. Yesod is one of the ten sephirot. Yesod is defined briefly in the Introduction to the Ten Sephirot in Appendix D.

Yod – Hebrew. Noun. Yod is the name of the tenth letter of the Hebrew alphabet, and is the starting letter of the Divine Root Name discussed in Chapter 11. The Divine Root Name is spelled with the Hebrew letters yod and hay and vav and hay.

Yiddish – English. Noun. Yiddish is a language that is a hybrid of German and Hebrew. For example, in German, "Jew" is "Jude" (pronounced "yoo-da"), and in Yiddish, "Jew" is Yidd (pronounced "yeed"). On the other hand, the Yiddish word "s'choirah" means "merchandise" from the Hebrew "s'chorah." (The Yiddish is pronounced "s-choi-rah" with "ch" as in the name of the musical composer Bach) Because of the combination of German and Hebrew, one could call Yiddish a pigeon language. In different countries where Yiddish was spoken over the centuries, words from the local language, and pronunciation of the vowels in the local language, often embedded themselves in local Yiddish.

YHVH – A depiction in English of the Divine Root Name, which consists of the Hebrew letters yod and hay and vav and hay. "Y" stands for yod, "H" stands for hay, "V" stands for vav, and the last "H" stands for hay.

YHWH – See "YHVH" above. "W" is sometimes used in place of "V" to depict the Hebrew letter vav in the Divine Root Name."

Za**chor** – Hebrew. Verb. Zachor means remember.

Zikr – Arabic. Noun. Zikr is a Sufi term meaning remembrance. Zikr is the Sufi practice of remembering our oneness with the divine, reconnecting with the Oneness, reconnecting with the root of our being, and reconnecting with the source of all life and being.

Zohar – Hebrew. Noun. Zohar means splendor and refers to a mystical commentary on the Torah that first appeared in the Jewish community in Spain during the twelfth century. See the "*Zohar*" section at the end of Chapter 2.

Appendix B

Guide to the Books of the Hebrew Bible

Two Torahs and a Third

There are two Torahs and a third: the Written Torah, the Oral Torah and the original Torah that emanated from God before creation. The Written Torah is the Hebrew Bible. This Appendix includes a brief description of each book of the Hebrew Bible.

The Oral Torah consists of all other Jewish spiritual and religious teachings. The Oral Torah was intended to remain oral so that it could be transmitted from mouth to ear and heart to heart, and so that it could retain fluidity within the spiritual and religious jurisdiction of the sages of each generation. During the Roman occupation, the persecution, torture and murder of Jews in general and Torah scholars in particular, rendered the Oral Torah at risk of extinction. Sages of succeeding generations wrote down to Oral Torah of the time—first in the Mishna, and later in the Gemara—to preserve it for future generations. This is explained in greater detail in Chapter 2.

The third Torah is the original Torah that emanated from God before creation.

Overview of the Hebrew Bible

The Hebrew Bible is called Tanakh, which can also be spelled Tanach. Tanakh is an acronym that stands for Torah-Nevi'im-Ketuvim. Torah refers to the Five Books of Moses. Nevi'im means Prophets and contains most of the Biblical books of the prophets. Ketuvim means Writings. Each of the books of the Torah, Prophets and Writings are described briefly below in the section to which they belong, and in the order in which they appear in the Hebrew Bible.

Christians refer to the Hebrew Bible as the Old Testament. The Old Testament contains the very same text as the Hebrew Bible. However, the books appear in a different order in the Hebrew Bible than in the Old Testament. In addition, a number of books of the Hebrew Bible are subdivided in the Old Testament. This is explained in the "Bible" entry in the Glossary of Terms.

The Hebrew Bible is written in Hebrew, except for parts of the Book of Daniel that are written in Aramaic. Hebrew appears to have been a living language during Biblical times. There are differences in the Hebrew of different Biblical books as result of having been written during different centuries.

Torah – Five Books of Moses

Book of Genesis - Sefer Bereishit - Bereishit means "in the beginning" or "at the beginning," and contains the Jewish creation myth and stories of the founding fathers and mothers of the Jewish people and many other peoples, and a few of the 613 commandments. The Book of Genesis opens with the words, "In the Beginning, God created the heavens and the earth." Rashi, a famous rabbi and scholar who lived in France in the eleventh century, wrote a commentary on the Torah and the Talmud. Regarding the opening words of the Book of Genesis, Rashi writes, "In the beginning, God created the heavens and the earth. This is the story of creation; the rest is commentary."

Book of Exodus - Sefer Shmot - Shmot means "names" and refers to the list of names of the Israelites who went from the land of Canaan to the land of Egypt to dwell during the time of Joseph. Exodus contains the stories of Israelite slavery in Egypt, God's call to Moses at the burning bush, the exodus from slavery, the parting and crossing of the Sea of Reeds, receiving the Ten Commandments at Mount Sinai, instructions for building the Tabernacle—a portable sanctuary—the building of the Tabernacle, and the receiving of many other of the 613 commandments.

Book of Leviticus - Sefer Vayikra - Vayikra means "He called" and refers to God, Who called Moses from the Tent of Meeting in the wilderness. Leviticus contains many levitical laws, that is to say, instructions for the how and what of animal sacrifices, grain sacrifices, and other sacrifices, instructions for anointing and installing Israelite priests, and a host of other priestly commandments, as well as agricultural commandments as well as commandments for living a holy life. The many commandments given in Leviticus are part of the 613 commandments.

Book of Numbers - Sefer BeMidbar - BeMidbar means "in the wilderness" and refers to the wilderness where the Israelites dwelled and wandered for forty years following slavery in Egypt and before entering the Promised Land. The English name "Numbers" refers to the census of the Israelites that is taken at the beginning of the book. The Book of Numbers contains stories about the adventures, successes, challenges and defeats of the years that the Israelites wandered in the wilderness, together with a summary of the places where the Israelites camped during their wandering. The Book of Numbers also contains a number of the 613 commandments.

Book of Deuteronomy - Sefer Devarim - Devarim means "words" and refers to the words of Moses to the people as they were assembled on the eastern shore of the Jordan River at the end of the forty years of wandering in the wilderness. Moses speaks to the Israelites for thirty-seven days, recounting events of their history and giving them many laws and teachings. Moses then blesses each of the twelve tribes of Israel, and then he goes up onto a mountain and passes from this world. God buries Moses and the Israelites mourn his passing, and thus the Torah ends. In addition to these stories, Deuteronomy contains many of the 613 mitzvot (commandments) contained in the Torah.

Nevi'im – The Books of the Prophets

Joshua – This Book, which bears the name of the successor of Moses, describes the conquests of the Israelites in the Promised Land, which we now call the Land of Israel.

Judges – When the Israelites first settled in the Land of Israel, their leaders were called judges. The Book of Judges includes stories of the judges and the Israelites during that period.

Samuel – Samuel was a prophet. The Book of Samuel opens with the story of his mother, Hannah, a barren wife who prays for a son and promises to give her son over to divine service. Samuel responds to the insistence of the Israelites that they have a king. Following divine guidance, Samuel anoints Saul as King of Israel, and later anoints David and brings Saul the message that he is no longer king.

Kings[231] – The Book of Kings includes stories from the latter years of the reign of King David through King Solomon. After the death of King Solomon, Israel became divided into two kingdoms. The Northern Kingdom was called Israel, and the Southern Kingdom was called Judea, which included Jerusalem and the Temple. The Book of Kings also includes stories about the kings of Israel and Judea from the separation of the two kingdoms through the destruction of each realm. The Book of Kings also includes stories of numerous prophets, including Nathan, Elijah and Elisha.

Isaiah – The Book of Isaiah contains Isaiah's prophecies concerning Judea and Jerusalem during the reigns of Kings Uzziah, Jothan, Ahaz and Hezekiah of Judea.

Jeremiah – The Book of Jeremiah contains Jeremiah's prophecies concerning Kings Josiah, Jehoiachim and Zedekiah of Judea. This is before and during Babylonian captivity of Judea and the destruction of the Kingdom of Judea.

Ezekiel – The Book of Ezekiel contains Ezekiel's prophecies during the Babylonian occupation and destruction of Judea. Ezekiel prophesied concerning the Jewish homeland and other regions.

Tray Asar – The Twelve.[232] Tray Asar is a single Book containing the booklets of twelve prophets, including:

Hosea, who prophesied during the reign of King Jeroboam of Israel and Kings Uzziah, Jothan, Ahaz and Hezekiah of Judea;

Joel, who prophesied regarding the Kingdom of Judea and Jerusalem;

Amos, who prophesied during the reign of King Jeroboam of Israel, and King Uzziah of Judea;

Obadiah, who prophesied after the destruction of Judea by the Babylonians, to whom he refers as the children of Esau;

Jonah, who prophesied to Nineveh. It is believed that Jonah may have lived in the Kingdom of Israel;

---

231 The Kingdom of Israel was destroyed by the Assyrians in 722 B.C.E. and most of its population was taken into captivity. The captives of the Northern Kingdom of Israel are known as the lost tribes. The Southern Kingdom of Judea included Jerusalem and the Holy Temple. The Kingdom of Judea was destroyed by the Babylonians in 586 B.C.E. and its population was taken into captivity. In 538 B.C.E., the Persians conquered the Babylonians and subsequently allowed the Judeans to return to rebuild the Temple and live on the land. The Second Temple stood for approximately five hundred years and was destroyed by the Romans in 70 C.E. Since the destruction of the Second Temple, there has always been a small continuous presence of Jews—from the word Yehudim, meaning Judeans—living on the land that is now modern Israel. However, Jews were not allowed to live on the land in large numbers until after the birth of the modern State of Israel in 1948.

232 According to Jewish scholars, the Hebrew Bible contains twenty-five books. Christian scholars refer to the Hebrew Bible as the Old Testament and to the stories and teachings of Jesus as the New Testament. According to Christian scholars, the Old Testament contains thirty-nine books. The difference in counting is due to the following: In the Christian Scriptures, each of the twelve booklets of the Trey Asar are considered to be a separate book; whereas, in the Jewish scriptures, all twelve are considered to be part of the one book called Trey Asar. Also, in the Jewish scriptures, first and second Kings, first and second Samuel, and first and second Chronicles are considered to be one book, whereas in the Christian scriptures each of these are counted as two books.

Micah, who prophesied during the reigns of Kings Jothan, Ahaz and Hezekiah of Judea;

Nahum, who prophesied about Nineveh;

Habakkuk, who likely lived in Judea and was a contemporary of Nahum and Jeremiah. He predicts the coming Babylonian invasion;

Zephaniah, who prophesied during the reign of King Josiah of Judea;

Haggai, who prophesied during the reign of King Darius of Persia. The Persians conquered Babylonia at a time when the Judeans were in exile in Babylonia;

Zechariah, who also prophesied during the reign of King Darius of Persia. Zechariah received prophecy from an angel. One of the angel's teachings was, "Not by might; not by power, but by My spirit, says the Lord of Hosts." This prophecy is read in modern times on the Sabbath during the festival of Chanukah; and

Malachi, who prophesized at the time of Nehemiah (whose story is in the Writings section of the Hebrew Bible). This was during the time of Persian rule in Babylonia and Judeans were welcome to return to Judea and Jerusalem. Malachi prophesizes that Elijah will return and turn the hearts of parents to children, and children to parents.

KETUVIM – THE BOOKS OF THE WRITINGS

Psalms – This Book of Psalms contains one hundred fifty spiritual poems, called psalms. Many of the psalms are attributed to King David, while some are attributed to Asaph, and some to the children of Korach, whose difficult story is told in chapter 16 of the Book of Numbers in the Torah.

Proverbs – The Book of Proverbs contains thirty-one proverbs, each containing wisdom teachings.

Job – The Book of Job includes the story of Job. After much pain and suffering, hopelessness and faith, Job is blessed with prosperity, and is surrounded by family and friends.

Song of Songs - The Song of Songs is love poetry attributed to Solomon. There was a great deal of controversy about whether Song of Songs would make it into the Bible, and in the end, it did. The imagery in Song of Songs is explicit about human love and is also said to refer to the love between God and the Jewish people, or love between God and humanity. Song of Songs is quoted in the Talmud and other rabbinic literature. The *Zohar* and other mystical texts focus considerably on the imagery of Song of Songs.

Ruth – The Book of Ruth tells the story of a Moabite woman married to an Israelite who dies at a young age. Ruth follows her husband's mother, Naomi, from the land of Moab to Naomi's homeland in the tribe of Judah, one of the twelve tribes of Israel. Ruth marries Boaz, a relative of her late husband, and they have a son together. Ten generations later, David is born into their lineage, and becomes king of Israel, a nation forged from the twelve tribes.

Lamentations – The Book of Lamentations is attributed to the Prophet Jeremiah, and contains a lament of the destruction of Judea and Jerusalem.

Ecclesiastes – The Book of Ecclesiastes is a brief philosophical treatise attributed to Solomon. It begins, "Futility, futility, all is futile," and ends, "The sum of the matter, when all is said and done; revere God and observe God's commandments, for this applies to all humankind."

Esther – The Book of Esther contains the story of Esther, a Jewish woman, who is chosen by King Ahashuerus of Persia to be his queen. Queen Esther saves the Jewish people from the tyrannical Haman, a chief advisor to the king who wants to annihilate the Jews.

Daniel – The Book of Daniel takes place during the Babylonian exile and contains stories of miracles, courage and prophecy. The early verses of chapter 12 contain overt teachings on resurrection.

Ezra – The Book of Ezra describes some of the events that took place in Persia during the reign of Cyrus who gave freedom to the Judeans, who had been living in captivity in Babylon.

Nehemiah – The Book of Nehemiah describes the return to Jerusalem.

Chronicles – This book chronicles the lineages from Adam to King Cyrus who receives word from God to encourage the Judeans to return to Judea and Jerusalem and to rebuild the Temple. It also contains stories of certain periods.

Appendix C

Index and Guide to Sacred Phrases

Some of the practices in this Index and Guide
are not found elsewhere in the book.

Pronunciations and melodies are available at http://rebpam.com/.

Shokkelen is defined in the Glossary of Terms.

Hadrat kodesh is defined in Chapter 11.

<u>Sacred Word or Phrase</u>   <u>Chapter</u>

Adonai Echad   12
Language: Hebrew
Pronunciation: Ado**nai** E**chad**
Meaning: God is One.
Repetition: See the section entitled, "YaH Echad" in Chapter 12.

Adonai Elohaynu Adonai Echad   12
Language: Hebrew
Pronunciation: Ado**nai** Elo**hay**nu Ado**nai** E**chad**
Meaning: God is our God, God is One.
Repetition: See "Zikrs of Shomer Yisrael" Chapter 12.

Adonai Hu HaElohim   11
Language: Hebrew
Pronunciation: Ado**nai Hu** HaElo**heem**
Meaning: God He is the God.
Repetition: See the section entitled, "YaH Hu HaElohim" in Chapter 11.

Adoshem   8, 9
Language: Hebrew
Pronunciation: Ado**shem**
Meaning and Use: Adoshem is a hybrid of Adonai and HaShem and is a name of God
that may be repeated in place of the Divine Root Name in ordinary conversation
and while teaching.
Repetition: Shokkel while chanting or reciting Adoshem, focusing Shem in the heart.

Sacred Word or Phrase   Chapter

Adoshem Hu HaElokim   11
Language: Hebrew
Pronunciation: Ado**shem Hu** HaElok**eem**
Meaning: God, He is the God. Or God is God.
Repetition: See the section entitled, "YaH Hu HaElohim" in Chapter 11.

Ahavah Rabbah   18
Language: Hebrew
Pronunciation: Aha**vah** Ra**bbah**
Meaning: Great love
Repetition:
   (1) Recite aloud in full voice, or whisper, or chant.
   (2) On the breath: Ahavah Rabbah on the in-breath, Ahavah Rabbah on the out-breath.
   (3) On the breath: repeat Ahavah Rabbah in the mind over and over until you
   have completed your in-breath, and Ahavah Rabbah over and over until you
   have completed your out-breath.
   (4) As a thought concentration while sitting or standing still,
   (5) As a walking practice: Ahavah as the right foot comes to the floor,
   Rabbah on the left foot.

Ahavat Olam   18
Language: Hebrew
Pronunciation: Aha**vat O**lam
Meaning: Ahavat Olam is a sacred phrase meaning eternal love.
Repetition:
   (1) Recite aloud in full voice, or whisper, or chant.
   (2) On the breath: Ahavat Olam on the in-breath, Ahavah Olam on the out-breath.
   (3) On the breath: repeat Ahavah Olam in the mind over and over until you have
   completed your in-breath, and Ahavat Olam over and over until you have
   completed your out-breath.
   (4) As a thought concentration while sitting or standing still,
   (5) As a walking practice: Ahavat as the right foot comes to the floor,
   Olam on the left foot.

Ahavat Adonai V'ahavat Kol Briyat Adonai   18
Language: Hebrew
Pronunciation: Aha**vat** Ado**nai** V'aha**vat Kol** Bri**yat** Ado**nai**
Meaning: Love of God and love of all God's creation
Repetition: See section entitled "Focus and Repetition" in Chapter 18.

Ahavat YaH V'ahavat Kol Briyat YaH   18
Language: Hebrew
Pronunciation: Aha**vat YaH** V'aha**vat** Kol Bri**yat YaH**
Meaning: Love of God and love of all God's creation
Repetition: See section entitled "Focus and Repetition" in Chapter 18.

Sacred Word or Phrase   Chapter

Ana Avda D'Kudsha Brikh Hu   21
Language: Aramaic
Pronunciation: **A**na **A**vda D'**Kud**sha **Brikh**-Hu
Meaning: I am a servant of the Holy One, blessed be He.
Repetition: Whisper while shokkelen, with head going up and down ever so slightly.

Atah Hu Gibbor   20
Language: Hebrew
Pronunciation: **A**tah-Hu Gi**bbor**
Meaning: You are power. (You refers to God)
Repetition: See Chapter 20.

Barukh HaShem   17
Language: Hebrew
Pronunciation: Ba**rukh** Ha**Shem**
Meaning: Thank God, or blessed is God
Repetition: See Chapter 17.

Barukh Shem Kevod Malkhuto L'Olam Va'ed   13
Language: Hebrew
Pronunciation: **Ba**rukh **Shem** Ke**vod** Mal**khu**to L'**Ol**am Va'**ed**
Meaning: Blessed is the Name, the Glory of His Kingdom is forever.
Repetition: See Chapter 13.

Bayh Ana Racheytz   21
Language: Aramaic
Pronunciation: **Bayh**-Ana Ra**cheytz**
Meaning: In God I trust.
Repetition: See Chapter 21.

Birkat Kohanim   26
See Priestly Blessings.

Blessings for Shabbes   24
See Chapter 24 for the blessings over candles, wine or juice, and challah, Shalom Aleichem (welcoming the angels) and other prayers and readings.

Blessing of God's Goodness   25
Language: Hebrew
Pronunciation and Meaning: See Chapter 25.

Brukha At YaH Shekhinah, Barukh Atah Elohim   16
Language: Aramaic and Hebrew
Pronunciation: Bru**kha** At-**YaH** Shekhi**nah**, Ba**rukh** **A**tah Elo**heem**
Meaning: Blessed are You Shechina, Blessed are You Elohim.
Repetition: See "Brukha At YaH" section of Chapter 16.

Sacred Word or Phrase   Chapter

Divine Root Name   8
Language: English.
Meaning: The Divine Root Name is an English translation for "Shem HaMeforash,"
and refers to the ineffable name of God, spelled yod and hay and vav and hay in Hebrew.

Echad Yachid U'meyuchad   19
Language: Hebrew
Pronunciation: E**chad** Ya**chid** U'myu**chad**
Meaning: One, singular and unique
Repetition: See Chapter 19.

El Nah Refa Nah Lah   22
Language: Hebrew
Pronunciation: **El Nah** Re**fa**-Nah **Lah**
Meaning: God please heal (please) her. Moses cried out to God with these words when his brother
Aaron pleaded with him to pray for the healing of their sister Miriam. Numbers 12:13.
Repetition: Chant or recite rhythmically while praying for healing. Also see Chapter 22.

El Nah Refa Nah Lanu   22
Language: Hebrew
Pronunciation: **El Nah** Re**fa**-Nah **Lanu**
Meaning: God please heal (please) us.
Repetition: Chant or recite rhythmically while praying for healing. Also see Chapter 22.

Elohim   8, 11
Language: Hebrew
Pronunciation: Elo**heem**
Meaning: God
Repetition:
  (1) Recite softly, lift head slightly to the right and say Elohim, feeling the sound
  in ketter. Lower head slightly to the left, feeling the sound in tiferet. Repeat.
  (2) Do the same in reverse: lower head slightly to the left and say Elohim, raise
  head slightly to the right and say Elohim.

Eyn Od   11
Language: Hebrew
Pronunciation: **Eyn Od** (with the vowels pronounced as in "raincoat")
Meaning: None else, or there is none else.
Repetition: See Chapter 11.

Eyn Od Milvada   11
Language: Hebrew
Pronunciation: Eyn (with the vowel pronounced like "rain") Od (with the vowel like "coat")
Milvada (with the vowels like "peel," "pod" and "pod"). **Eyn Od Mil**va**da**
(with slightly more emphasis on "da" than "mil").
Meaning: There is nothing but Her, or there is none else but Her, or there is none but Her.
Repetition: See Chapter 11.

Sacred Word or Phrase   Chapter

Eyn Od Milvado   11
Language: Hebrew
Pronunciation: Eyn (with the vowel pronounced like "rain") Od (with the vowel like "coat")
Milvado (with the vowels like "peel," "pod" and "code"). **Eyn Od Mil**vado
(with slightly more emphasis on "do" than "mil").
Meaning: There is nothing but Him, or there is none else but Him, or there is none but Him.
Repetition: See Chapter 11.

Eyn HaChayyim   8
Language: Hebrew
Pronunciation: Eyn-HaCha**yyeem**
Meaning: Source of life
Repetition: Recite softly. Lower the head on Eyn, and aim the sound in tiferet.
  Raise the head on HaCha, and aim the sound of yyim in ketter. Head may be lowered
  and lifted straight up and down; or up and slightly to the right, down and slightly
  to the left.

Hadrat Kodesh   11
Language: Hebrew
Pronunciation: **Had**-rat **Ko**-desh
Meaning: holy majesty, or holy splendor
Hadrat Kodesh is a sacred phrase from Psalm 29, described in the "Hadrat Kodesh" and
"Hadrat Kodesh Movement" sections of Chapter 11.

Halleluyah with Emphasis on "ha" - *Pronunciation:* **Ha**lleluyah   15
Halleluyah with Emphasis on "ha" and "ya" - *Pronunciation:* **Ha**lleluyah
Halleluyah with Emphasis on "lu" - *Pronunciation:* Halle**lu**yah
Language: Hebrew
Pronunciation: See *Pronunciation* for each Halleluyah with different emphasis above
Meaning: Praise God! or Let us praise God!
Repetition: See Chapter 15.

HaShem   8
Language: Hebrew
Pronunciation: Ha**Shem**
Meaning: God
Repetition:
  (1) Recite softly. With head looking forward, say Ha, feeling the sound in da'at. Lift head
  slightly to the right and say Shem. Feel the sound in ketter. Lower head, say Ha. Feel the
  sound in da'at. Lift head slightly to the right and say Shem. Feel the sound in ketter. Repeat.
  (2) Do the same in reverse: Raise head slightly to the right on Ha, feeling the sound
  in ketter. Lower the head on Shem and feel the sound in tiferet and da'at.
  (3) Lift head slightly to the right, say HaShem, feeling the sound in ketter. Lower
  head and say HaShem, feeling the sound in tiferet. Da'at is awakened by this practice
  as well as ketter and tiferet.
  (4) Do the same in reverse: Say HaShem, feeling the sound in tiferet. Lift head slightly
  to the right, say HaShem, feeling the sound in ketter. Da'at is awakened as well.

Sacred Word or Phrase   Chapter

L'sheym Yichud Kudsha Brich Hu U'Shekhintay   19
As a practice
Language: Aramaic
Pronunciation: L'sheym-**Yi**chud-Kudsha **Brich-Hu** U'She**khin**tay
Meaning: In the name of unity of the Holy One, blessed be He, and the Shechina.
Repetition: Recite L'sheym-Yichud-Kudsha Brich-Hu U'Shekhintay softly
  with an attunement to the interior feeling. Don't rush. Feel it.

L'Sheym Yichud Kudsha Brikh Hu U'Shekhintay   19
Yod Hay Vav Hay, Yod Hay Vav Hay
Language: Aramaic and Hebrew
Pronunciation: L'sheym-**Yi**chud-Kudsha **Brich-Hu** U'She**khin**tay
  Yod-Hay Vav-Hay Yod-Hay Vav-Hay
Meaning: See Chapter 19.
Repetition: This is a chant. The first line repeats four times. The second line repeats twice.
  The first line is sung to the low part of the melody, and the second line is sung to the
  high part.

L'Takeyn Olam B'Malkhut Shaddai   23
Language: Hebrew
Pronunciation: Letakeyn Olam BeMalkhut Shaddai
Meaning: To repair the world in the sovereignty of the divine.
Repetition: See Chapter 23.

May All Beings Be Well   26
Language: English
Meaning: Buddhist prayer
Repetition: May all beings be well. May all beings be happy. Peace, peace, peace.

May the Blessings of God Rest Upon You   26
See Priestly Blessings

Mishebeyrakh for Healing   22
Language: Hebrew and English
Pronunciation: See Chapter 22.
Meaning: See Chapter 22.
Repetition: See Chapter 22.

M'maleh Kol Uhl'min   19
Language: Hebrew and Aramaic
Pronunciation: M'maleh Kol Uhl'min, Vesoveyv Kol Uhl'min, Umibaladecha
  Eyn-Shum M'tziyut Klal
Meaning and Repetition: See Chapter 19.

New Jewish Invocation   25
Language: Aramaic and Hebrew
Pronunciation and Repetition: See Chapter 25.

Sacred Word or Phrase   Chapter

N'vareykh Et Eyn HaChayyim (also see Eyn HaChayyim)   8
Language: Hebrew
Pronunciation: N'vareykh Et-Eyn HaChayyim
Meaning: Let us bless the Source of Life.
Repetition: Moving the head forward slightly and then upright or slightly back,
  say N'vareykh with head forward, Et Eyn Ha as you lift the head, and Chayyim
  with head upright or slightly back.

Priestly Blessings   26
Language: Given in Hebrew in the Torah (Book of Numbers 6:22-26), Given in this book
  In English translation, and Pir-O-Murshid Hazrat Inayat Khan's
  midrashic (interpretive) rendition.
English Translation:
  The Lord bless you and protect you.
  The Lord shine His face upon you and be gracious unto you.
  The Lord lift his face to you and grant you peace.
Hazrat Inayat Khan's Rendition:
  May the blessings of God rest upon you.
  May God's peace abide with you.
  May God's presence illuminate your heart now and forever more.
  (For slight variations in the way this blessing was given and is used, see the footnote in Chapter 26.)
Repetition: See the website listed in the Key to Pronunciation

Shema   11, 12, 13, 14
Practices using forms of the Shema are contained in Chapters 11, 12, 13 and 14.

Shema Yisrael Adonai Elohaynu Adonai Echad   11
Language: Hebrew
Pronunciation: Shema Yisrael Adonai Elohaynu Adonai Echad
Repetition: See Chapter 11.

Shema Yisrael Adoshem Elokaynu Adoshem Echad   11
Language: Hebrew
Pronunciation: Shema Yisrael Adoshem Elokaynu Adoshem Echad
Repetition: See Chapter 11.

Shema Yisrael HaShem Elokaynu HaShem Echad   11
Language: Hebrew
Pronunciation: Shema Yisrael HaShem Elohaynu HaShem Echad
Meaning: Listen Israel, God is our God, God is One.
Repetition: See Chapter 11.

Shema Yisrael YaH Elohaynu YaH Echad   11, 14
Language: Hebrew
Pronunciation: Shema Yisrael YaH Elohaynu YaH Echad
Meaning: Listen Israel, God is our God, God is One.
Repetition: See Chapters 11 and 14.

Sacred Word or Phrase	Chapter

Shema Yisrael YaH Hi Elohaynu YaH Hi Echad   11
Language: Hebrew
Pronunciation: Shema Yisrael Ya Hi Elohaynu Ya Hi Echad
Meaning: Listen Israel, God is our God, God is One.
Repetition: See Chapter 11.

Shema Yisrael YaH Hi HaElohaynu YaH Hi HaEchad   11
Language: Hebrew
Pronunciation: Shema Yisrael Ya Hi HaElohaynu Ya Hi HaEchad
Meaning: Listen Israel, God is our God, God is One.
Repetition: See Chapter 11.

Shema Yisrael YaH Hu Elohaynu YaH Hu Echad   11
Language: Hebrew
Pronunciation: Shema Yisrael Ya Hu Elohaynu Ya Hu Echad
Meaning: Listen Israel, God is our God, God is One.
Repetition: See Chapter 11.

Shema Yisrael YaH Hu HaElohaynu YaH Hu HaEchad   11
Language: Hebrew
Pronunciation: Shema Yisrael Ya Hu HaElohaynu Ya Hu HaEchad
Meaning: Listen Israel, God is our God, God is One.
Repetition: See Chapter 11.

Shema (insert your own name in place of the word "Yisrael")   11
Practices inserting one's own name into the Shema are in Chapter 11

Takeyn Olam B'Malkhut Shaddai   23
Language: Hebrew
Pronunciation: Takeyn Olam BeMalkhut Shaddai
Meaning: Repair the world in the sovereignty of the divine
Repetition: See Chapter 23.

Tamid Echad   19
Language: Hebrew
Pronunciation: Tamid Echad
Meaning: Always One.
Repetition:
  (1) Recite or chant Tamid Echad being still.
  (2) Recite or chant Tamid Echad, leaning the upper body ever-so-slightly forward,
  and back to almost upright; repeat Tamid Echad while forward; silent while back.
  (3) Using the movement described in (2), chant over and over with a melody like this:
  Tamid Tamid Tamid Tamid Tamid Tamid Echad
  Oy Tamid Tamid Tamid Tamid Tamid Tamid Echad
  Echad Echad Echad Echad Tamid Tamid Echad
  Echad Echad Echad Echad Tamid Tamid Echad

Sacred Word or Phrase   Chapter

There is Nothing, Nothing, Nothing only God   18
See Chapter 18.

Todah La'Eyl   17
Language: Hebrew
Pronunciation: Todah La'Eyl
Meaning: Thank God or thank you God or thanks to God
Repetition: Move the head forward and then upright. As the head goes down,
    aim the sound of Todah in tiferet, with dah as a gentle tap to open the heart. Let the
    head rise almost automatically in response to the focus of dah in the heart, and say
    La'Eyl as your head rises, feeling Eyl in ketter.

YaH   8
Language: Hebrew
Pronunciation: YaH!
Meaning: God
Repetition:
    (1) Repeat YaH, focusing the sound in tiferet. Lift head slightly after each repetition,
    and lower it to focus the sound of the next YaH as if it were a gentle tap opening tiferet.
    (2) Lift the head, repeat YaH, focusing the sound in ketter. Lower head slightly after
    each repetition, and raise it to focus the sound as if it were a gentle tap to open ketter.

YaH Echad   12
Language: Hebrew
Pronunciation: YaH Echad
Meaning: God is One.
Repetition: See section entitled "YaH Echad" in Chapter 12.

YaH Elohaynu YaH Echad   12
Language: Hebrew
Pronunciation: YaH Elohaynu YaH Echad
Meaning: God is our God, God is One.
Repetition: See Chapter 12.

YaH Hi   16
Language: Hebrew
Pronunciation: YaH Hi
Meaning: God She, or God is.
Repetition: See section entitled, "YaH Hi" in Chapter 16.

YaH Hi Elohaynu YaH Hi Echad   12
Language: Hebrew
Pronunciation: YaH Hi Elohaynu YaH Hi Echad
Meaning: God, She is our God, God, She is One.
Repetition: See Chapter 12.

Sacred Word or Phrase   Chapter

YaH Hi Elohaynu YaH Hi HaEchad   12
Language: Hebrew
Pronunciation: YaH Hi Elohaynu YaH Hi HaEchad
Meaning: God, She is our God, God, She is the One.
Repetition: See Chapter 12.

YaH Hu   16
Language: Hebrew
Pronunciation: YaH Hu
Meaning: "God, He is our God" or "God, He is the One."
Repetition: See "YaH Hu" section of Chapter 16.

YaH Hu Elohaynu YaH Hu Echad   12
Language: Hebrew
Pronunciation: YaH-Hu Elohaynu YaH-Hu Echad
Meaning: God, He is our God, God, He is the One.
Repetition: See Chapter 12.

YaH Hu HaEchad   12
Language: Hebrew
Pronunciation: YaH Hu HaEchad
Meaning: God, He is the One.
Repetition: See section entitled, "YaH Echad" in Chapter 12.

YaH Hu HaElohaynu, YaH Hu HaEchad   12
Language: Hebrew
Pronunciation: YaH Hu HaElohaynu, YaH Hu HaEchad
Meaning: God, He is our God, God, He is the One.
Repetition: See Chapter 12.

YaH Hu HaElohim   11
Language: Hebrew
Pronunciation: YaH Hu HaEloheem
Meaning: God (alone) is the (true) God.
Repetition: See section entitled, "YaH Hu HaElohim" in Chapter 11.

YaH Hu YaH Hi   16
Language: Hebrew
Pronunciation: YaH-**Hu** YaH-**Hi**
Meaning: "God He, God She." or "God is."
Repetition: See section entitled, "YaH Hu YaH Hi" in Chapter 16.

YaH Hu Elohaynu YaH Hu Echad   12
Language: Hebrew
Pronunciation: YaH Hu Elohaynu YaH Hu Echad
Meaning: God, He is our God, God, He is God.
Repetition: See Chapter 12.

Sacred Word or Phrase   Chapter

YaH Hu HaElohim   11
Language: Hebrew
Pronunciation: YaH Hu HaElohim
Meaning: God, He is God.
Repetition: See section entitled, "YaH Hu HaElohim" in Chapter 11.

YaH Hu HaGibbor   20
Language: Hebrew
Pronunciation: YaH Hu HaGibbor
Meaning: God, He is the Powerful, or God, He is the Strength (or the Powerful One or the Strong One)
Repetition: See Chapter 20.

Yom Kippur Traditional Sacred Closing Chant   13
Language: Hebrew
Pronunciation: She**ma** Yisra-**el** Ado**nai** Elo**hay**nu Ado**nai** E**chad**
        Ba**rukh** Shem Ke**vod** Mal**khu**to L'Olam Va'**ed**
        Ado**nai Hu** HaElo**him**
Meaning: See "Sources of the Zikrs of Yom Kippur" in Chapter 13.
Repetition:
  Recite or chant once: Shema Yisrael Adonai Elohaynu Adonai Echad
  Recite or chant three times: Barukh Shem Kevod Malkhuto L'Olam Va'ed
  Recite seven times: Adonai Hu HaElohim (recite or chant seven times)

Yom Kippur Sacred Closing Chant according to Reb Zalman   13
Language: Hebrew
Pronunciation: Shema Yisrael YaH Elohaynu YaH Echad
Barukh Shem Kevod Malkhuto L'Olam Va'ed
YaH Hu HaElohim
Meaning: See "Sources of the Zikrs of Yom Kippur" in Chapter 13.
Repetition:
  (1) Chant or recite once: Shema Yisrael YaH Elohaynu YaH Echad
  Chant or recite three times: Barukh Shem Kevod Malkhuto L'Olam Va'ed
  Chant or recite seven times: YaH Hu HaElohim
  (2) Recite as a Zikr, repeating each phrase until completed,
  and then repeat the next phrase.

You   18
Language: English
Pronunciation: As in ordinary English
Repetition: A song to be sung.
"You" is a poem, written in Yiddish, and attributed to Rabbi Levi Yitzhak of Berdichev.

Sacred Word or Phrase	Chapter

Zikr   11, 12, 13, 15, 16
Language: Arabic
Pronunciation: **z'**kr
Meaning: Zikr is a Sufi term meaning remembrance.
Repetitions: See the various practices in Chapters 11, 12, 13, 15 and 16.

Appendix D

The Ten Sephirot

The Ashrey Tree

The Teachings section divider before Chapter 1 includes a decorative tree that I have dubbed the "Ashrey Tree." Ashrey means "happy" or "happy are" and is the name of a prayer recited numerous times each day during traditional Jewish worship.[233] The Ashrey Tree displays all the letters of the Hebrew alphabet—together with the final form of those letters that look different in the beginning and middle of a word than at the end of a word—with the exception of the final letter nun. The absence of final nun from the Ashrey prayer—and hence the Ashrey Tree—is explained at the end of the Introduction to the Hebrew Letters in Appendix H. The lovely Ashrey Tree is meaningful and symbolic. However, it is not a depiction of the Kabbalistic Tree of Life and it does not display the Ten Sephirot.

Defining Sephirah

A sephirah is an energy, attribute or emanation. Sephirah is a Hebrew word and is pronounced "sfeerah," with little to no pause between the "s" and "f." It may also be spelled in English as s'phira, s'fira, sefirah, sephira and in other ways. The plural of sephirah is sephirot.

According to the Kabbalah,[234] God created the universe with the ten sephirot and the twenty-two letters of the Hebrew alphabet. The names of the sephirot and their location on the Tree of Life are described in brief below and depicted in Charts 1 and 2 on the pages that follow. The letters of the Hebrew alphabet are listed in Charts 4 and 5 in Appendix H.

Brief Description of the Ten Sephirot

Ketter - Ketter literally means crown, as in the diadem worn by royalty. Ketter is the crown center in relation to the body and the universe. It is located just above the crown of the human head and at the top of the Tree of Life. (Also see the section entitled "Da'at" later in this appendix.)

Chokhmah - Chokhmah means wisdom. Chokhmah is on the Tree of Life below and to the right of ketter (crown), across from binah (understanding) and above netzach (mastery or victory).

Binah - Binah means understanding. On the Tree of Life, binah is both understanding and also refers to the womb within manifestation and in the upper worlds. Binah is the sephirah from which creation pours forth into existence, just as a baby enters the world from its mother's womb. (See also Yesod.) Binah is on the Tree of Life below and to the left of ketter (crown), across from chokhmah (wisdom) and above hod (splendor or grace).

---

233 The Ashrey prayer is a compilation of the following chapters and verses from the Biblical Book of Psalms: 84:5, 144:15, 145:1-21, and 115:18.
234 This is a teaching of Jewish Kabbalah. Christian Kabbalah and the Kabbalistic teachings that are part of the occult may rely upon different teachings, principles and scriptural references.

Chesed - Chesed means kindness or loving-kindness, and is associated with the right arm. Chesed is on the Tree of Life directly below chokhmah (wisdom), above netzach (victory, mastery) and across from gevurah (strength, severity, boundaries). Chesed is also slightly higher than, and to the right of, tiferet (heart, harmony, beauty).

Gevurah - Gevurah means strength, and it may also be translated as severity. As a sephirah, gevurah may be understood as strength, severity and boundaries. Gevurah is associated with the left arm. On the Tree of Life, gevurah is directly below binah (understanding), above hod (splendor, grace) and across from chesed (loving-kindness). Gevurah is also slightly higher than, and to the left of, tiferet (heart, harmony, beauty).

Tiferet - Tiferet means beauty, and may also be understood as harmony and love. Tiferet refers to the heart center in the human body, as well as the spiritual heart. Tiferet is depicted at a central point on the Tree of Life. In modern Israeli Hebrew and in Sephardi Hebrew, it is pronounced "teef-eh-ret." In Yiddish and Ashkenazi Hebrew, it may also be pronounced "tiferes" and "siferes." On the Tree of Life, tiferet is directly below ketter/da'at (crown, knowledge) and above yesod (foundation, procreation). Charts 1 and 2 each depict a different placement for tiferet in relation to the sephirot that are on the left and right side of the Tree of Life. (See "Tree of Life According to the Ari HaKodesh and the Gra.")

Netzach - Netzach literally means victory. As a sephirah, netzach may also be understood as mastery, such as mastering a skill or a spiritual practice. Netzach is associated with the right leg. On the Tree of Life, netzach is directly below chesed (loving-kindness) and across from hod (splendor, grace). Netzach is above and to the right of yesod (foundation, procreation). It is also to the right of tiferet (heart, beauty, harmony); in Chart 1, netzach is to the right and above tiferet, whereas in Chart 2, it is to the right and below tiferet.

Hod - Hod literally means splendor. As a sephirah, hod may also be understood as grace, such as a gift—whether spiritual or material—that is received or achieved without effort. In truth, of course, everything we receive is through grace, regardless of whether we invest effort toward attaining it. Hod is associated with the left leg. On the Tree of Life, hod is directly below gevurah (strength, severity, boundaries) and across from netzach (victory, mastery). Hod is slightly above and to the left of yesod (foundation, procreation). It is also to the left of tiferet (heart, beauty, harmony); in Chart 1, hod is to the left and above tiferet, whereas in Chart 2, it is to the left and below tiferet.

Yesod - Yesod literally means foundation, and may be understood as the foundation upon which an intuition, thought, feeling or action is based—or from which it is launched. Yesod includes the genitals, procreation and reproduction. (See also Binah.) Yesod is parallel to the second chakra in the Hindu chakra system. Yesod is the foundation, or launching pad, from which creation emanates. However, it is not the genesis of creation, nor is it the path or goal of creation. Yesod is directly below tiferet (heart, harmony, beauty) and above malkhut (sovereignty, kingdom, queendom). It is also below netzach (victory, mastery) and hod (splendor, grace).

Malkhut - Malkhut means kingdom, and is at the bottom of the Tree of Life, directly below yesod. The following quotation from a teaching of Rabbi Shimon Lieberman may be helpful in understanding malkhut:[235]

> When we think of a king or a kingdom, we imagine a dictator imposing his will on a helpless populace, draining them of their resources to be used for his own personal aggrandizement. Even if we picture him as a benevolent despot, he is at best an efficient bureaucrat.
>
> When we speak of God and the concept of kingdom, we refer to a completely different model. The model we have in mind is of a king who has a picture of good and bad, an ideology of right and wrong, and [who] teaches the society around him those ideas and values. That society is then awakened to what is really right and structures itself and its institutions accordingly. When society has finished this process, it thereby amplifies and proclaims those values that the king had in his heart and mind.
>
> That society is thereby not only expressing the king's norms and values, but showing that these norms and values are really the inner norms and values of the people in the country.
>
> While we do not live with kings and it might be difficult for us to picture this, we can definitely use the illustration of a good teacher. A teacher who allows the students to "do as they wish" is not a teacher at all. The students have not received anything from him.
>
> On the other hand, a teacher who forces his students to do as he says has merely imposed external shackles on them…. The real teacher is the one who inspires his students, so that they realize that their own real feelings and values are those espoused by their teacher.

This is *malkhut*[236] in the true sense. It is God's actions and attributes—not as expressed by God, but rather as human beings express them. It is as if God's actions have struck a resonant chord in us, and we thereby act in a similar manner.

The sephirah of malkhut is also associated with ruach hakodesh, the spirit of divine holiness, and is considered to be connected with the divine name Adonai. According to the *Zohar*, Adonai is connected with the Shechina, the feminine divine presence found within manifestation. One might, therefore, translate malkhut as "queendom." As we know from human history, both queens and kings may be despots. For this reason, Rabbi Lieberman's teaching quoted above is relevant regardless of whether we choose the masculine or feminine translation of malkhut.

---

235 Excerpted from a teaching by Rabbi Shimon Lieberman, Kabbalah 101, Lesson 23, Aish HaTorah, May 6, 2012 <http://www.aish.com/sp/k/48971776.html>. Aish HaTorah is a Jewish outreach organization founded in Jerusalem by Rabbi Noah Weinberg, of blessed memory, in 1974. See <http://www.aish.com/> for additional teachings by Orthodox scholars and theologians.

236 "Malkhut" is generally spelled with "ch." To adhere to Reb Zalman's preferred method of delineating between the Hebrew letters kaf and kuf, I have spelled it as "malkhut" in this book; both spellings are correct.

Tree of Life According to the Ari HaKodesh and the Gra

Rabbi Isaac Luria, of blessed memory, is known as the "Ari," meaning "Lion," or "Ari HaKodesh," meaning "the Holy Lion." The Ari HaKodesh lived in the sixteenth century and taught in Tzefat, an ancient city located in present day Northern Israel. The Ari HaKodesh is considered one of the greatest Kabbalists of all time.[237] He made a careful study of a short text entitled *Sefer Yetzirah*, which is best translated as "Book of Formation" or "Book of Creation." The authorship of the original *Sefer Yetzirah* is uncertain. Many scholars attribute it to Abraham, the first patriarch of Judaism; and many attribute it to Rabbi Akiva, a famous teacher and sage who lived during the first century and the beginning of the second century of the common era. In the sixteenth century, when the Ari HaKodesh lived and taught, there were a multitude of versions of the *Sefer Yetzirah* available in manuscript form. The Ari HaKodesh studied and made selections from various versions and assembled a manuscript of the *Sefer Yetzirah* whose teachings are in concert with the *Zohar* (discussed in Chapter 2). This work is known as the Ari version of the *Sefer Yetzirah*.

In the eighteenth century, Rabbi Eliahu, the Gaon (Sage) of Vilna,[238] studied the Ari's version of the *Sefer Yetzirah* and made final edits and published it. Rabbi Eliahu's version is known as the Gra-Ari version, or the Gra version of the *Sefer Yetzirah*.[239]

In the 1970's, Rabbi Aryeh Kaplan wrote a book entitled *Sefer Yetzirah*. This scholarly work contains a number of versions of the *Sefer Yetzirah* in English and one version in Hebrew, together with history, commentaries, diagrams and other valuable information. Rabbi Kaplan's book is highly recommended to scholars and mystics whose appetite is whetted for study of the *Sefer Yetzirah* as an accessible esoteric Jewish text.

Chart 1 in this appendix presents the ten sephirot, together with da'at, in a compilation based upon the Ari version of the Tree of Life. Chart 2 presents the same ten sephirot, also with da'at, in a compilation based upon the Gra-Ari version of the Tree of Life. These versions of the Tree of Life are based upon the teachings the respective versions of the *Sefer Yetzirah* discussed above.

---

237 Aryeh Kaplan. *Sefer Yetzirah, The Book of Creation*, Revised Edition. (York Beach, Maine: Samuel Weiser, Inc. 1997), xxv.
238 Vilna (or Vilnius) is a city in Lithuania. Sometimes called the "Jerusalem of Lithuania," Vilna was a center of Jewish life and Kabbalistic study for centuries, and produced more than one gaon (sage) of Jewish mysticism, practice and thought.
239 Gra is an English depiction of the Hebrew abbreviation composed of the letters gimmel, resh and alef, which are the first letters of Gaon Rabbi Eliahu.

Da'at

In modern Hebrew, Da'at means knowledge. In the Hebrew Bible, da'at is also used to refer to specific types of knowledge, intention and capacities. For example, in the story of the Garden of Eden, there are references to the tree of knowledge of good and evil.[240] In that context, da'at is the Hebrew word for knowledge and it seems to also encapsulate an intellectual and moral capacity to discern between good and evil.[241]

After Adam and Eve were banished from the Garden, it states in the Bible, "Now Adam knew Eve his wife and she conceived and bore Cain...."[242] In that sentence, da'at seems to refer to human sexuality. This knowing is not just intellectual knowledge of sexuality. Rather, it seems to encapsulate the actual act of sexuality. Rabbi Avraham Ibn Ezra states in his commentary on the Garden of Eden story:

The "Tree of Knowledge" gave rise to sexual desire, and it is for this reason that the man and his wife covered their private parts... When Adam ate from the Tree of Knowledge, he knew his wife, this knowledge being a euphemism for sexual relations. This is called [knowing] on account of the Tree of Knowledge. When a youth "knows good and evil," then his sexual desire begins.[243]

In addition to the knowledge of good and evil, and the act of human sexuality, da'at is also used in relation to knowledge of God and empathy with the poor, as well as discernment, judgment and the ability to lead.[244] An example of this use of da'at is found in the prophecy of Jeremiah concerning King Shallum of Judea, who was the son of King Josiah. The prophet Jeremiah states,[245]

> Do you think you are more of a king because you compete in cedar? Your father ate and drank and dispensed justice and equity— Then all went well with him. He upheld the rights of the poor and needy— Then all was well.[246]

> Is this not truly knowing me, declares God.[247]

> But your eyes and your mind are only on ill gotten gains, on shedding the blood of the innocent, on committing fraud and violence.[248]

---

240 See *Genesis* 2:9 and 2:17.

241 Judith Z. Abrams. "Categorization, Disabilities and Persons with Disabilities," *Judaism and Disability: Portrayals in Ancient Texts From the Tanach Through the Bavli* (Washington D.C.: Gallaudet University Press, 1998) 131.

242 *Genesis* 4:1.

243 Rabbi Avraham Ibn Ezra's commentary to Genesis 3:6, as cited in "Lecture 10: The Tree of Knowledge "Original Sin"? by Rabbi Chaim Navon, published by the Israel Koschitsky Virtual Beit Midrash of Yeshivat Har Etzion located in Gush Etzion in the West Bank 1997-2012, May 7, 2012 <http://vbm-torah.org/archive/bereishit/10bereishit.htm>.

244 *Judaism and Disability*, page 132.

245 The prophecy begins in the Book of Jeremiah, chapter 22, verse 11 and continues through verse 17.

246 Jeremiah 22:15-16, *JPS Tanakh*, Philadelphia: The Jewish Publication Society, 1999, page 1064.

247 The phrase from Jeremiah 22:16 is translated by the Author.

248 Jeremiah 22:17, *JPS Tanakh*, page 1064.

Rabbi Judith Abrams is a modern Reform rabbi, a Biblical and Talmudic scholar and a teacher of clergy students in a number of settings, including in the Jewish Renewal Movement. Rabbi Abrams puts this latter use of da'at into perspective when she states, "The main way to gain access to da'at is through the study of God's teachings."[249] Rabbi Abrams brings, as evidence, two verses from the prophet Hosea:

> Listen [to the] word of God, Children of Israel, because God has a dispute with the inhabitants of the land, because there is no truth and no loving kindness and no knowledge of God in [the] land....[250]

> My people are destroyed for lack of the knowledge, because you have rejected the knowledge...[251]

Rabbi Abrams goes on to teach us that there is yet another use of the word da'at in the Hebrew Bible, which is the quality of acting intentionally. According to Rabbi Abrams, this intentional action is, "a metaphorical extension of the primary meaning of da'at as discernment and judgment."[252] The examples she brings are in the negative. The Hebrew expression is bivli da'at, meaning unintentional, or not premeditated. The following is a quote from Deuteronomy 4:41-42:

> Then Moses separated three cities on the eastern side of the Jordan [River] to which a manslayer who killed a person unintentionally [bivli da'at] could flee, if he did not recently hate the person [whom he killed];[253]

The next quote is from the Book of Joshua 20:1-3:

> When they [the Israelites] had finished dividing the land, the Lord said to Joshua: Speak to the Israelites: Designate the cities of refuge—about which I commanded you through Moses—to which a manslayer who kills a person by mistake, unintentionally[254] may flee.[255]

---

249 Judith Z. Abrams. *Judaism and Disability*, page 132.
250 Hosea 4:1, translation by the Author.
251 Hosea 4:6, translation by the Author.
252 Judith Z. Abrams. *Judaism and Disability*, page 133.
253 Deuteronomy 4:41-42, translated by the Author.
254 The expression for "unintentionally" in Hebrew is biv'li da'at, which literally means "without knowledge"
255 Joshua 20:1-3, JPS Tanakh, page 500.

According to the teachings of Rabbi Shneur Zalman of Liadi, the founder of Chabad Chassidus,[256] da'at is an aspect of the sephirah of ketter (crown center). The prominence and importance of da'at is apparent in the very name of Chabad Chassidus. Chabad is an acronym. The consonants chet, bet and dalet (represented by "ch," "b" and "d") are the initial consonants of the Hebrew words chokhmah (wisdom), binah (understanding) and da'at (knowledge). In Chabad Chassidus, one finds da'at to be listed on the Tree of Life, together with the ten sephirot. In Jewish Renewal sources, one may sometimes also find da'at listed on the Tree of Life. Da'at is also found occasionally in the depictions and descriptions of other Jewish scholars, mystics and theologians.

If one imagines the Tree of Life superimposed on a drawing of a human being sitting in what one might call "yoga posture," one can imagine da'at in the area of the throat center of the body. Da'at also relates to the throat or center of expression in the universe. I believe that ketter is realization of the transcendent, or transcendent realization; whereas da'at is applied realization, or realization as it manifests through knowledge and expression.

---

[256] Rabbi Shneur Zalman was a disciple of the Maggid of Mezrich, who was, in turn, a disciple of Rabbi Israel Baal Shem Tov, who was known as the Baal Shem Tov. The Baal Shem Tov lived in the eighteenth century and was the father of modern Chassidism (as opposed to ancient Chassidism mentioned in the Talmud). Rabbi Shneur Zalman studied in the company of such Chassidic luminaries as Rabbi Levi Yitzchak of Berdichiv (whose teachings are mentioned in the sections entitled "You" in Chapter 18, "Which is the Best Path" in Chapter 23, and "Blessing of God's Goodness" in Chapter 25 of this book.); Reb Elimelekh of Lizhensk and Reb Zusia of Anypol (See Chapter 24 of this book). Rabbi Shneur Zalman was the founder of the Chassidic dynasty known as Chabad or Lubavitch. As of this writing, Chabad maintains over three thousand centers worldwide, each run by a rabbi. Chabad rabbis perform outreach to Jews, and in some locales, they run programs to help all people regardless of their religious affiliation. For example, as of this writing, in Los Angeles, California, Chabad runs a drug and alcohol treatment center that is open to the public. The outreach of Chabad to Jews who are affiliated with other streams of Judaism is sometimes welcome and sometimes extremely controversial. Controversy is particularly prevalent in communities with small Jewish populations where Chabad and non-Chabad congregations are vying for the same members whose involvement is needed for the community's existence and success.

Chart 1

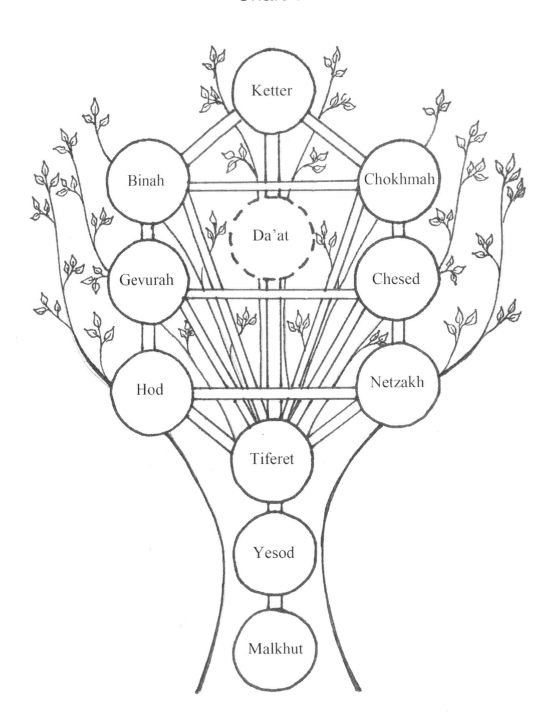

Tree of Life
Based upon the teachings of the Ari HaKodesh (Rabbi Isaac Luria)

Chart 2

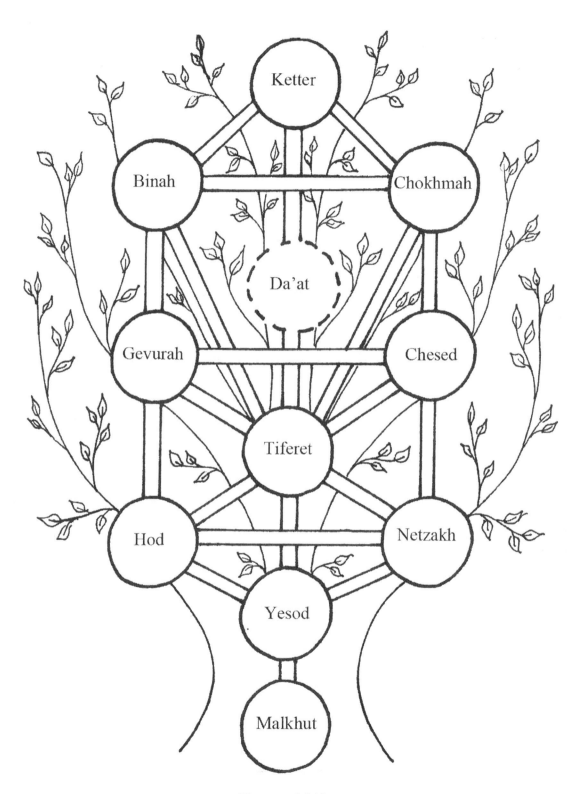

Tree of Life
Based upon the edits of the Gra (Rabbi Eliyahu, the Gaon of Vilna),
upon the teachings of the Ari HaKodesh (Rabbi Isaac Luria)

Appendix E

Introduction to the Jewish Calendar

The Jewish calendar consists of twelve months, with a leap year that occurs every two or three years. During a leap year, the Jewish calendar has thirteen months, with the twelfth month—called Adar—occurring twice. The two Adars are called Adar Aleph, meaning "Adar One," and Adar Beyt, meaning "Adar Two." If a person is born or gets married during Adar Beyt, the birthday or anniversary is celebrated in Adar Aleph in ordinary years, and in Adar Beyt during leap years. Yahrzeits (anniversaries of passing) for those who die in Adar Beyt are observed similarly.

Each Jewish month begins on a day close to the "molad," meaning the "birth" of the new moon. Thus, the Jewish calendar is lunar, and similar to the Muslim calendar. At the same time, there are seven Jewish leap years in every nineteen years, which allows the Jewish calendar to stay in relative alignment with the sun. The leap years allow each Jewish holiday to occur during the same season each year, and this keeps the Jewish calendar in alignment with the Gregorian calendar.

During the period of the Second Holy Temple in Jerusalem (516 B.C.E. to 70 C.E.), the Jewish calendar was intercalated by a special committee of the Sanhedrin, the Jewish high court, with the president of the Sanhedrin serving as chair of the committee. This practice continued for approximately three hundred years following the destruction of the Second Temple. At that point, persecution threatened the very existence of the Sanhedrin, creating the risk that the Jews, who by then were scattered all over the known world, would find themselves celebrating the Jewish holidays at different times because there would be no central authority for the intercalating of the calendar. To avoid this, the patriarch Hillel II applied certain rules by which astronomical facts are combined with religious requirements in order to sanctify all months in advance, and intercalate all future leap years in perpetuity, or until such time as a new Sanhedrin might be established. Those interested in studying the considerations that went into Hillel II's system are referred to the introductory sections of *The Comprehensive Hebrew Calendar* by Arthur Spier.[257]

The names of the Jewish months are listed in Hebrew and English on Chart 3 in this appendix. Chart 3 also includes the sephirah, or divine quality, associated with each month. (The sephirot are discussed in Appendix D.) In addition, Chart 3 lists the form of the Divine Root Name that corresponds with each month. (The Divine Root Name is discussed in Chapter 8.) For each Hebrew month, the four consonants of the Divine Root Name are permutated—in other words, their order changes—and vowels are added for the purpose of meditation and concentration. Chart 3 includes these permutations.

The Hebrew letters and vowels are discussed in Appendix H. Some letters are also discussed in the Key to Pronunciation at the beginning of this book.

---

257 Spier, Arthur. *The Comprehensive Hebrew Calendar* (Twentieth to Twenty Second Century). Jerusalem: Feldheim Publishers, 1986.

The Hebrew spelling of the Hebrew months in Chart 3 comport with *The Complete Hebrew English Dictionary* by Reuven Alcalay (Tel Aviv: Miskal - Publishing and Distribution, Ltd., 1996). The months of Nisan, Iyar, Sivan, Tamuz, Tishrei, Heshvan, Kislev, Tevet, and Shevat have more than one English spelling. The vowels in the Divine Root Name and the assigning of the sephirot to each month comport with *Sefer Yetzirah, The Book of Creation* by Aryeh Kaplan (York Beach, Maine: Samuel Weiser, Inc., 1997), page 202.

Chart 3 - Hebrew Months, Sephirot and Divine Root Name Permutations

Order of Month	Name of Month		Sephirah		Divine Root Name	Without Vowels	Divine Root Name	With Vowels
1	יָסָן	Nissan	Chesed	Loving-kindness	יהוה	YHVH	יְַהָוְָה	Yi-hahv'-ha
2	אִיָּר	Iyyar	Gevurah	Strength Boundaries	יההו	YHHV	יְִהַהְו	Yi-hah-hahv'
3	סִיוָן	Sivvan	Tiferet	Beauty Eternity	יוהה	YVHH	יְוַהָה	Y'vu-hah-hah
4	תַּמּוּז	Tammuz	Netzakh	Mastery Victory	הוהי	HVHY	הֶוַיֹהִי	Heh-vay-ho'hi
5	אָב	Av	Hod	Grace Splendor	הויה	HVYH	הַוְיִהַה	Hah-vu-yi-hah
6	אֱלוּל	Elul	Yesod	Foundation	ההוי	HHVY	הֻהִוַיִ	Hu-hi-va-yi
7	תִּשְׁרִי	Tishrey	Chesed	Loving-kindness	והיה	VHYH	וַהֹיַַהַה	Va-ho-ya-hah
8	חֶשְׁוָן	Cheshvan	Gevurah	Strength Boundaries	וההי	VHHY	וֻהַהַהְי	Vu-hah-hah-y'
9	כִּסְלֵו	Kisleyv	Tiferet	Beauty Eternity	ויהה	VYHH	וַיֹהַַהַה	Vah-yo-ha-hah
10	טֵבֵת	Teyveyt	Netzakh	Mastery Victory	היהו	HYHV	הַיְהֻוְ	Hah-yi-hu-'v
11	שְׁבָט	Shvat	Hod	Grace Splendor	היוה	HYVH	הַיְוְֻהֻ	Hah-y'-v-hu
12	אֲדָר	Adar	Yesod	Foundation	ההיו	HHYV	הִהְיְוַה	Hi-h'-y'-vah

163

Appendix F

Translating the Invocation Toward the One
Into The Hebrew of the Jewish Tradition

By Rabbi Zalman Schachter-Shalomi and Netanel Miles-Yepez[258]

> Toward the One,
> The Perfection of Love, Harmony, and Beauty,
> The Only Being,
> United with All the Illuminated Souls,
> Who Form the Embodiment of the Master,
> The Spirit of Guidance.

Years ago, when I first began saying the *Toward the One* prayer of the Sufi Master *Hazrat* Inayat Khan, I found that I was often unable to get beyond the opening words. For even as I was speaking, I would be lifted "Toward the One" to regions of "Love, Harmony, and Beauty" where my feet no longer touched the ground of materiality, but instead were grounded in "The Only Being." I was overwhelmed by the energetic *qurb*—'proximity' to the One—in the words themselves. There was such holy precision in them and manifest spiritual energy that my heart could not fail to respond to them. And, as with other things that touched me powerfully from outside of the Jewish tradition, I immediately wanted to translate it into Hebrew, the language of my spiritual upbringing.[259]

In the years since I originally made this little translation for myself in the 1970's, other Hebrew translations of *Toward the One* have appeared in various places. This is in no way meant to imply criticism of other Hebrew translations, but only to offer another version. The beauty of a translation is the access it gives to a 'message' originally given in another language, but we must always understand that it is an interpretation of that 'message.' For each language has a beauty and sophistication of its own which resists translation. There is no one-to-one equivalence for the cultural understandings of words translated from one language into another. Thus, there is a practical truth to what Muslims say when they speak of the miraculous *ijaz* ('inimitability') of the Arabic *Qur'an*. And when they say that a *Qur'an* in English is not *the Qur'an*, they are also right. It is an interpretation.

This is not to say that the spirit of the 'message' is not conveyed in the translation, only that there is variation between one and the other. And just as a translation is an interpretation of the original, different translations sometimes yield quite different interpretations. Thus, it is possible that there will be some who will find value in my particular Hebrew interpretation of *Toward the One*.

---

258 "I" in this article is Reb Zalman. Mu'in ad-Din Netanel Miles-Yepez is a student of Reb Zalman, a Sufi Murshid, the Pir-O-Murshid of the Inayati-Maimuniyya Order of Sufis, and the successor to Reb Zalman, who founded the Order. Mu'in ad-Din has co-authored numerous books and articles with Reb Zalman. This article is published by Seven Pillars House of Wisdom at <http://www.sevenpillarshouse.org/article/translating_the_invocation_toward_the_one/>, and is reprinted here with the permission of Reb Zalman and Mu'in ad-Din. All rights reserved.
259 In the tradition of Jewish mysticism, there is a formula in Aramaic that is said before carrying out various commandments, which is similar to the Toward the One: L'Sheym Yihud Kudshah Berikh Hu u'Shekhintei b'Dehilu u'Rehimu l'YaHed Shem Y"H b' V"H b'Yihudah Shelim b'Shem Kol Yisra'el. We have "interpreted" this in English as: "I do this for the sake of the conscious-uniting of the transcendent holy One with the manifest Presence, Yud Heh with Vav Heh, thus giving pleasure to the act of Creation."

Appendix F - Translating Toward the One Into the Hebrew of the Jewish Tradition

This is why I am now hoping to make this translation available, for I have noticed that the Hebrew translations of the *Toward the One* I have seen are interpretations into *modern* Hebrew. This is good, and I am delighted to see them, just as I am pleased to see renderings into modern Spanish, German, French, and Arabic. But with this translation I intended to render *Toward the One* into a Hebrew that has a resonance with the liturgical Hebrew of the *beit midrash*, where Jews traditionally prayed and studied.

For today, there is both a traditional Hebrew of Judaism and a secular Hebrew of social discourse.

For Israelis (who have often been raised in a secular environment), modern Hebrew obviously makes more sense and is far more palatable, but for others who are more oriented toward the Hebrew of prayer and study, there are certain words and phrases in modern Hebrew that are foreign to traditional Judaism and do not come across as authentically Jewish. Thus, I labored to translate *Toward the One* in such a way that those who have solid footing in Jewish tradition may add it to their prayers without it feeling like something foreign.

Here is my translation of *Toward the One* into traditional Hebrew:

> *Liqrat ha'ehad,*
> *Ha'yahid ha'ehad v'ha'm'yuhad,*
> *Shleymut ha'emmet, ha'tzedeq v'ha'tif'eret,*
> *Hannimtza ha'yahid,*
> *Ha'kolel kol hann'shamot ha'ne'orot,*
> *Yotzrey hag'shammat harrabbi,*
> *Ha'ruah hakodesh.*

Of course, some of the words will be the same in nearly all translations into Hebrew, but there will also be critical differences, and in this case, even additions.

First of all, the phrase *Liqrat ha'ehad* is a fairly direct translation of 'Toward the One' into Hebrew. But if we wish it to impart more of the sense intended by *Hazrat* Inayat Khan, and to connect with how the Jewish tradition expresses this notion, we have to include another phrase here. In Hasidism, there is a distinction between *ehad ha'manuy*, the number one, and *ehad v'eyn sheyni*, the One that has no other, no two or three. The phrase in traditional Hebrew that best expresses this notion comes from the Italian Kabbalist and *hakham* ('sage'), Rabbi Moshe Hayyim Luzzatto (1707-1747), the author of the *Mesillat Yesharim* ('Path of the Upright'), who gives us *Ehad, yahid, u'meyuhad*, 'One Uniquely Simple Unity.'[260] But since this phrase cannot follow *Liqrat ha'ehad* in a natural way, I created a kind of echo of it with *Ha'yahid ha'ehad v'ha'm'yuhad*.

In the next line, we have *Shleymut ha'emmet, ha'tzedeq v'ha'tif'eret*, which is quite different from what we have in the English and requires some explanation. First of all, *shleymut*, 'wholeness,' is simply the word that best conveys the notion of 'perfection' in Hebrew,[261] but *ha'emmet, ha'tzedeq*

---

260 In Arabic, this is paralleled by Ahad, Wahid, wa-Samad.
261 The Hebrew takhlit, 'ultimate,' does not feel right in this context.

166

v'ha'tif'eret actually translates to 'truth, righteousness, and beauty.' Somehow, *emmet*, 'truth,' struck me as a better choice from within the Jewish tradition to put in this trilogy of words.[262] Nevertheless, I think *ahavah*, 'love,' (*ha'ahavah* if put into the whole phrase) would still be acceptable here. I chose to use *tzedeq*, 'righteousness' for 'harmony' because 'righteousness' in Hebrew carries with it the sense of balanced scales.[263] Now, *tif'eret* is in fact the Hebrew for 'beauty,' but it is also a word that is loaded with meaning in the world of Jewish mysticism (*kabbalah*). In a very simple sense, *tif'eret* is what balances and completes the forces of Love and Justice in the Universe.

The next three lines are fairly straightforward. *Hannimtza ha'yahid* is basically, 'the only one who can be found,' 'the only existent.' *YaHid* is also the One Infinite Being, the Simple Unity without separation or parts, the God without limits. *Ha'kolel kol hann'shamot ha'ne'orot* is 'Who contains all the souls that have been illuminated.' *Yotzrey hag'shammat harrabbi* is 'Forming the actualization of the master,'[264] the *rebbe*, in Hasidic parlance.

Finally, in the last line, I chose not to translate the words, "The Spirit of Guidance," but to replace them with the parallel concept from the Jewish tradition, *Ha'ruah hakodesh*, 'the Spirit of Holiness,' or Holy Spirit. This is the phrase most often used in the Talmudic and Midrashic literature to denote prophetic inspiration. And while there are statements in the tradition that say that *ruah hakodesh* departed after the passing of the prophets Haggai, Zachariah and Malachi, Hasidim clearly believe that it is still available, even today.

If one were to translate this Hebrew *Toward the One* back into English, it would probably come out something like this:

> Toward the One,
> Unique, One, and Unified,
> The Wholeness of Truth, Righteousness, and Beauty,
> The Only One in Existence,
> Who contains all the Illuminated Souls,
> Forming the actualization of the Master,
> The Spirit of Holiness.

As you can see, there is clear variation in the sense of the words, but I believe that the Message is still available in them. The English prayer of *Hazrat* Inayat Khan is so precise and beautiful that all attempts at translation will fail in one way or another. It has its own miraculous *ijaz* and will stand forever among the great prayer-creations of the English language. Nevertheless, I offer this rendering into Hebrew as a way for those who wish to pray in Hebrew, but who are also committed to the Message, to add this to their other prayers in a way that will feel natural in the prayer-space of Judaism.

---

262 The Hebrew word, emmet, is actually comprised of three letters—aleph-mem-tav—the beginning, middle and last letters of the Hebrew alphabet. In Jewish mysticism, this seeming coincidence is understood to suggest that emmet, 'truth,' is the beginning, middle, and the end, all and everything. And it is this notion that seemed to parallel 'love' in the Sufi tradition as a kind of ground concept, underlying all things.
263 There is no true parallel for 'harmony' in Hebrew. Of course, I could have used ahdut, 'oneness,' but it is a very modern word.
264 This has the sense of 'Who form—thickening into shape—the master.'

Appendix G

Quotation from

"A Journey for Those Who Wish to Take It" by Yael Unterman

The following is a quotation from an article by Yael Unterman[265] entitled, "A Journey for Those Who Wish to Take It," published in *HaAretz,* an Israeli daily newspaper that appears both in print and on the Internet, and in Hebrew and English. The original article is a book review of *A Heart Afire: Stories and Teachings of the Early Hasidic Masters*, by Zalman Schachter-Shalomi and Netanel Miles-Yepez.[266]

> ....[the book] is more than a collection of tales. It also incorporates ideas from non-Jewish sources of wisdom, ranging from the Buddha to Jung to the Greek-Armenian mystic G.I. Gurdjieff....
>
> Believing that Judaism – indeed, the world – was in the midst of a paradigm shift to a more expanded consciousness, Schachter-Shalomi founded what was later to become the Jewish Renewal movement, aiming to infuse Judaism with universal spiritual and creative practices....
>
> Of all the sources of wisdom included, Sufism is particularly prominent. This too is not unexpected, both due to some shared history with Judaism (for example, Abraham Maimuni, the son of Maimonides, who recommended adopting certain Sufi practices, believing them to stem from the Hebrew prophets), and to Sufism's open-hearted mystical approach. But the penny drops when we read on the cover that Miles-Yepez and Schachter-Shalomi co-founded the Inayati-Maimuni Tariqat, which is an inter-spiritual fellowship of seekers committed to both the Sufi and Hasidic paths, and the world's only Jewish order of Sufis. At this point we realize that the proportion of outside material present in "A Heart Afire" is not, in fact, so considerable, in light of where the authors are coming from. Whether this is a plus or a minus depends on the reader's enjoyment of such interjections....
>
> ...May these authors and others treat us to more wonderful unities of paradoxes, where old Jews speak to new and new Jews to old, in a voice that began at Sinai and that we hope shall never cease. [267]

---

265 Yael Unterman is a writer and educator. Her book *Nehama Leibowitz: Teacher and Bible Scholar* (Urim Publications) was a finalist for a 2009 National Jewish Book Award.
266 Zalman Schachter-Shalomi and Netanel Miles-Yepez, *A Heart Afire: Stories and Teachings of the Early Hasidic Masters* (Philadelphia: Jewish Publication Society of America, 2009).
267 Yael Unterman, "A Journey for Those Who Wish to Take It," *HaAretz*, February 4, 2010, May 20, 2012 <http://tinyurl.com/629dhrs> or <http://www.haaretz.com/culture/books/a-journey-for-those-who-wish-to-take-it-1.262771>.

Appendix H

Introduction to the Hebrew Alphabet

There are twenty-two letters in the Hebrew alphabet, each of which is described on Chart 4. Please note that Chart 4 appears in two parts, with each part being on a separate page.

All of the Hebrew letters are consonants. Hebrew may be written with and without vowels. Hebrew vowels are called "nikudim,"[268] and are composed of dots and dashes that appear above, within or below a Hebrew letter. The Hebrew vowels are described in Chart 5.

The letter vav serves both as a consonant and a vowel. The letter yod serves both as a consonant and as a vowel enhancer. For these reasons, vav and yod are listed on Charts 4 and 5.

Like all languages that are spoken in different parts of the world, Hebrew letters and vowels are pronounced differently by different Hebrew speakers. The pronunciations described on Charts 4 and 5 are for modern Hebrew spoken in the land of Israel today. To be sure, there are many Israelis who were born and raised in other countries, or whose mother tongue is not Hebrew. These speakers may pronounce certain letters and vowels differently. Ultra Orthodox (haredi) Jews generally use Yiddish for ordinary speech and Hebrew for prayer, study and when reading sacred texts. Haredi Jews use the Yiddish pronunciation of Hebrew letters and vowels rather than the ones on Charts 4 and 5. Those who are interested in Hebrew linguistics are encouraged to find a Hebrew teacher and inquire about pronunciation and other usage.

As discussed in Chapter 5, Gematria is the study of Hebrew numerology. Chart 4 includes the numeric value of each Hebrew letter according to gematria. The Hebrew letters kaf, mem, nun, pay and tzadi are written in one form in the beginning and middle of a word, and in a different form at the end of a word. The ending forms are called "sofit," meaning "final" or "ending." Kaf sofit, mem sofit, nun sofit, pay sofit and tzadi sofit are listed toward the bottom of Chart 4, Part 2. In some situations, these final letters have their own value in gematria as depicted on Chart 4, but in other situations, they do not. For example, when writing the year on the Hebrew calendar, the final kaf, mem, nun, pay and tzadi are not used to denote a different numeric value from the form of these letters that appear at the beginning or middle of a word. On the other hand, when calculating the numeric value of a verse of scripture or other sacred phrase, the final letters are counted by some using the values listed next to them on Chart 4.

The Hebrew alphabet is phonetic. Thus, when one learns the letters and vowels, and the rules for reading and using them, one may read any voweled text in Hebrew regardless of whether one understands the words. This is different from English where one needs to know a great many idiosyncrasies in order to be able to pronounce what one is reading. For example, there is no rule that will help one to know how to pronounce "gh" in tough, cough and through, or the "l" in alm, calm and palm.

---

268 The singular of the word "vowel" in Hebrew is nikud and the plural is nikudim. N'kudah means "dot" or "point" and may also be used to refer to a vowel. The plural of n'kudah is n'kudot.

Chart 4, Part 1

Hebrew Letters Alef to Nun

Hebrew Letter	Name of Letter	Sound	This form of the letter may appear in these places within a word	Numeric Value in Gematria (Jewish numerology)
א	alef	silent	everywhere	1
ב	beyt	"b" and "v"	everywhere	2
ג	gimmel	"g"	everywhere	3
ד	dalet	"d"	everywhere	4
ה	hay	"h"	everywhere	5
ו	vav (Vav may also be a vowel.)	"v" and sometimes "w"	everywhere	6
ז	zayin	"z"	everywhere	7
ח	chet	"ch" as in the musical composer "Bach"	everywhere	8
ט	tet	"t"	everywhere	9
י	yod (Yod may also be a vowel enhancer.)	"y" and sometimes silent	everywhere	10
כ	kaf	"k" and "ch" as in the musical composer "Bach"	beginning or middle	20
ל	lamed	"l"	everywhere	30
מ	mem	"m"	beginning or middle	40
נ	nun	"n"	beginning or middle	50

Chart 4, Part 2

Hebrew Letters Samech to Tzadi Sofit

Hebrew Letter	Name of Hebrew Letter	Sound of Hebrew Letter	This form of the letter may appear in these places within a word	Numeric Value in Gematria (Jewish numerology)
ס	samech	"s"	everywhere	60
ע	ayin	silent or glottal stop	everywhere	70
פ	pay	"p" or "f"	beginning or middle	80
צ	tzadi	"ts" as in "cuts"	beginning or middle	90
ק	kuf	"k"	everywhere	100
ר	raysh	"r"	everywhere	200
ש	shin	"sh" or "s"	everywhere	300
ת	tav	"t"	everywhere	400
ך	kaf sofit	"k" or "ch" as in the musical composer "Bach"	end	500
ם	mem sofit	"m"	end	600
ן	nun sofit	"n"	end	700
ף	pay sofit	"f" or "p"	end	800
ץ	tzadi sofit	"ts" as in "cuts"	end	900

Chart 5

The Hebrew Vowels

Hebrew Vowel	Name of Vowel	Vowel with Letter Alef	Pronunciation of Vowel (In this chart, the letter aleph is silent.)
_	patach	אַ	"ah" as in "hoorah"
ָ	kamatz	אָ	"uh" as in "cut"
ֶ	segol	אֶ	"e" as in "met"
ֵ	tzeyreyh	אֵ	"ay" as in "day"
ִ	chirik	אִ	"ee" as in "peek"
ֹ	cholam	אֹ	"o" as in "go"
וֹ	cholam maley	אוֹ	"o" as in "go"
ֻ	kubutz	אֻ	"oo" as in "boot"
וּ	shuruk	אוּ	"oo" as in "boot"
ֲ	chataf patach	אֲ	"ah" as in "hoorah," but with the emphasis on another syllable
ֳ	chataf kamatz	אֳ	"uh" as in "cut," but with the emphasis on another syllable
ֱ	chataf segol	אֱ	"e" as in "met," but with the emphasis on another syllable
יַ	patach with yod	אַי	"ai" as in "Adonai"
יָ	kamatz with yod	אָי	"ai" as in "Adonai"

Because Hebrew is phonetic, one may davven (worship) in Hebrew and become quite fluent in davvenen without understanding the words as one pronounces them. Jewish prayer books that provide translations into English, Spanish, Russian and other languages allow the worshipper to read the Hebrew and gain an understanding of its meaning through the translation. This is also true for those who read the Bible in Hebrew and rely upon a translation into another language to understand its meaning.

Acrostics

An acrostic is a poem or prayer or other writing in which each line or section begins with a subsequent letter of a meaningful word, or with all of the letters of the alphabet in alphabetical order. For example, there is an old show tune that begins, "A, you're adorable. B, you're so beautiful," etc. The words to that song are an acrostic, with each new saying beginning with the successive letter of the English alphabet. Another example is greeting cards that use a key word such as "mother" or "love" and include a series of sayings that begin with each successive letter of the word featured on the card.

The traditional Kiddush recited over wine or grape juice in the home on Friday evening begins with the Biblical words, "Yom hashishi, vay'khulu hashamayim v'ha'aretz," meaning, "The sixth day, and the heavens and the earth were completed." The first four words in Hebrew begin with the Hebrew letters yod and hay and vav and hay in that order. These are the letters of the Divine Root Name in the order in which it appear countless times in the Torah. Kiddush is a prayer that sanctifies the Sabbath and the wine or grape juice that Jewish people drink as they usher in the Sabbath day each week. However, in order to remember to have the Divine Root Name in our consciousness as we make Kiddush, we begin the Kiddush at home by reciting the closing two words of the Biblical story about the day before the Sabbath, namely the sixth day, which is called "yom hashishi."[269]

A number of Biblical psalms are composed of acrostics, with the first letter of each verse being the successive letter of the Hebrew alphabet. The body of Psalm 34 contains such an acrostic and is part of the Shabbat morning liturgy in many Jewish prayer books. Another example is Psalm 145, which contains an acrostic of all the Hebrew letters in alphabetical order except the letter nun. As one can see in Chart 4, nun comes between the letters mem and samech. In Psalm 145, the word "noflim," meaning "fallen ones" appears in the verse that begins with the letter samech. The Hebrew is "Someych Adonai l'khol ha'noflim, v'zokeyf l'khol hak'fufim," meaning "God supports all who stumble, and lifts up all who are bowed down." There is a teaching that says that King David, to whom Psalm 145 is attributed, embedded the letter nun in the verse that begins with the letter samech in order to say "someych (l'khol ha') noflim," meaning "supports (all the) fallen."[270]

Psalm 145 forms the major portion of a prayer known as Ashrey that is traditionally recited numerous times each day during Jewish worship. The central verses of Ashrey begin sequentially with each letter of the Hebrew alphabet, except nun, as explained above. Like the Ashrey prayer, the Ashrey Tree that adorns the Teachings section divider just before Chapter 1 contains all the Hebrew letters—including the final letters depicted toward the bottom of Chart 4, Part 2—except for nun. The Ashrey Tree was conceived by the author and created by the interior illustrator of this book.

---

269 When making Kiddush on Friday evening during worship services in the synagogue, the Kiddush begins one paragraph later, namely with the prayer boray pri hagafen. If one is going to have a meal at the synagogue, however, then the Kiddush recited at the synagogue also begins with "yom hashishi."
270 I learned this teaching from Rabbi Micah Hyman.

The Relationship between Adonai and the Divine Root Name

As discussed in Chapter 8 and elsewhere, Adonai is a Hebrew name of God. Adonai means Lord or my Lord,[271] it implies the One who provides sustenance and it also refers to the Shechina, the feminine aspect of the One Being, or God in manifestation.

As also discussed in Chapter 8, the Divine Root Name is the ineffable name of God and consists of the four Hebrew letters yod and hay and vav and hay. The Divine Root Name is considered to be ineffable, but we do give it a pronunciation when praying, blessing, reading scripture, teaching and having a discussion. The pronunciations of the Divine Root Name include Adonai, YaH, HaShem, Shem Hameforash, Shem Havayah, Adoshem, Yahweh, Jehovah and Ya-hu-va. These pronunciations are discussed in Chapter 8.

The Divine Root Name is sometimes abbreviated with two yods and accompanying vowels as depicted in Chart 6. This abbreviation appears across the Jewish denominations in prayer books published during the twentieth century,[272] and in most renditions of Targum Onkelos.[273] Onkelos was a Roman convert to Judaism who translated the Hebrew Bible into Aramaic. Targum Onkelos—meaning the Translation of Onkelos—was accepted by the rabbis as authoritative, and there are many Torah commentaries that refer to Onkelos' translation of a particular word or phrase as a clue, or as evidence, of how to understand it.

Chart 6 also depicts the intertwining of the Divine Root Name with the divine name Adonai. This intertwining is found in some sacred texts and mystical prayer books as well as on sacred wall hangings. It conveys a sense that the Divine Root Name is the name at which we gaze and "Ah-doh-nai" is the way we pronounce it. The Jewish Sabbath is viewed mystically as a time when God, depicted in the Divine Root Name, has yichud (union) with the Shechina. The intertwining of the letters of the Divine Root Name and the divine name Adonai may be seen as a symbol of that union.[274]

---

271 In modern Hebrew, Adon means mister. For example, Adon Goldberg means Mr. Goldberg. Adoni would be translated as sir in American English and as my lord in British English. The divine name Adonai has an implied plural just like the divine name Elohim. In Hebrew, ordinary plural nouns are used in sentences and phrases together with the plural form of verbs. However, Adonai and Elohim are used with the singular form of verbs, and this supports the linguistic and theological notion that God is One and God's greatness is expounded in a kind of plurality that is impossible to describe or define or encompass in words.

272 The following are examples of Reform, Orthodox, Conservative and Haredi (Ultra Orthodox) prayer books that include the abbreviation of the Divine Root Name with two yods and attendant vowels. **Reform:** "Services for the New Year" and "Services for Day of Atonement," *The Union Prayerbook for Jewish Worship* (New York: The Central Conference of American Rabbis, 1962); **Orthodox:** *Shilo Siddur T'filah L'khol Hashanah L'vatay Knesset Ul'vatay Sefer* (New York: Shilo Publishing House, Inc., 1980); **Conservative:** *Sabbath and Festival Prayer Book with A New Translation, Supplementary Readings and Notes* (The Rabbinical Assembly of America and The United Synagogue of America, 1982); **Haredi:** *Machzor for Yom Kippur (According to the custom of those who pray Nusach Ha-Ari Zal as arranged by Rabbi Shneur Zalman of Liadi, English Translation by Rabbi Nissen Mangel)* (Brooklyn: Merkos L'Inyonei Chinuch, Inc. 1991).

273 One such example is the following Hebrew text of Torah, Targum Onkelos and the commentary of Rashi (Rabbi Shlomo Yitzhaki, an outstanding Biblical commentator of the middle ages): *Chumash Kolel Chamishah Chumshei Torah B'Otiyot G'dolot Me'od, Im Peyrush Rashi, V'Tirgum Onkelos, Haftarot, V'Chamesh Megillot* (New York: Hebrew Publishing Co.)

274 The *Zohar*, a mystical commentary on the Torah, refers to Adonai as the Shechina and as the divine name linked with the sephirah of Malkhut. (*Zohar*, Shechina and Malkhut are defined in the Glossary of Terms in Appendix A. The *Zohar* is also introduced in the "Mystical Texts" section of Chapter 2. Shechina is discussed briefly in the "Background on Brukha At YaH Shekhinah, Barukh Atah Elohim" section of Chapter 8 and elsewhere. The sephirah of Malkhut is discussed at some length in Appendix D.)

As demonstrated in Chart 6, the abbreviation of the Divine Root Name begins with the yod from the Divine Root Name itself, together with its attendant vowel; and it ends with the yod from Adonai and the vowel that precedes it.

Like seeing a token of our beloved that melts our heart, viewing these two yods together with their vowels during prayer and study of scripture reminds us of the yichud (union) of the beloved we call God with God's counterpart, or "other half," as it were, namely, the Shechina. Since God is One, this is all metaphor and cannot be fully comprehended with the mind. At the same time, since humans are said to be created in the image of God, and since human love and physical union are seen in Judaism as mirrors of divine love, the depiction of the two yods in Biblical texts and prayer books as a placeholder for yod and hay and vav and hay creates a mnemonic device that draws us into the consciousness of our own union with God, which is called devaykut. Devaykut is a Hebrew expression meaning stick-to-it-iveness, or adhering to, or being glued to the Oneness.

Chart 6

Adonai and the Divine Root Name

(The teachings in this chart are contained in the section entitled, "The Relationship between Adonai and the Divine Root Name" in Appendix H. If you are not familiar with the Hebrew letters, please also see the "Introduction to the Hebrew Alphabet" in Appendix H.)

The Divine Root Name is sometimes abbreviated as

יְיָ

In the Sefer Torah (the scroll of the Torah rolled onto two handles), everything is written with consonants and no vowels, and the Divine Root name is depicted like this:

יהוה

The Divine Root Name with vowels looks like this:

יְהֹוָה

The consonants of Adonai look like this:

אדני

Adonai with vowels looks like this:

אֲדֹנָי

Sometimes, on a sacred wall hanging or a graphic in an esoteric Hebrew text, one finds the Divine Root Name and Adonai written as one word with their letters intertwined, like this:

י א ה ד ו נ ה י

The abbreviation of the Divine Root Name with two yods that appears at the beginning of this chart includes the yod and its vowel from the beginning of the full Divine Root Name, and the yod and its vowel from the end of Adonai.

Index

A footnote is indicated by "n." Consecutive footnotes are indicated by "nn."

Index

Index

Index

About the Author

Rabbi Pamela Frydman is the founder and Director of the Holocaust Education Project of the Academy for Jewish Religion in California. She was the founding rabbi of Or Shalom Jewish Community of San Francisco, now a Reconstructionist congregation. She was a co-founder of OHALAH, the international association of Jewish Renewal rabbis and cantors, and the first woman to serve as its president. She also served on the Academic Board of the ALEPH Ordination Program.

Rabbi Pam was a co-founder and serves on the Rabbinic Advisory Council of Shalom Bayit, Jewish Women Working to End Domestic Violence. She organized and co-chaired Rabbis for Women of the Wall, a campaign to raise consciousness about women's rights at the Kotel (the Western Wall in Jerusalem), and served as co-organizer of Women of the Wall's Legal and Education Fund. She organized and, together with 59 rabbinic colleagues, co-chaired one of the many campaigns to free Gilad Shalit.

She received a bachelor's degree in linguistics and psychology from Tel Aviv University and rabbinic ordination from B'nai Or Religious Fellowship, predecessor to the ALEPH Ordination Program of the Jewish Renewal Movement.

Prior to entering the rabbinate, she studied Sufism, Buddhism and Theosophy. She served as a spiritual teacher in the Sufi Ruhaniat International, a leader of the Dances of Universal Peace and a Board member of the San Francisco Lodge of the Theosophical Society. Along with her universal spiritual pursuits, she served as a founding member and leader of the Aquarian Minyan of Berkeley.

She is also the proud mother of two wonderful young men: her son Josh and stepson Terry.

Published under Pamela Frydman Baugh

Reflections: A High Holy Day Machzor, second edition (Or Shalom Jewish Community,1997-98). Soon to be republished under Pamela Frydman. Check http://rebpam.com/ for details.

"Unseemly, Very Unseemly," Patti Moskovitz, *The Minyan, A Tapestry of Jewish Life* (San Jose: Writers Club Press, 2002).

Aley T'filah, Leaves of Prayers, Sabbath Morning Prayer Book (Or Shalom Jewish Community, 2002). Soon to be republished under Pamela Frydman. Check http://rebpam.com/ for details.

*Seasons of Freedom, A Passover Haggadah, fifth edition (*Or Shalom Jewish Community, 2004). Soon to be republished under Pamela Frydman. Check http://rebpam.com/ for details.

"A Renewal Ritual of Divorce to Supplement a Traditional Gett," OHALAH/Resources/Rituals/Divorce, Winter 2007, <http://ohalah.org/> and Spring 2012 <http://rebpam.com/>.

"Her Brother's Sandals," *Poetica Magazine*, August 2009. Reprinted Spring 2012 <http://rebpam.com/>.

"A Blessing from my Grandmother," *Zeek Magazine,* October 2009, <http://zeek.forward.com/articles/115540/> and Spring, 2012 <http://rebpam.com/>.

39112348R00121

Made in the USA
Lexington, KY
08 February 2015